D1796504

Hitler or Hippocrates

Medical experiments and euthanasia in the
Third Reich

HITLER OR HIPPOCRATES

Medical experiments and euthanasia in the Third Reich

Paul Hoedeman

Translation from the Dutch by
Ralph de Rijke

Foreword by
Dr E.A. Cohen

The Book Guild Ltd.
Sussex, England

For Carla

This book is sold subject to the condition that it shall not, by way of trade or otherwise, be lent, re-sold, hired out, photocopied or held in any retrieval system, or otherwise circulated without the publisher's prior consent in any form of binding or cover other than that in which this is published and without a similar condition including this condition being imposed on the subsequent purchaser.

The Book Guild Ltd.
25 High Street,
Lewes, Sussex.

First published 1991
© Paul Hoedeman 1991
Set in Baskerville
Typesetting by Ashford Setting & Design,
Ashford, Middlesex.
Printed in Great Britain by
Antony Rowe Ltd.,
Chippenham, Wiltshire.

British Library Cataloguing in Publication Data
Hoedeman, Paul
  Hitler or Hippocrates: medical experiments and euthanasia
  in the Third Reich
  1. German war crimes. Role of doctors, history
  I. Title
  364.1380943

ISBN 0 86332 544 0

CONTENTS

Glossary   6

Foreword   7

Preface   11

Introduction   15

Chapter 1   Himmler and his SS   31

Chapter 2   The Experiments at Ravensbrück   51

Chapter 3   Conti and Brandt   75

Chapter 4   Euthanasia   96

Chapter 5   The Buchenwald and Natzweiler Experiments   120

Chapter 6   The Dachau Experiments   150

Chapter 7   The Auschwitz-Birkenau Experiments   183

Notes   245

Bibliography   257

GLOSSARY

SS Ranks And Their Army Equivalents

COMMISSIONED RANKS

Oberstgruppenführer	General
Obergruppenführer	Lieutenant General
Gruppenführer	Major General
Brigadeführer	Brigadier General
Oberführer	(no army equivalent)
Standartenführer	Colonel
Obersturmbannführer	Lieutenant Colonel
Sturmbannführer	Major
Hauptsturmführer	Captain
Obersturmführer	First Lieutenant
Untersturmführer	Second Lieutenant

NON-COMMISSIONED RANKS

Oberscharführer	Senior non-commissioned rank
Unterscharführer	Equivalent to Sergeant
Rottenführer	Equivalent to Corporal

FOREWORD

We have always wanted doctors to work to high moral standards, and concern ourselves with 'medical ethics'. Perhaps this is why the accounts of how Aryan Germans doctors transgressed these norms during National Socialism are so striking.

Most behaved no worse than their fellow citizens. No one protested when Jewish colleagues were thrown out of work; they quietly moved into the vacancies.

No protests were heard either when Jewish doctors were forbidden to treat Aryan patients; Aryan doctors accepted the subsequent growth of their practices without complaint. It remains difficult to fathom that German doctors behaved according to the precepts of National Socialism. Some were physicians for whom I too had great respect. My own medical education was based almost entirely on German textbooks.

The German medical world carried out Hitler's decisions, so they murdered psychiatric patients labelled '*nutzlose Fresser*' — useless hungry mouths — and called it euthanasia. They co-operated in the '*Endlösung der Judenfrage*' — the final solution, a camouflage for the extermination of the Jews, for were not the Jews an inferior race and the cause of all world's evils?

The Jews were murdered by *Einsatzgruppen* and in the gas chambers of Chelmno, Sobibor, Belzec, Treblinka.

Auschwitz, too, saw murder on a vast scale, but not before German doctors had picked out the *Arbeitsfähige* — the able-bodied for work — men and women over fifty, mothers with children, invalids, the sick and the frail were sent straight to the gas chambers.

While some doctors needed alcohol to perform this criminal task, most regarded it as a necessity.

Lagerarzt SS Obersturmführer Dr F. Klein's justification was: 'Just as I remove a festering appendix to make the patient healthy again, I must destroy the Jews to make mankind healthy again!'

For over a year Dr Klein and I were at Auschwitz together. I was witness to the playful, friendly and smiling way in which he carried out his own selections in the Auschwitz hospital. Once a fortnight he came to inspect my ward; I had to present the patients together with my diagnosis and treatment, which thanks to lack of medicines existed only on paper. Finally I had to answer the crucial question — how long it would be before the patient was *arbeitsfähig* once more.

There stood the patient, not much more than skin and bones. My answer should have been: 'With good care, good food and hygiene, a year!'

But this would have been useless.

'Two weeks,' was my reply.

Any other answer would not have helped; the patient was sent as a rule to the gas chambers. Only a few patients were allowed to live.

To this day I blame myself for having assisted in these selections. I would go so far as to call it collaboration. I shall not employ the excuse that all doctors did it, for I believe that I am responsible for my own actions. Dr Klein's conduct is mentioned in this book, as is Dr Münch's comment on the horrors and the selections:

'You get used to it!'

At Auschwitz he was considered a good doctor.

The prisoners at these concentration camps were considered inferior beings whose only function was to obey orders.

They were without rights, suffered filth, lice, hunger, cold; they had insufficient clothing and the hygiene was a travesty.

They were forced into hard labour. By the time they were entirely emaciated, the gas chamber was waiting: once worked out, Nazi Germany had no more use for them. This went under the name *produktive Vernichtung* — productive destruction. At the Nuremberg trials the German doctors denied all blame, claiming *Befehl ist Befehl* -orders are orders. They thrust all responsibility back to the man who was conspicuous by his absence: Reichsführer SS Heinrich Himmler.

This also applies to those doctors who had carried out experiments on camp prisoners, although several had actually requested such human guinea pigs.

There is no doubt in my mind: these guinea pigs were not

volunteers, and did not consent to the experiments performed on them.

There cannot be anyone left on earth who considers that the fifty Jewish men and women, picked out and killed that their skeletons might augment to the collection of one Professor Hirt in Strassburg, had been asked whether they might like to co-operate. Professor Hirt knew that his activities had been criminal. When the Allies were advancing rapidly on Strassburg, he gave orders that the bodies should vanish. Who would now defend Dr Kurt Heismeyer, who carried out tuberculosis experiments on twenty Jewish children aged between five and twelve? To cover his tracks completely, he had them all killed. An SS Kommando led by SS Obersturmführer Arnold Strippel put them to death in the cellar of the Hamburger Schule Bullenhuserdamm in the night of 20-21 April 1945.

During the Nuremberg trials the judges, who had no concentration camp experience, often deliberated over the extent to which the test persons had 'volunteered'. Speaking as an ex-concentration camp prisoner I have always found it to be self-evident that the power to choose had not existed.

Medical experiments took place in many concentration camps. The results were discussed at doctors' conferences where the absence of loud remonstration was not even noticed.

We might perhaps seek to understand the behaviour of these experimental doctors as being somehow what one might expect of the dregs of the medical world. Again this would be mistaken, for it is a sad truth that prominent physicians were involved.

Did they feel guilty afterwards? On the contrary. German doctors did not differentiate themselves from the rest of German citizenry.

They denied all blame. Refinement, education, knowledge do not set a man apart from the crowd. The doctors of Nazi Germany have made this sufficiently clear.

The ground covered in this book has been published before, but as the author correctly points out, from an exclusively medical point of view.

This is why, in my opinion, it is a welcome development that such matters as 'euthanasia' and forced medical experiments upon people be illuminated from an historical perspective. The author has furnished hitherto unpublished interviews with criminals and victims. It is especially important that this takes place while these people are still alive.

The perpetrators and the victims alike will all be dead one day, and these terrible events will pass into history.

This applies to everything that happened under Nazi rule, but especially to the *Endlösung der Judenfrage*.

In this book the author accomplishes this important task.

Dr E.A. Cohen

Former prisoner physician at Auschwitz concentration camp and author of *Human Behaviour in the Concentration Camp* and *The Abyss*.

PREFACE

This book is concerned with the medical experiments and the 'euthanasia' in Nazi Germany. I began to write it more than ten years ago, but for many reasons, I have only recently completed the work.

This book describes, in broad terms, how euthanasia was applied, under what circumstances the experiments took place, and with what aim. My original intention had been to restrict myself to the scientific study of a small number of experiments; but as I worked, the idea that the material should be made available to a wider public was growing. That is not to say that the scientific rigour was relaxed but rather that a number of medical and legal details had to be sacrificed. While I am aware that this introduces the risk of incompleteness, it is simply the logical consequence of the above-mentioned objective.

Up to now, the historical material has been examined principally by doctors; Bayle, Cohen, Ternon, Helman, Menges, Mitscherlich and Mielke have all written excellent (and detailed) studies, of which I have gratefully made use of during the preparation of this work. However, these studies do not, in my opinion, lend themselves to those looking for a general overview, since they are written from a specialist, and especially a medical point of view.

These works are, nevertheless, strongly to be recommended to those who, having read this book, wish to examine the material more closely. One of the greatest authorities on the *Endlösung*, Miriam Novitch, supported the idea of my work most clearly when, at the end of a long conversation with me, she remarked:

> Detailed studies are very important, but their disadvantage is that they are read by very few and more in very limited circles. I know this from my own

11

experience. Everyone knows that the German doctors performed experiments in the camps. But what sort of experiments, and for what purpose, is almost always unknown. In my opinion, the widest possible audience should be informed of this affair . . .

A former SS physician reacted similarly:

The only reason I have talked with you is so that as many people as possible hear the story. Make sure you show clearly how easily and how far people can fall . . .

In the course of writing this book, I spoke with many people who were directly or indirectly involved. While some of those who provided me with information did not want their names to be used, some of those who did I would like to acknowledge are: Miriam Novitch, who encouraged me to continue with the study and who introduced me to various people and institutions involved, directly or indirectly, with the euthanasia and experiments.

Albert Speer, Hitler's former minister of armaments, who gave me much information about Himmler, Karl Brandt and the nature of medical affairs and of the decision-making in Hitler's immediate circle.

The American researchers Drs Jerry and Wendy Nessel, who provided much useful information and material for the chapter on euthanasia.

Dr Hans Münch, who has been an important source of information about many SS doctors (himself included) at Auschwitz, and about the psychological climate in which the personnel worked.

Dr Kazimir Smolen, former prisoner and director of the Auschwitz museum who provided general information and who made much source material available.

Dr Elie Cohen, former prisoner-doctor at Auschwitz and author of the unsurpassed standard work on the German concentration camp in which the medical and psychological conditions of the prisoners and of the personnel is described, for the valuable information he supplied about the work and position of the prisoner-doctor.

Dr Ellis Hertzberger who was forced to do bacteriological research at Auschwitz and Dachau who shared his wide store of knowledge in response to my many questions concerning his work as prisoner-bacteriologist.

The Buchenwald Museum, Mahn-und Gedenkstätte Sachsenhausen and the Dachau Museum for the general information and photographic material they provided.

A special acknowledgement is due to Eva Mozes Kor, founder and president of the organization CANDLES (Children of Auschwitz Nazi Deadly Lab Experiments Survivors) for the information she gave me concerning Mengele and his twin experiments.

The National Archives in Washington DC, the German National Archives in Nuremberg, the Zentrale Stelle der Landesjustizverwaltungen in Ludwigsburg, the Zentrale Landesjustizverwaltungen in Munich, the Centre du Documentation Juive Contemporain in Paris, the Institut für Zeitgeschichte in Munich and the Staatsanwaltschaft bei dem Landgericht München for the help they extended, and finally, Robert Perry, for reading over and typing the manuscript.

INTRODUCTION

In 1947 Dr Heinz Baumkötter, former doctor-in-charge at the Sachsenhausen concentration camp, was put on trial. He had to justify his acts before a Russian tribunal, and the dialogue with the prosecutor went as follows:

'In what capacity did you work at Sachsenhausen?'

'At executions on the trestle (prisoners were forced to lie on a trestle and were beaten or whipped to death) or by firing squad, and at hangings or gassings, I had either to be present in person or to nominate my representative. In addition, I had to draw up lists of sick prisoners and those unfit for work, who had to be transferred to other camps, and finally I was ordered to carry out experiments.'

'How many invalid and sick prisoners were transported to their death at other camps?'

'Over the years, very many. About 50,000 ...'

'And how many were sent to other camps and to their death thanks to your selection, your initiative?'

'Ask Rehn that question!'

'Were these lists drawn up by you or by Rehn?'

'The lists were drawn up on my orders after I had received instructions from superiors ...'

'Then you must know how many, because Rehn transported only those who were on your list ... ?'

'Yes, that is correct.'

'So, I must ask you and not Rehn to answer that question. How many were sent to their death in other camps as a result of your selection, your initiative?'

'About 8,000 prisoners were transported under my instructions.'

'Dr Baumkötter, why did you, and the camp doctors subordinate to you, order prisoners to genuflect *after* they had been tortured on the trestle?'

'It was customary in Sachsenhausen and it improved their blood circulation!'

'Then why did the prisoners not kneel voluntarily? Why did they have to be forced?'

'I found that prisoners kneeled voluntarily ... .'

'So, you dare to assert that prisoners might, after appalling torture on the trestle, actually voluntarily kneel to you?'

'Yes ... I think so ... maybe they did it also because they would otherwise be punished further.'

'Dr Baumkötter, was this not, in truth, simply an additional form of torture?'

'I must now regard it as such.'

'As you undoubtedly know, there was, in Sachsenhausen, an execution room camouflaged as a doctor's room. Before prisoners were murdered, they were examined by the doctors. For what purpose?'

'The prisoners were checked for gold teeth or fillings and this check served to prevent the prisoners from finding out about the real purpose ...'[1]

SS Hauptsturmführer Heinz Baumkötter was in fact merely an unimportant pawn on the medical chessboard of Nazi Germany. Why then draw attention to this camp doctor at Sachsenhausen? Official sources reveal that he must have been one of the first Nazi doctors to perform medical experiments on non-volunteers.[2] Baumkötter himself speaks of 'orders to perform experiments', but the sources reveal nothing of the sort. It is more likely that he began the tests on his own initiative. As a matter of fact, a camp doctor enjoyed a privileged position in comparison with doctors working near the front. The camp doctor who gave the impression of being engaged in an important project stood a smaller chance of being called to the front than his idle colleague. To perform experiments *in vivo* (on living material) was one way to steer clear of such a summons. As an illustrative example, the Baumkötter case is interesting for another reason. After the war, the Soviet Union transferred him to Bonn as 'not pardoned'. In Bonn he was immediately released and given 6,000 DM as a *Spätheimkehrer*.[3] His war history was forgotten and the erstwhile Hauptsturmführer worked as a respectable doctor in the Elizabeth Hospital in Iserlohn for quite some time.[4]

The historian Léon Poliakow, renowned for his studies on the Third Reich, plainly states in his study of the Auschwitz concentration camp: 'Of all wrongdoers, the criminal doctor is certainly the most dangerous.'[5]

The medical experiments that took place in the German concentration camps make for some of the blackest pages in the history of the Second World War. During the so-called 'Doctors' Trial' in Nuremberg, Brigadier General Telford Taylor of the US army, Chief of Counsel for war crimes did not mince his words when describing the characters of the doctors experimenting in the concentration camps:

> 'The defendants in this case are charged with murders, tortures, and other atrocities committed in the name of medical science. The victims of these crimes are numbered in the hundreds of thousands. A handful only are still alive; a few of the survivors will appear in this courtroom. But most of these miserable victims were slaughtered outright or died in the course of the tortures to which they were subjected. (. . .) None of the victims of the atrocities perpetuated by these defendants were volunteers, and this is true regardless of what these unfortunate people may have said or signed before their tortures began. Most of the victims had not been condemned to death, and those who had been were not criminals, unless it is a crime to be a Jew, or a Pole or a gypsy, or a Russian prisoner of war . . . it is a fundamental and inescapable obligation of every physician under any known system of law not to perform a dangerous experiment without the subject's consent . . . .
>
> I fervently hope that none of us here in the courtroom will have to suffer in silence while it is said on the part of these defendants that the wretched and helpless people whom they froze, drowned, burned and poisoned were volunteers. If such a shameless lie is spoken here, we need only remember the four girls who were taken from the Ravensbrück concentration camp and made to lie naked with the frozen and all but dead Jews who survived Dr Rascher's tank of ice

water. One of these women, whose hair and eyes and figure were pleasing to Dr Rascher, when asked by him why she had volunteered for such a task replied: 'Rather half a year in a brothel than half a year in a concentration camp . . . .' (. . .) The defendants in the dock are charged with murder, but this is no mere murder trial. We cannot rest content when we have shown that crimes were committed and that certain people committed them. It is our deep obligation to all peoples of the world to show why and how these things happened. It is incumbent upon us to set forth with conspicuous clarity the ideas and motives which moved these defendants to treat their fellowmen as less than beasts. The perverse thoughts and distorted concepts which brought about these savageries are not dead. They cannot be killed by force of arms. They must not become a spreading cancer in the breast of humanity. (. . .)

This case is a striking demonstration not only of the tremendous degradation of German medical ethics which Nazi doctrine brought about, but of the undermining of the medical art and thwarting of the techniques which the defendants sought to employ. The Nazis have, to a certain extent, succeeded in convincing the peoples of the world that the Nazi system, although ruthless was scientifically efficient; that although savage, it was completely scientific; that although entirely devoid of humanity, it is highly systematic — that 'it got things done'.

The Nazi methods of investigation were inefficient and unscientific, and their techniques of research were unsystematic. These experiments revealed nothing which civilized medicine can use. It was indeed ascertained that phenol or gasoline injected intravenously will kill a man inexpensively and within sixty seconds. This and other 'advances' are all in the field of 'thanatology' (. . .). Apart from these deadly fruits, the experiments were not only criminal but a scientific failure. It is indeed as if a just deity had shrouded the solutions which they attempted to reach with murderous means. In short, this conspiracy was a ghastly failure as well as a hideous crime. The creeping paralysis of Nazi superstition spread through the medical profession and just as it destroyed character and morals, it dulled the mind.'[6]

And the consultant to the secretary of War and to the Chief of Counsel for war crimes, Leo Alexander, stated that:

'The arch crime to which the SS was committed was the genocide of non-German peoples and the elimination by killing, in groups or singly, of Germans who were considered useless or disloyal. In effecting this two-fold programme Himmler demanded and received the co-operation of physicians and of German medical science. I have proposed the term 'ktenology', the science of killing, for this trend of Nazi research.'[7]

The accused doctors took a completely contrary view. Their standard defence was that they had simply behaved according to the principle 'orders are orders' and that the tests had been performed on prisoners already sentenced to death whose co-operation offered them the chance of a pardon. Whenever the prosecutors dwelt on Hippocrates' oath and the defendants social and ethical conscience, they retorted with extensive arguments about the relationship between the individual and the state.

They regarded themselves as ordinary soldiers with a duty towards the society that they represented, and wished to be treated accordingly. Why should a doctor who performs tests on a prisoner who has been condemned to death be labelled a criminal when the pilot of a bomber that flattens a town is not? Both act on orders, so why hold the one to be guilty and the other innocent? On what grounds can we assume that a doctor should have refused to perform experiments, but that the pilot should have agreed to the bombing?[8]

Were the medical experiments so much more criminal than the bombing of Hamburg or Dresden, or the use of the atomic bombs on Hiroshima and Nagasaki?

These bomb attacks, whose military necessity had by no means been established, had indeed been called into question, had claimed the lives of thousands of innocent women and children.

These and many other questions were considered between 21 November 1946 and 20 August 1947 in the course of the greatest medical trial in human history: the United States of America v. Karl Brandt et al, Case 1, the 'medical case' which comprised one of the twelve Nuremberg trials of German war criminals.

The charges against the twenty-three suspects, amongst them twenty doctors, comprised four points: common design or conspiracy (this part of the indictment was withdrawn for lack of jurisdiction); war crimes; crimes against humanity; membership of criminal organizations.[9] In Taylor's words:

> 'The twenty physicians in the dock range from leaders of German scientific medicine, with excellent reputations, down to the dregs of the German medical profession. All of them have in common a callous lack of consideration and human regard for, and an unprincipled willingness to abuse their power over the poor, unfortunate, defenceless creatures who had been deprived of their rights by a ruthless and criminal government.'[10]

That there were, among the defendants in the dock, seven professors of medicine, need not be surprising when one realizes that the NSDAP distributed the professorial chairs.

Historically, the change in the attitudes of the medical profession is even more remarkable because in the last hundred years Germany was the medical centre of the world. Many German professors enjoyed world renown, and their scientific and intellectual integrity was widely lauded. In fact, at the end of the last century the history of German medical science had reached its zenith. There was Max Pettenkofer, the great cholera specialist, Erich Martini, the malaria expert, Max Taute who distinguished himself in the field of tropical diseases, Reinhard Köhler, one of the first cancer researchers and many more.[11]

There was no field of medical science in which German doctors had not won their spurs convincingly. Marburg, Heidelburg, Frankfurt am Main and Berlin were medical Meccas in the 1920's and exerted a powerful attraction on qualified doctors from all over the world. With the arrival of National Socialism, a new chapter opened in the history of German medical science.

In 1929, the National Socialists set up their own medical league, which, with its numerous subsidiary organizations, began to erode the independence of the existing medical organizations, a process which accelerated when Hitler came to power in 1933.

The first decree, its form premonitory of the series to follow, appeared on 8 September 1937. Jewish doctors' organizations were forbidden, and with the exception of war veterans, they were forbidden to work in practices together. Access to German hospitals was also denied. One year later, on 3 August 1938, they were no longer allowed to exercise their profession. Jewish war veterans could continue their practices, provided their nameplates carried a blue David's star. These decrees formed only a small fraction of the large number of measures by which the Nazis slowly but surely took control of the medical world.

Where scientific achievements had once provided the basis for medical qualifications, now loyalty to Nazi doctrine often decided the issue instead. Fervent Nazi students whose work did not really merit medical qualification had the rules bent for them and became doctors. Opposition to these practices was brutally stifled and professors who resisted were replaced by more ideologically suitable candidates. But it should not be assumed that all doctors who performed experiments came from this generation. At all times the distinction should be made between the ordinary doctor and the ideologically instated SS doctor, between the ordinary professor and the one affiliated with the SS. Within these categories, as we shall see, further nuances can be revealed.

Doctors who performed tests on prisoners all had different sets of premises, from personal glory to the social value of their work. Many automatically blended the two. But the German doctors in the Second World War were conspicuous for the way they performed their tests. The number of medical men (including university professors and lecturers) involved in concentration camp experiments was 350 — that is one out of every 300 members of the German medical profession.[12]

A mixture of personal curiosity, general interest and cruelty was the hallmark of these doctors, and the last named aspect was predominant. There were doctors who from the outset had performed their experiments in a cruel manner and had never shown the smallest consideration for the prisoners, and there were also those who had demonstrated a lifelong respect for the ethical norms for medical tests only to cast them aside during the war. A good example of such a doctor is Klaus Schilling .

In 1898, at the age of twenty-seven, this specialist in tropical diseases and professor of parasitology in the faculty of medicine at Berlin University, began his life's work: the search for a vaccine against malaria. He secured international respect as an accomplished scientist and was selected from a long list of candidates as the director of the Malaria Commission of the League of Nations. In the years before the war he had been given financial backing for this research by the Rockefeller foundation, and by the Kahn foundation in Paris. When he retired in 1936, his research had made but little progress. One of the reasons was a chronic lack of human test-subjects. The days of Ronald Ross and Giovanni Battista Grassi, the two great malaria pioneers who experimented on themselves in their endeavours to fathom the secrets of the disease, were long gone.

Schilling needed healthy human subjects, but who in the 1930's would have volunteered for such experiments? Who would have risked being infected with the dreaded disease so that doctors could test various medicines?

In 1942 he was put in touch with Himmler, who recruited him to do research at Dachau into the possibilities of immunizing the human body against malaria. The Germans too had a malaria problem. Hundreds of German soldiers in Africa lay in improvised field hospitals and the army officers were desperate. Himmler's appeal pleased Schilling and he leapt at the offer; he was after all seventy-three and time was no longer on his side. Besides, this was a unique opportunity to put a crown on his life's work. That he would have to work in a concentration camp did not trouble him in the slightest. Nobody would later demand *how* a particular result had been obtained, since it would be considered much more important *that* it had been obtained. Such must have been Schilling's thoughts when he took up his post in the Dachau concentration camp in the summer of 1942. By the end of the war he had subjected 1,000-1,100 prisoners to malaria tests. There was no question of voluntary co-operation. The majority of his human guinea pigs were Polish clergymen aged between twenty and forty-five years.

Dr Eugène Ost from Luxemburg, who was the prisoner-Schreiber (recorder) at the malaria establishment in Blocks 1 and 3, secretly compiled a list from notes taken by him out of

Dachau Museum

Klaus Schilling

filing cabinets destroyed before the camp was liberated and from this, it emerges that Schilling's experiments were directly responsible for the death of ten prisoners, the other subjects who died being victims of other diseases.[13] There can be no doubt about the nature of the tests that took place; the Dachau trial in November 1945 incontestably proved their criminality.

Schilling himself selected his subjects from among the prisoners chosen by the *Arbeitseinsatz*. He was assisted by an SS doctor, at first Dr Bracht and then SS Hauptsturmführer Dr Kurt Plötner. But Plötner later returned to his post as camp doctor. In 1960 a juridicial inquiry was held into Plötner's past. There was, however, not enough evidence to bring charges against him. Exactly twelve years later the case was reopened, but again grounds were insufficient to justify pursuing it.

Nevertheless, it is interesting to note that the German Ministry of Justice refused to state why the grounds were insufficient.[14] Plötner himself had no comment to make to the author.

What actually happened in a malaria experiment?

The Polish priest Leo Michialowsky:

> 'I was a subject of the malaria — and high-altitude experiments. As for the malaria experiments, I can tell you this. One day thirty prisoners, myself included, were picked out to do 'easier work'. Instead of that they brought us to the camp hospital where we had to undress and where X-rays were made. For two days, I had a little box containing mosquitoes fixed to my hand so I would be stung. Only five weeks later did this become clear because I started showing the first signs of malaria. I was given Néosalvarsan and quinine injections. I felt as if my heart was being torn in two. I went crazy and could not utter a word . . . . I was given injections again and again and when, after eight days, I could speak again I told the nurse that I didn't want any more of them. Then Dr Plötner came; he examined me and gave me two pills for the dreadful pain in my head and kidneys. Just before he left he instructed the nurse to give me the rest of the injections. I refused, to which he retorted,
> "I am responsible for your health and future. You aren't." Then I was given the injections. Soon after I was shuddering with fever . . . .'[15]

Schilling treated hundreds of prisoners in this way. He infected them with malaria and tested various substances for their medical properties. Several prisoners died as a result of these tests but during later hearings Schilling refused to recognize this fact. He then delegated his responsibility to Himmler, admitted that it would have been dangerous for the prisoners to disobey his order (which, according to him were 'requests'), and emphasized the nobility of the goal towards which his tests had been directed.

> 'When the prisoners came to you, were they told that they were free not to take part in these tests?'
> 'No.'

'Did you know that the prisoners at Dachau were obliged to obey orders from superiors?'

'I presume that this was the case in every concentration camp.'

'The camp administration supplied you with test persons. Did you just take them and begin your tests?'

'Yes.'

'Suppose that you had refused Himmler's orders to perform the experiments, what would have been the result?'

'I would probably have been sent to a concentration camp myself.'

'What would have happened to prisoners refusing to take part in your experiments?'

'They would have been punished.'

'Had you, before you came to Dachau, ever performed experiments on people?'

'Yes, on mentally retarded people in an institution. In those days I also experimented on fourteen or fifteen German students from Berlin who voluntarily put themselves at my disposal.'

'Were you aware of the nationality of the test persons?'

'No, I would have needed an interpreter for that.'

'Did you know that you experimented on Polish priests?'

'Polish priests? I didn't know. I can only tell you that I did what I was told .... .'

'Dr Schilling, a large number of prisoners refused to take part in your work and protested .... .'

'There were only three or four. I explained to them exactly what I was going to do and promised that nothing would befall them.'

'Now, how could you give such guarantees?'

'As for that, I can tell you that we cured about one hundred percent within two or three months. The most effective method was to give them two five-day courses of atebrine with a rest period of ten days in between, the drug in a dose of three grammes per day. After this cure there was another cure using atebrine .... .'

'Were there deaths as a result of these experiments?'

'I don't know . . . that is to say . . . prisoners died, but not of malaria. These people died of lung infections or of TB. I have here a list which gives the causes of death in these cases.'

'Something else now, do you believe in God?'

'Yes, I believe in God.'

'Did you, upon qualifying, take the Hippocratic oath?'

'No, I didn't.'

'Is it not true Doctor, that one should not experiment upon a person without his consent unless there is a risk of death which an experiment might avert?'

'Yes, that is well known.'

'But, that is what you did. Why?'

'Because I wanted to develop a method whereby the lives of millions of people could be saved . . . that is the only reason.'

'So, only the final results mattered?'

'Yes, and nothing else!'[16]

Nevertheless Schilling was condemned to death. Before his execution he wrote a letter to the President of the United States in which he appealed against his sentence on the grounds that he should be allowed to continue his research 'which was almost finished'. This appeal was refused. Schilling was hanged at Dachau.

At the same time a huge trial was opening in Krakow against the personnel of the Auschwitz concentration camp. Amongst the defendants was the former SS doctor and head of the Hygiene-Institute of the camp, Dr Hans Wilhelm Münch.[17] Of the defendants in the dock he was the only one who had adhered to the principles of medical ethics throughout his period of service at Auschwitz and who had clearly not given way to the unrestrained brutality towards the prisoners. Whenever it was possible he had tried to improve the prisoner's conditions and, as a doctor, had treated rather than maltreated them.[18] The former prisoner Alfred Fiderkiewicz:

'The camp physician Thilo had a nervous

breakdown, though it was said that he was on leave. His place was taken by Dr Hans Münch from Rasjko and he behaved with extraordinary decency but could offer no help in anything. When he asked me one day how I treated my cases I answered: '*Mit Sonne und Luft*' (with sun and air), as I had no medicines. He looked at our pneumothorax apparatus and left. Our work with him was most pleasant as he relied on our diagnoses . . . .'[19]

Münch's case contrasted strongly with those of his co-defendants who were, one by one, accused of the most gruesome crimes. He was, accordingly, the only defendant whose demeanour during the war ensured his acquittal by the tribunal.

He was also the only defendant to speak forthrightly of the terrible things that happened at Auschwitz-Birkenau. However, during his frequent visits to Germany during the war he carefully avoided talking about his work at Auschwitz.

That subject was taboo. Münch:

'It would have been useless to attempt talking about Auschwitz. The Gestapo would have picked me up together with my family and have liquidated us; they were so well organized, and the warnings, sent to all SS members, to keep secret anything to do with the human destruction at Auschwitz were so clearly formulated that everyone avoided the subject, even with their closest friends. Experience soon taught us that anyone who did speak out in any way was soon discovered . . . .'[20]

After his acquittal in Poland, Münch returned to Germany and opened a general practice in a small village in Bavaria. Unlike Plötner, he was not reluctant to talk about the past with the author:

'Your most important question, why I ever went to work in Auschwitz but nevertheless took no part in the Nazi practices, is actually quite simple to answer. I come from a family of natural scientists and doctors. My upbringing was tolerant, without religious or ideological leanings. One of my best friends at school was a Jew. My relationship with the Nazi party and ideology was really limited to a membership dating from 1937. Every young man in Germany who wanted to build a career was obliged to do that. I ended up at Auschwitz, not as a qualified Nazi-doctor, but as a physician with experience in bacteriology and epidemiology. My SS career, that is to say, the Waffen SS, was actually rather unusual.

In 1939, I was twenty-eight, I had not yet performed my national service and my chances of being called were substantial. In fact, as a younger man I had wanted to do my national service but, in the preceding two years, all sorts of circumstances had prevented me. I applied several times and only in 1942 did I have any success. The Waffen SS was prepared to accept me, the only reason being that, in my application, I had not stated any special preferences; I would be happy with any army Division. So I ended up in Waffen SS and after a short military training, eight weeks, I was called to the Waffen SS Hygiene-Institute where I ran into a former colleague, Bruno Weber.[21] We had worked together at the Hygiene-Institute in Munich in 1937 and 1938. I noticed that Weber was pleased to see me again. He was head of the South-East Hygiene-Institute of the Waffen SS, which was responsible for the medical activities at Auschwitz-Birkenau.

I had never heard of Auschwitz and when Weber asked me if I wanted to work there, I raised no objections. Weber was just as apathetic a Nazi as I was and supported my exertions not to take part in inhuman activities.[22] However, I could not shirk my ordinary duties in the camp. It wasn't always easy to withdraw one's co-operation, but on the other hand it wasn't so difficult as people usually suppose either. The best example I can give you, and you mentioned him just now, was Dr Caesar. He was an SS führer who sincerely and, moreover, officially resisted the way things were done at Auschwitz. He went to Himmler and said: 'If there is no way to leave there

(Auschwitz) then I want my own camp, a camp for which I alone am responsible'.

He got it and worked there from 1941 until the end of the war. (Dr Joachim Caesar was the manager of the agricultural enterprises connected with the concentration camp Auschwitz and the prisoners who came into his care enjoyed excellent treatment: author).

'There was another doctor who did not agree with the working methods used at Auschwitz: Dr Delmotte, a young doctor who had come straight from university. He too resisted the Auschwitz methods and did not succumb to the ideological pressure put on him by older officers.[23] After the war he committed suicide. These two people are actually more interesting than myself. Dr Delmotte's name cannot be found in the Auschwitz literature and the same goes for Dr Caesar. No tribunal was willing to decorate them for their services. No one who saw it, and this applies both to prisoners and to members of the SS, could describe Auschwitz as it was ... as it actually was. We will have to be content with collecting facts, and as you will no doubt have discovered, it's a difficult business. In times to come, people will regard these facts in a clearer light, just as we now regard historical events from our own viewpoint ... .'

Collection Author

Auschwitz-Birkenau Concentration Camp

1

Himmler and his SS

'In the public imagination Himmler is a real and
terrible figure, a cold-blooded inhuman ogre ruthlessly
exterminating millions of helpless prisoners by every
refinement of sadistic torture; not a man, but an
impersonal abstraction, a creature to whom the
weaknesses of pity and forgiveness are unknown; an
inexplorable monster whose cold and malignant rage
no prayers, no human sacrifices can ever for one
moment appease,'[1]

wrote Professor Trevor-Roper in his study of the last days of
the Third Reich.

Given the large amount of available source material, it might
be thought no hard task to analyse Himmler's character, but
perhaps it is in fact difficult for this very reason: a plethora of
details makes it difficult to draw a clear picture. Many Nazi
chiefs made use of their time in prison to write memoirs, albeit
often just to plead for their freedom. One of the few exceptions
in this respect is Hitler's former architect and minister of
Armaments, Albert Speer.

Trevor-Roper:

'His (Speer's) conclusions are never naive, never
parochial; they seem always honest; they are often
profound. If he seems sometimes to have fallen too
deeply under the spell of the tyrant whom he served,
at least he retained the capacity to examine himself
and the honesty to declare both his errors and his
convictions.'[2]

'It is true', wrote Speer in his memoirs, 'that the

31

Reichsführer SS (Himmler) sometimes seemed to be a visionary whose intellectual flights struck even Hitler as ridiculous. But Himmler was also a sober-minded realist who knew exactly what his long-term political aims were. In our discussions, he displayed a friendly courtesy that seemed slightly forced and never cordial. And he always made a point of having a witness from his staff present. He had the patience to listen to his visitor's arguments — a gift rare in those days. In the discussions, he often seemed petty and pedantic and had apparently thought out beforehand everything he wanted to say. He was obviously not concerned with the impression this made. His office worked with the precision of a well oiled machine, which was probably an expression of his own impersonality'.[3]

Himmler is usually regarded as the great ideologist of the Third Reich, but to what extent was he taken seriously? Speer:

'Hitler had little sympathy with Himmler in his mythologizing of the SS. "What nonsense!", he said. "Here we have at least reached an age that has left all mysticism behind it, and now he wants to start all over again. We might just as well have stayed within the church. At least it had tradition. To think that I may be turned into an SS saint. Can you imagine it? I would turn in my grave." '[4]

Speer had this to say about Himmler's ideological obsession:

'Himmler was going his own absurd way, which was compounded of beliefs about an original German race, a brand of élitism, and an assortment of cranky health-food notions. The whole thing was beginning to assume far-fetched and pseudo-religious forms. Goebbels, with Hitler, took the lead in ridiculing these dreams of Himmler's, with Himmler himself adding to the comedy by his vanity and obsessiveness. When, for example, the Japanese presented him with a samurai sword, he at once discovered kinships between Japanese and Teutonic cults and called upon scientists to help him trace the similarities to a common racial denominator.'[5]

A more palpable image is drawn by the Swedish Count Folke Bernadotte who on behalf of the Red Cross, negotiated the release of prisoners with Himmler in 1945;

'When he suddenly appeared before me he looked most of all like some unimportant functionary. Had you met him in the street, you would never have paid him any heed. He had small delicate hands. I found them well manicured considering that this was forbidden within the SS. He behaved startlingly civilly (. . .) Of the cold hard gaze, of which I had heard so much, I could see nothing. Heinrich Himmler behaved, during the interviews, as a very ordinary man. It was a singular experience to hear this man, who had by means of the most scandalous schemes sent millions to their death, speak warmly of the "gentlemanly" warfare between the English and the Germans in France in the summer of 1944, when hostilities were broken off at their height to allow both parties the opportunity to tend to their wounded. I can only say that Himmler had the most complicated nature I have ever met.'[6]

Professor Karl Gebhardt, one of Himmler's few close friends, they had grown up together, stated during the medical trial:

'Himmler considered himself to be the General of an order which knew only one law: Adolf Hitler. Though he wanted to camouflage it, he made no secret of the fact that his orders came directly from Hitler. For Himmler the state was the highest good, to which the individual was entirely subordinated . . . .'[7]

Finally, and again in the words of Albert Speer, this time addressing himself to the author:

'It is extremely difficult to come to an agreement about the character of Heinrich Himmler. He was

National Archives

Heinrich Himmler

taciturn and, all in all, a reticent type. Everyone was frightened of him, because they all appreciated the power of the dossiers that he had had prepared on practically everybody. Who had no guilty conscience? Who could safely assert that they had nothing at all to fear from Gestapo?'

Heinrich Himmler was born on 7 October 1900 into a Bavarian family and was raised in an orthodox, middle-class environment. His father was a well-placed and well-respected schoolmaster in Munich. He was a studious, pedantic man, very conscious of the social prestige he had gained from the patronage of the Bavarian household of Wittelsbach. For when he had finished his education at the University of Munich where he had studied philology and languages, he had been appointed tutor to Prince Heinrich of Bavaria, after whom he had named his son. By the time he was seventeen Heinrich had but one aim: a career in the armed forces. He had to wait until 1917 before he could volunteer but the budding soldier would never see the front. The First World War came to an end and Himmler was forced to suppress his ambitions to wear uniform for a while. This was a great disappointment for the boy who had dreamed of being a second Frederick the Great. His carefully-kept diary speaks for itself. 19 February 1922:

'If only there were battle again, war, advances . . .
11 June 1922: Maybe I'll get into the services somehow or other. For in my heart I am a soldier. But first I must do my exams . . . .'[9]

Himmler had by now entered the Technical High School of the University of Munich. The decision to study agriculture had been taken at his father's suggestion, which in turn had been prompted by his observations of the boy's interest in collecting botanical books and laying out a plant garden. In this way Himmler found himself in the turbulent student world of Munich, where he got himself a managerial post at the student club *Apollo*. Nevertheless, he remained an eccentric, for in the obligatory duelling and drinking he took no part. The first was forbidden by the church and the second by his health.

However, we see him break slowly with his religious beliefs.

Although on 15 December 1919 he had written in his diary:

> 'Come what may I shall love God, pray to him,
> remain loyal to the Catholic church, and even remain
> in its defence should it ever reject me.'[10]

Less than four years later he had broken with the church.
Faith had given away to another reality: politics.

It must have been during his student days that he came under
the influence of Ernst Röhm, the head of the SA (Assault
Sections). The *Sturmabteilungen* were set up in 1921 for political
ends and had a paramilitary organization. At that time the SA
was the strong arm of the NSDAP and was also entrusted with
propagation of nationalist socialist views. The military character
of the SA must have been especially fascinating to Himmler.

It was Röhm who introduced this young student to the political
arena, though his pupil still gave much of his time to study and
amusement.

In 1922 Himmler graduated and got a job as a laboratory
assistant on the staff of a firm in Schleissheim specializing in
the development of fertilizers. Schleissheim was barely fifteen
miles north of Munich and this meant that Himmler did not
lose touch with the centre where Hitler was breeding his own
particular form of nationalism which already led to the formation
of the Nationalist Socialist party.

Himmler found little joy in the work, and as time went on
his interests came to centre more and more around politics.
Eventually he resigned, and took on a full-time position within
the NSDAP. Röhm made him the party courier and Himmler
rode a Swedish motorcycle from village to village, spreading
the National Socialist gospel. Gradually he came under Hitler's
spell, and in 1925 the latter made him responsible for the
Schutzstaffeln (Protection Squads). The SS, an élite within the
SA, had been formed on the pretext of the necessity to protect
Party leaders and to take immediate counter-action if there was
any show of violence.

The SS at this time was, in fact, little more than a platoon
which, despite its special duties, was subordinate to the SA.
Himmler had only about 200 men at his disposal but he gave
himself completely to the cause of Nazism. After Hitler's rise
to power, another task was soon added, *i.e.* that of keeping an

eye on Röhm's SA. The greatly inflated ranks of the SA, about 100,000 men by 1930, rising to around three million by 1933-1934, were necessary at this stage to give the party its shock-troops among the voters and to put up a formidable front against the Communists on the streets. But Hitler was well aware of the danger he was in from his own SA forces. They could only too easily get out of hand. In the end a clash between the SA and the party was unavoidable. In 1934 the contest was decided.

In the so-called 'Night of the Long Knives' the leaders of the SA were murdered on Hitler's orders, and from then onwards the SS enjoyed the monopoly.

With inextinguishable zeal, Heinrich Himmler, Reichsführer SS, expanded his army. At the outbreak of the war the SS was a crack corps, organized on military lines, with about a quarter of a million members. Himmler left no doubt about its aims and the methods that were to be used:

> 'I know that there are some people in Germany who feel sick when they see the black uniforms; we understand the reason for this and do not expect to be loved by all; those who come to fear us in any way or at any time, must have a bad conscience concerning the Führer and the nation. For these persons we have established an organization called the Security Service.
>
> Without pity we shall wield the sword of justice. Each one of us knows he does not stand alone, but that this tremendous force of men, who are bound together by oath, gives him immeasurable strength. We assemble and march according to unalterable laws as a National Socialist military order of predominantly Nordic men, and as a sworn community on our way to a far future . . . ancestors of later generations, and necessary for the eternal life of the Germanic people. Only good blood, Nordic blood can be considered. I said to myself that should I succeed in selecting as many men from the German people, a majority of whom possesses this valued blood, and teach them military discipline and in time, the understanding of the value of blood and the entire ideology that results from it, then it will be possible to create such an élite

organization which will successfully hold its own in all cases of emergency (. . .). We are more valuable than the others who do now, and always will, surpass us in numbers. We are more valuable because our blood enables us to invent more than others, to lead our people better than others. Let us clearly realize, the next decades will involve a struggle leading to the extermination of the subhuman opponents in the whole world who fight Germany, the basic people of the Northern race, bearer of the culture of mankind . . . .'

The Reichsführer was a consistent man. He held up his own life as an example to his followers of the attitude he expected of them. The core of the philosophy underlying his lectures was not 'What am I doing?' but 'What do I have to do?'

Himmler formulated his thoughts in a striking manner in the famous meeting of his SS Major-Generals at Posen on 4 October 1943:

'Thinking in terms of generations, it need not be regretted; but in terms of the here and now it is deplorable because of the loss of labour — that prisoners died in tens and hundreds of thousands from exhaustion and hunger. We must be honest, decent, loyal and comradely to members of our own blood, but to nobody else. What happens to a Russian or to a Czech, does not interest me in the slightest. What the nations can offer in the way of good blood of our type, we will take, if necessary by kidnapping their children and raising them here among us.

Whether nations live in prosperity or starve to death interests me only in so far as we need them for slaves for our "*Kultur*"; otherwise, it is of no interest to me. Whether 10,000 Russian females fall down from exhaustion digging an anti-tank ditch interests me only in so far as the anti-tank ditch for Germany is finished . . . . It is a crime against our own blood to worry about them and give them ideals, thus causing our sons and grandsons to have a more difficult time with them. When somebody comes to me and says:

"I cannot dig the anti-tank ditch using women and children, it is inhuman because it will kill them," then I must reply: You are a murderer of your own blood, because if the anti-tank ditch is not dug, German soldiers will die and they are the sons of German mothers. They are our own blood. That is what I want to instill in to the SS and what I believe I have instilled into them as one of the most sacred laws of all foreign, non-Germanic peoples .... .'[12]

The moral principle was simple. There were people, superior beings with good or pure blood and there were inferior beings in human form but of unsound composition, genetically undesirable elements of the species. In the same speech Himmler continued:

'Among ourselves it should be mentioned quite frankly, but we will never speak of it publicly, just as we did not hesitate on 30 June 1934 to do what we were told to do and put up against the wall those comrades who had been backsliding (who had failed) and shoot them, and we have never spoken about it, likewise we will never speak of this .... . I mean the cleaning out of the Jews, the extermination of the Jewish race. It is one of those things one can easily talk about .... . The Jewish race is being exterminated ... it is our programme, and we're doing it. And then there are these eighty million Germans, and each one of them knows this one decent Jew. Of course the others are vermin, but this particular Jew is a first-rate man .... . Most of you must know what it means when a hundred corpses are lying side by side, or five hundred or a thousand.

To have persevered and at the same time, apart from exceptions cause by human weakness, to have remained fellows, that is what has made us so hard. This is one of the glorious pages in our history that has never been written and will never be written ... . We are a product of the law of selection. We have made our choice from a cross-section of our people. This people came into being aeons ago, through generations and centuries . . . .

Alien peoples have swept over this people and left their heritage behind them . . . but it has . . . still has the strength in the very essence of its blood to win through. This whole people is held together by Nordic-Phalian-Germanic blood (. . .). We must remember our principle: blood, selection, austerity.' [13]

Still, Himmler himself turned out to be a victim of the human weakness he so despised. In 1941 he attended a mass execution in East Poland at the end of which he had to vomit. After this his tour was cancelled.[14]

He literally idolized Hitler; his devotion was religious. His Finnish masseur, Felix Kersten, tells us:

'If Hitler had ordered him to hang himself at the stroke of twelve, he would have done so, and right on time. If I had been there and asked him why, he would have answered: "You have no right to ask that sort of question. The Führer's will is the highest law; if he gives me an order, he knows what for. My only duty is to follow the order to the letter". He would probably have added "Heil Hitler" as he put his head through the noose.'[15]

Himmler was no doubt convinced that Hitler could depend on him more than on anyone else, but this does not justify Kersten's amusing hypothesis. Ideologically he was aligned with Hitler, but this itself made him no willing tool. Himmler radicalized the ideology, no more. Speer too exaggerates when he says that Hitler poked fun at Himmler's ideas, for many sources agree that Hitler cherished a deep affection for his Reichsführer. Of course, Hitler made the odd joke about the Reichsführer's aspirations, but this was reciprocal. Unless they came from Goebbels or Bormann, Hitler would not allow Himmler to be made fun of; even these two were expected to keep their quasi-jocular comments to a minimum. So did Himmler actually invite ridicule? Perhaps. One of his SS divisions consisted of a team of skilled colleagues engaged in the 'momentous' study of Rosicrucianism, Freemasonry, the symbolism of the suppression of the Ulster Harp, and the occult significance of Gothic pinnacles and Eton top-hats.

The SS scientific laboratories laboured in vain to isolate 'pure' Aryan blood. An explorer was sent to Tibet to discover traces of supposed pure Germanic race, believed to preserve the ancient Nordic mysteries in those inaccessible mountains. As late as April 1945, when the Reich lay in ruins, Himmler was contemplating the colonization of the Ukraine with a new religious sect.[16]

> 'Himmler was an elementary believer',[17] Trevor-Roper states. It all invited hilarity which everyone was careful to conceal; Himmler wielded terrible power and in his heart there dwelled a cynical '*Realpolitik*'.

'Work is my passion' read Himmler's motto, and it suited him. The Reichsführer carried out his work from three headquarters, Berlin, Hochwald and a fourteen-wagon train, the '*Sonderzug Heinrich*', later renamed the '*Sonderzug Steiermark*'. Behind Himmler the bureaucrat stood Himmler the scholar, well-read and well informed in German and Indo-German culture. Notions such as 'culture', 'people' and 'race' had a magical effect on him. Deeply absorbed in the subject, he was convinced that it would be possible to breed a German super-race of the purest kind. The racially pure stock lay ready to hand; only 100 per cent Aryans were admitted to the SS, and they needed permission from SS command to get married. For that matter, Himmler considered marriage a fiendish invention of the Roman Catholic church; the husband was compelled in advance to be unfaithful since men found it difficult to share their whole lives with one woman only. Many marriages remained childless for reasons of incompatibility and Himmler saw this as a danger to the nation, and judged that the state had the right to intervene in a couple's life at this point. To give form to these ideas, though participation was voluntary at this time, he set up the Lebensborn project. Himmler:

> 'Beyond the boundaries of bourgeois laws and customs which may in themselves be necessary, it will now become the great task, even outside the marriage bond, for German women and girls of good blood, not in frivolity but in deep moral earnestness, to become

mothers of the children of soldiers going to war . . . .'[18]

The Lebensborn project offered selected SS men as prospective sires to those women whose husbands were sterile. Selection procedure for this SS breeding élite was strict; a medical test, racial purity, loyalty to the Reichsführer, and at least the Iron Cross first class. Lebensborn had at its disposal large and well-equipped maternity clinics where women could give birth anonymously. Mother Crosses were given to SS wives who had given birth to seven or more children and special leave was to be given to married SS men to encourage procreation. In his conduct of the Lebensborn movement, Himmler's racial obsessions combined with his genetic fantasies and reflected the strange humanitarianism that always lurked in Himmler's nature and which he satisfied through his relations with children, beginning with his own and extending to his nation-wide family of god-children.

In Himmler's eyes, children of sound racial background should be rescued from parents who for political or other reasons were undesirable, and placed in the rehabilitation centre of a Lebensborn home. Public reaction to Lebensborn was often critical. Because the homes were full of unmarried mothers many people thought they were brothels set up for the SS. The church, in particular, opposed the homes.

In May 1944 Himmler spoke informally about the Lebensborn movement and the attacks that had been made upon it, and on himself for advising his SS men to procreate:

> 'At first these Lebensborn homes, like every new idea, became the object of scandalmongers by the score. They called them breeding ground, human stud farms and so on. In fact, in these homes we merely look after mothers and children, some of them legitimate, some not. I would say the ratio is about fifty-fifty, more likely sixty-forty in favour of the legitimately born babies. In these homes every woman is addressed as Frau Marta, or Frau Elisabeth, or whatever her name happens to be. No one bothers whether their babies are legitimate or illegitimate. We look after mother and child, protect them, help them in their problems. In these homes, there is only one

thing unforgivable: if a mother fails to care for her child as a mother should. Towards the end of 1939, as soon as we knew that there would be war in the West, I issued an order which, at the same time, caused quite a controversy and got the scandalmongers going again with loads of abuse, directed largely at me. That order simply said: before going to the front, every SS man should procreate. This seemed a thoroughly simple and decent order to me, and by now, after many years of terrible losses sustained by the German people, those who failed to understand my order at the time will have come to see that it makes sense. After all, I gave these matters a great deal of careful thought. I simply reasoned as follows: it's a law of nature that the most valuable blood will be lost to the nation if there are no children. It stands to reason that the man who is racially the most valuable will be the bravest soldier, and the one most likely to be killed in action. A nation which, in the course of twenty-five years has lost millions of its best sons, simply cannot afford such a loss of its blood; hence if the nation is to survive, and if the sacrifice of its best blood is not to be wasted, something has to be done about it . . . .'

Reinhard Tristan Eugen Heydrich was born on 7 March 1907 in Halle an der Saale. His father was the director of a music school and Reinhard, a talented violinist, stood at the brink of a brilliant career in music. Then came the crisis of 1929; the German economy was in deep trouble. For the sake of security Reinhard chose a career in the Navy. However he was dishonourably discharged because he had seduced and jilted the daughter of a prominent industrialist who had the ear of Grand Admiral Raeder. In 1931 Himmler was approached by one of his officers, the Freiherr von Eberstein, with a request that he interview a young man who had recently joined the SS in Hamburg. His name was Reinhard Heydrich; he was of good family and had, until recently, been a lieutenant in the Navy. Heydrich was a godson of Eberstein's mother. Himmler agreed and the first meeting between these two men whose strange relationship was to constitute the direct threat to the well-being of Europe after its conquest by Hitler, took place on 4 June 1931. Himmler understood that Heydrich had been a Naval Intelligence officer, and he had a particularly important task in mind which he felt might be carried out by a man with this kind of training and background. Heydrich gave Himmler a detailed picture of how he thought an efficient espionage ring ought to operate. The Reichsführer was impressed enough to decide to appoint the ex-naval officer to the task of creating an Intelligence or security service within the SS to conduct secret research into those members of the party, particularly among the leaders of the SA, whose ambitions seemed hostile to the SS. It turned out to be an excellent choice; besides being a devoted National Socialist, Heydrich showed himself to be a skilled organizer. Within a few years he had set up one of the most dreaded instruments of fear in Nazidom; the *Sicherheitsdienst* or SD. Furthermore, in 1936 he was given command of the *Geheime Staatspolizei*, the Gestapo.

It was not Himmler but Heydrich who created the efficient machine for the deportation and extermination of whole peoples and in so doing became the perpetrator of genocide. It is difficult to overrate Heydrich's significance.

> 'More intelligent by far than Himmler, he (Heydrich) was the chief exponent of the *Endlösung*, the first diabolical mass-murder in European history, whose murders were but the means to the glorification of an end. His rule meant life or death, independent of any legislator. Heydrich's power reached out far beyond the borders of Germany, and his organization carried out Hitler's, Himmler's and his own secret orders most co-operatively. His empire was a dark one, hidden, murky, and armed with an unaccountable and uncontrolled authority . . . .'[20]

He hated Jews even more than Himmler did, which might, interestingly, have been the result of his own background;[21] it was said that he was partly Jewish himself and this would certainly throw light on his pathological anti-semitism. Heydrich himself had endeavoured to destroy all the evidence which pointed to the fact that his maternal grandmother was Jewish. Nonetheless he was forced to take legal action against various individuals on the ground that they were slandering him. The effect of all this was that he became schizophrenic. The historian Graber:

> 'On the one hand he was extremely ambitious, cruel and vain. On the other, he was driven by self-hatred, induced by the knowledge that his blood was impure. In exterminating the Jews, therefore, Heydrich was eradicating in himself that aspect of his make-up which he found most repellent.'[22]

Nevertheless he formed the classic example of the Aryan type: tall, slim, blond and blue-eyed. Those who crossed his path saw a retiring, reticent official, whose power they would never have suspected. Heydrich had an aversion to publicity, but thanks to his untiring efforts to avoid it, he made himself conspicuous.

> 'This handsome, refined and courageous man did not have a single friend. Heydrich's work, and the aura it might have imparted to him, are really insufficient explanation. Other high-placed Gestapo officers, who specialized in the most inhuman activities — for example Müller, chief of the department responsible for arrests and interrogations, who was a notorious torture specialist — had friends with whom they shared their joys and troubles. Heydrich had chosen loneliness. People were interesting to him in so far as they were useful to his work and to his career. Otherwise he ignored them. He only lived for his glory. Any one who had anything to do with him was frightened off by his character and behaviour.'[23]

The Nuremberg tribunal said about his organization, the SD:

> 'Mankind shall not quickly forget the revolting story of these wretched murderers, whose own stomachs turned over at the horrible sight when the doors of the death-wagons were opened next to the graves. These were the same men who, sitting on the edge of anti-tank ditches with cigarettes in their mouths, coolly shot their victims in the neck with automatic pistols. These

were the men who, according to their own
bookkeepers, murdered two million men, women and
children. These were the men of the SD ... .'[24]

Himmler's pupil grew slowly but surely in influence and his
aspirations went further than the Reichsführer liked. At whatever
Heydrich turned to, he found it necessary to excel. In many
ways he succeeded. A man of this type would never accept being
number two, and it is not too far-fetched to claim that he
considered himself Hitler's logical successor.

At the beginning of 1942 he deemed the time ripe for solving
the 'Jewish question' once and for all. The issue was discussed
on 20 January in the country-house district of Berlin, the
Wannsee. Heydrich chaired the meeting and did most of the
talking to the thirteen persons present, who represented both
State and party-apparatus. On this wintery day, the fate of
millions of Jews was decided. The *Endlösung*, or final solution,
became a reality. Heydrich had reckoned that eleven million
Jews would have to be exterminated. Adolf Eichmann took
minutes of the meeting and, after the visitors had left, enjoyed
the special privilege of remaining with Heydrich and Gestapo-
Müller for further informal chats, recalled during his trial:

'I remember well how, after the so-called Wannsee
conference, we gathered around the hearth for a while,
Heydrich, Müller and myself ... not to talk of
business, but to relax a little after those tiring hours.
I remember too, that was the first time I had ever seen
Heydrich smoking ... and I thought: "Hello,
Heydrich is smoking, I've never seen that before."
And he drank alcohol, which I hadn't seen him do
in years, as he usually never indulged in alcoholic
drinks ... .'[25]

Thus, in this genial and informal atmosphere, the procedure
of the extermination was settled and 'the Satanic programme
could begin'.[26]

Under the inspiring leadership of the SS and the SD, Jews
were herded together and deported eastwards to the gas
chambers. Heydrich was an example to his troops, and behaved
with indescribable cruelty to the Jews in Bohemia and Moravia.

The Czech government-in-exile in London decided to get rid of him, and on 27 May 1942, they made an attempt on Heydrich's life.

Mortally wounded, he was taken to the City Hospital in Bullouka where Czech surgeons removed dozens of pieces of shrapnel from his body.

Consternation ran high in Berlin. On Hitler's orders, the cream of the German medical world was immediately flown to Bullouka to do all that could be done. Responsibility for this operation fell to Professor Karl Gebhardt; on his shoulders rested the heavy task of saving Heydrich's life. He recalled:

> 'I arrived too late. The operation had already been carried out by two leading surgeons. All I could do was to supervise subsequent treatment. Naturally, in the extraordinary excitement and nervous tension which prevailed, and which was not diminished by daily personal telephone calls from Hitler and Himmler asking for information, a great many suggestions were made; I was practically ordered to call in my own teacher and Morell, who wanted to intervene in his own fashion with his own remedies. I refused. The two gentlemen from Prague had already operated, they had done a first-rate job of the operation and had also administered sulphonamide. I think that if anything endangers a patient it is nervous tension at the bedside and the appearance of too many doctors getting in each other's way. I refused, in reply to direct demands, to call in any other doctor, not even Morell. Heydrich died within fourteen days ... .'[27]

'A catastrophe for the country, equal to the loss of two divisions'[28] ran Hitler's first reaction. He summoned the erring Gebhardt to Berlin to account for his non-compliance, but at the last moment refused to see him and sent him to Himmler instead. Hitler's doctor Morell had suggested to the Führer that had his own sulphonamide preparations been used, Heydrich might have stood a better chance. This brought Gebhardt into disrepute, for which he saw one remedy: rehabilitation. To this end he appealed to Himmler for permission to perform a series of experiments concerning the therapeutic effect of sulphonamides. At the same time these experiments lay within a wider framework. German soldiers at the front frequently fell victim to wound infections, and whether these soldiers should be treated with medicines alone, surgery alone or with a combination was still a debatable issue in the German Medical World.

In 1933 Himmler gave orders for an organization to be established whose goal would be the determination of the origins, the spirit, the exploits and the heritage of the Aryan race. It would also have to inform the public of the results of this research in an interesting way.

This *Ahnenerbe* (Ancestral Heritage Community) turned away from it's original task within a short time and became a scientific research centre particularly involved with medical research in the concentration camps. The *Ahnenerbe* financed the experiments, supplied the necessary materials or arranged their supply.

The guidance of this society was entrusted to the ex-bookdealer Wolfram Sievers, who attested at Nuremberg that the *Ahnenerbe* contained no less than forty-six scientific departments and fifteen research commissions. The thirty professors who Sievers claimed were also on its wage sheet would never be exposed, as all the *Ahnenerbe* archives were destroyed shortly before Germany capitulated. In any event, it can incontestably be established that the part the *Ahnenerbe* played in the experimentation was hardly as trivial as Sievers would have liked the court to believe.

In Nuremberg, he claimed in mitigation that he had always acted on orders only and moreover, that, he had been a member of a resistance group which had at some time professed the wish to see Hitler and Himmler brought down. The court waived these excuses and condemned him to death.

> 'If we suppose that these claims were founded in truth, we still would not know to what extent they comprised a defence. For it remains a fact that with the collaboration of the *Ahnenerbe*, thousands of unprotected concentration camp prisoners, who had not the slightest chance of defence, were murdered.

And Sievers led the programme on which grounds the murders were committed.'[29]

Large number of doctors and professors performed experiments on people in the last three years of the war under instructions from the *Ahnenerbe*. 'Tests which had not scientific worth whatsoever'[30] according to Desoille and Lafitte.

Prosecutor Taylor also confirmed this during his opening address in Nuremberg:

'The tests were not only criminal but also, from the scientific point of view, incompetent.'[31]

In the years before the war, German doctors were bombarded with Nazi ideology. In 1935 Dr Arthur Gütt, director of the Department of Public Health within the ministry of Internal Affairs, wrote a book — *The structure of public health in the Third Reich*[32] in which he proclaimed, for example, that charity should disappear, especially towards inferior or anti-social elements of society; and that the highest duty of the state was to grant life and support only to the healthy, genetically untainted part of the nation, in order to preserve a genetically and racially pure people for all eternity.[33] Doctors in public service were often obliged to attend the '*Führerschule für Germanische Aerzte*' in Mecklenburg several times a year to receive instruction in national socialist racial theory. Only Aryans were permitted to study medicine and all medical students were obliged to become members of the *National-Sozialistische Studentenbund*; a medical student who exhibited inadequate familiarity with German race theory was simply dropped.

It is dangerous to pass judgement on all German doctors indiscriminately, but in general, according to Cohen:

'In this way German doctors were invested with Nazi ideas and they allowed it to happen, for it must not be forgotten that the German medic was also a German, subjected to the same influences as all the other Germans, for example, during their education.'[34]

Himmler provided a special place for these doctors within his

programme. By means of the *Ahnenerbe*, he offered unprecedented
opportunities to perform medical experiments in the service of
the State. That in doing so ethical boundaries would be crossed
he considered a logical consequence, but did not trouble him.
Heinrich Himmler was a man of disquieting mediocrity and
of equally disquieting contrasts. And a man whose importance
was no less disquieting.

In his famous speech in Posen he concluded:

> 'We must remember our principle: blood, selection,
> austerity . . . .'[35]

2

The Experiments at Ravensbrück

In Mecklenburg, about fifty miles north of Berlin, there is marshy area with several lakes. Here, near the Furstenbergersee, a new concentration camp was built, shortly after the outbreak of the war in 1939. It became known as Ravensbrück, and consisted of a main camp and several subsidiary camps. The main camp was meant for women only, and from its establishment until the liberation by the Russians, 123,000 female prisoners were interned here. A large number of these were French; which is why the camp came to be known as '*L'enfer des femmes*'.[1]

The treatment of the camp prisoners was aimed specifically at crushing them bodily as well as spiritually. A survivor recounts:

> 'The whole camp system had just one purpose and that was to destroy our humanity and our conscience; the weaker individuals sank to the lowest, most animal instincts were awakened whilst higher motives withered for lack of opportunity to express them. Even the stronger ones amongst us, those who came out of the camp alive, are marked by unnatural traits which can never disappear; they have lost faith in goodness and in justice. The degree of infestation with vermin was incredible, the barracks were so full of lice one often saw them floating in the soup. Both sewage and water supply systems were faulty and the camp looked like an enormous farmyard consisting of one great dungheap. We seldom, if ever, changed our clothes or underclothes, and if we were given underclothing, it was always full of lice. It was, for

me, a scene from Hell, not because I saw terrible
things happening but because, for the first time in my
life, I beheld human beings but could not tell whether
they were men or women. Their heads were shorn,
they were thin ... dirty ... miserable. But that did
not strike me the most. What struck me the most was
the expression in their eyes. They had what I can only
describe as "dead eyes".'[2]

In this 'first class concentration camp',[3] as the superintendent
Dr Percy Treite described it, Gebhart could carry out his
experiments.

The medical supervision of the camp was the responsibility
of Dr Oskar Schiedlausky, whose substitute and first assistant
was the above mentioned Treite. This Treite, an Englishman
by birth, who described himself during his trial as an
'insignificant camp medic'[4] was by no means a typical member
of the brutish SS.

'He was somehow an inexplicable mixture of
culture and inhumanity, morally more guilty than any
of his colleagues; for he was a young man of good
background and upbringing; no vulgar, bestial moron
like Binder, no trained villain like Schwarzhuber, no
sadistic creature like Binz; and if he sinned, he sinned
entirely consciously.'[5]

On his own initiative, this gynaecologist carried out
sterilization experiments on young gypsy girls and thereafter
he did research on typhus.

Just as remarkable as Treite was Dr Lucas, sent to
Ravensbrück in 1941. Once installed as a camp doctor, he
refused to make selections from the newly arrived
transportations. This was apparently not in accordance with his
understanding of medical ethics. On the other hand, he had no
objections when Treite asked him to assist in the sterilization
experiments.[6] Nevertheless, Lucas is one of the few doctors to
come out well in the memoirs of ex-prisoners. In the short time
that he worked in this camp he showed himself to be a doctor
in the true sense of the word. His refusal to carry out the
selections was to prove detrimental to his career: as a disciplinary

measure he was transferred to the eastern front.

Oskar Schiedlausky's story is less ambiguous: In 1933 he became a member of the SS, two years after his graduation. He came to Ravensbrück in 1941 and stayed until December 1943, when he was transferred to Buchenwald. He took with him two years of experience in the perpetration of inhuman acts and he showed himself so worthy of the promotion to his new post that, together with Ilse Koch and his other colleagues, he would have been sentenced to death by the American courts deciding the Buchenwald trials, had he not already been condemned to the same fate by the English court that judged his crimes in Ravensbrück. [7]

In December he was transferred. A few months before his departure he chose ten entirely healthy women as subjects for experimental operations involving gangrene (a condition in which parts of the body die and decay as a result of cold and infection). He did not stop in Buchenwald. Schiedlausky admitted that he performed experiments with gangrene, and moreover confessed that, with his foreknowledge and approval, deadly injections were given to patients whose illness was serious though not incurable; and that he performed experimental bone transplants on healthy women, whereby pieces of bone were taken from the shin and transplanted to other parts of the body.

In 1942 Dr Rolf Rosenthal arrived at Ravensbrück and he made an indelible impression upon all survivors.

> 'Rosenthal outdid all the other doctors in inhuman behaviour towards the sick. At one sickness report some of the patients were so weak that they had to lean against a wall in order to remain upright. Rosenthal kicked them several times and sent them away without further examination. For him there was only one diagnosis: "Bugger off". He was present when Schiedlausky chose a large number of healthy women for experiments, and he assisted in this.' [8]

A year after Rosenthal's arrival, Hauptsturmführer Dr Hellinger made his appearance at Ravensbrück. As a dentist, he was charged with the recovery of gold from the mouths of the corpses. In 1945 he was arrested and charged. During his trial he asserted that the removal of gold fillings under such macabre circumstances:

> 'While it wounded certain feelings of piety, was not really an absolute offence, and (that) in practice there were historical precedents.'[9]

National Archives

Karl Gebhardt

This was the environment and this the company in which Gebhardt had to re-establish his damaged reputation. Gebhardt, born in Haag in Bavaria in 1897 was one of the leading medical figures in the Third Reich. He had grown up and gone to school with Himmler. After his medical studies at the University of Munich, he specialized in surgery and developed a keen interest in sports injuries. Apart from being Himmler's personal physician, he was also made senior medic of the German team during the Olympic Games. His medical skills gave him international repute; knee injuries were just one of his specializations. The Belgian industrialist Danny Heineman and the Belgian King Leopold III did not hesitate to employ his services. Many prominent Germans were under his care. In 1938 he became Professor of Surgery. A year later Himmler decorated him with the highest rank in the SS: SS Oberstgruppenführer. In the same year Gebhardt opened a medical clinic in Hohenlychen near Ravensbrück, with a thousand beds. In January 1945, Hitler made him the director of the German Red Cross. That a man of his calibre co-operated in experiments upon non-volunteers was for many doctors a sign of legal, if not ethical sanction. Gebhardt:

'Hitler approved of the idea to carry out medical experiments upon people because he considered it important to the state. The moment a doctor began an experiment he was protected by the law. Hitler thought, as did Himmler, that concentration camp prisoners could not simply be left undisturbed while soldiers were dying at the front and their wives and children suffered air attacks and bombardments. The doctor who carried out experiments was not subject to sanctions, on the contrary, the doctor who refused an order to perform an experiment was punished . . . .'11

The first tests were carried out on 20 July 1942. Seventy-five women, nicknamed 'rabbits', were assigned to Gebhardt by the camp-administration. Assisted by Dr Fritz Fischer and Dr Herta Oberheuser, Gebhardt began his rehabilitation programme. The women were subjected to all sorts of tests: they were given wounds and sulphonamide drugs. Bone transplant

experiments were also begun.
Wladislawa Karolewska:

'On 22 July 1942, seventy-five prisoners of our transport from Lublin were called to see the camp commandant. Later we were sent back to the block where we were to await further instructions. On 25 July all the women who had come with the transport from Lublin were called together by Mandel who told us we were not allowed to work outside the camp. The next day, seventy-five women were called again and had to stand outside the camp hospital. Present were Schiedlausky, Oberheuser, Rosenthal, Koegel and a man I later recognized as Dr Fischer. On that day we did not know why we had been called before the camp physicians. But that same day ten of the twenty-five girls were transferred to the hospital, though we did not know for what purpose. Four came back but six remained in the hospital, after having received some sort of injection; but we did not know what kind of injection it was.

On 1 August, these six girls were again called to the hospital, the six who had received the injection. They were detained in the hospital, and we could not get in touch with them to find out why they had been taken to the hospital. A few days later one of my fellow inmates succeeded in getting close to the hospital and heard from one of the prisoners that they were all in bed, their legs in casts.

On 14 August of the same year I myself was called to the hospital and my name was on a sheet of paper. I did not know why. In addition to me, eight other girls were called to the hospital. We were called at a time of day when executions were usually carried out and I was sure I would be executed, since, shortly before, several girls had been shot down. In the hospital, we were put to bed and the room was locked. We were not told why we were in the hospital and when one of my fellow inmates asked, she got no reply at all. The only reaction was a sarcastic grin. A German nurse then came and gave me an injection in my leg. After this injection I vomited and grew weak. I was then placed on a wheeled stretcher and taken to the operating room. There Dr Schiedlausky and Dr Rosenthal gave me a second intravenous injection into my arm. Shortly before, I had seen Dr Fischer leave the operating room. He had been wearing surgical gloves. I then lost consciousness and when I awoke I noticed that I was in an ordinary hospital room. After some time I regained consciousness and felt severe pains in my leg .... . I noticed that my leg was in a cast from ankle to knee. The pains in my foot were very severe and I had a high fever. I also noticed that my leg was swollen from toe to hip. The pains increased more and more and the temperature rose too, and the next day I noticed that some fluid was trickling (being drained) from my leg.

On the third day I was placed on a wheeled stretcher and taken to the dressing room. There I saw Dr Fischer again. He wore an operating gown and rubber gloves. A blanket was drawn over my eyes and I had the impression that something was being cut out of my leg. Present were Drs Schiedlausky, Rosenthal and Oberheuser. When the dressing had been changed I was taken back to the ordinary dressing room. The dressing was changed by Dr Fischer with the aid of the doctors mentioned, my eyes having been covered. I was taken back to the operating room again, and put on the operating table. The dressing was removed and for the first time I saw my own leg again. The incision was so deep that I could see the bone itself. We were told that the Hohenlychen physician, Dr Gebhardt, would come to examine us. We waited three hours for his arrival while lying on the tables. When he came, sheets were spread over our eyes. Then we were taken back to our rooms.

On 8 September, I was sent back to the block. I could not walk. Pus flowed out of my leg. In the block, I stayed in bed for a week. Then I was again called to the hospital, and since I could not walk, my fellow inmates carried me. In the hospital I met a few of my fellow prisoners who had also been operated on. I was sure I would now be executed. For outside the hall I saw the ambulance drawn up which was used by the Germans to take away people selected for execution. We were taken to the dressing room where Drs Oberheuser and Schiedlausky examined our legs. We were again put to bed.

That same afternoon I was taken to the operating room and the second operation on my leg was performed. As before, I was put to sleep by means of an injection. This time I again saw Dr Fischer. I woke up in the ordinary hospital room. I felt still sharper pain and was running a temperature. The symptoms were the same. The leg was swollen and full of pus (...). While I lay in the hospital, Dr Oberheuser treated me with extreme cruelty ... .'[12]

This is the sad story of one of the survivors subjected to the sulphonamide experiments. Wounds had been deliberately made in both her legs and had been infected with splinters of wood and glass. The scientific value of these tests was small, despite the fact that Fischer discovered that sulphonamide molecules could be spread by using an electrical current — a process still used in analytical science today under the name 'electrophoresis' — since he did not succeed in presenting the results of his work convincingly.[13]

An objective and clear picture of the tests is given by the Polish Dr Sofia Magzka, who had worked in the camp hospital as a nurse. Foreseeing that one day she might be a witness in a tribunal, she secretly prepared accurate notes on the nature and the number of experiments carried out. At the same time, she wrote down the names and numbers of the victims and the doctors. She denounced the 'medical care' in the camp in the strongest terms possible, and criticized the ethical ideas of Gebhardt's assistants Dr Fischer and Dr Oberheuser. She described in detail the bone operations performed by Gebhardt and Fischer:

'As far as I know about thirteen prisoners were operated on several times, as a result of which two of them died. The muscle operations were very important. Certain muscles were hereby removed from the leg, which then became thin and weak. I never understood the point of these tests, neither was it clear to me what then happened to the muscles once they were removed. I don't know whether they were taken to Hohenlychen. The experiments on the mentally defective is another story. I can still remember two incidents very well. They amputated someone's leg. The nurses took her to the operating room, and afterwards she did not return, but was brought to the special department to which the dead were normally transferred. Together with a friend, who also worked in the camp hospital, I went to have a look; we saw a corpse, from which one leg had been amputated, covered by a sheet. A little while later the nurses returned and, with no help from other prisoners, put the body into a coffin; this is how it was kept secret . . . . Later, another mentally defective woman was taken in to the operating room; shortly thereafter Dr Fischer also went in. A little later he returned with a large parcel under his arm, the length of an arm, and he left for Hohenlychen by car. Shortly afterwards one of the prisoners came up to me and said: "Do you know what's happened? They amputated her arm, together with the shoulder blade!" I still remember these two incidents very well . . . .'

Dr Magzka at once dismissed the suggestion that the prisoners upon whom the above-mentioned experiments were performed had volunteered.

'They did not! and nothing came of the promises to extend pardons to the test subjects either. I can recall only one instance of a pardon being granted; that happened to a certain Miss Okaniewka.'[14]

Dr Herta Oberheuser was the only woman in the Nuremberg dock. In 1940 she had applied for the job of camp doctor, and because of her experience in skin and sexually transmitted diseases, she had been taken on. In a long opening speech to the court she described her duties and did her level best to fend off the charges against her.

National Archives

Herta Oberheuser

'Of the 3,000 women about seventy-five percent were criminals, prostitutes or other offenders. The number of political prisoners was small and the number of Jewesses negligible (!). When I was appointed camp doctor, the administration made it clear to me that I was to maintain a certain distance between myself and the prisoners. The bulk of the German doctors and nurses were SS members and formed a clique that I detested. The situation changed with the arrival of Professor Gebhardt and Dr Fischer. The circumstances in the camp were getting worse all the time. I did all I could to improve the situation but this was very difficult as I had absolutely no authority. One of the worst problems was the scarcity of medicines. The only way out of this situation was to accept Gebhardt's offer. He told me that he had come to perform a number of experiments upon prisoners who had been condemned to death. I shuddered but he immediately added that the experiments had been ordered by high-ranking authorities and were entirely in order. The test subjects would by their co-operation, improve their chances of receiving a pardon. Moreover, Gebhardt assured me that the tests were completely harmless and he asked me to assist him. That a man of his calibre was prepared to perform tests on prisoners made my decision all the easier and I agreed to help.

In the medical preparations, the initial discussions and selections I took no part. I only knew that the women upon whom the tests would be carried out were staying in a specially guarded block; they had been convicted of espionage — Gebhardt told me: "You will have to obey only those orders that are concerned with nursing and you will receive these from myself or from Dr Fischer". From the camp administration I received the impression that they were happy with the treatment that I gave them. I performed no operations myself; I am a skin specialist, not a surgeon. Once I did assist in the administration of an anaesthetic. I did my work after the operation. I took care of the post-operative checks, medicines, blood, urine and so on, and attended to the patient's general condition.

The patients were lying in small sickrooms and enjoyed excellent care; day and night a nurse was in attendance, and they did not lack anything . . . .'[15]

When later during the trial the prosecutor confronted Dr Oberheuser with Dr Magzka's evidence, she replied:

'The women who had been operated on were under continuous medical scrutiny. Reports were regularly sent to Hohenlychen and Drs Gebhardt and Fischer came regularly to examine the patients. The accusation that I grossly ignored the sick is nonsense. The general care for the patients was entrusted to prisoner-nurses, mainly Polish women. Whether there were individual instances of maltreatment or whatever, I cannot say, I know nothing about it. I do remember that between August and October 1942 there were several serious cases; Dr Gebhardt and Fischer stopped their tests and extended their care to these patients. They devoted themselves to the rescue of these cases . . . alas, three died . . . (. . .). I treated all the prisoners in the same way and I deny utterly that I ever maltreated a prisoner. Professor Gebhardt came regularly and certainly did not tolerate maltreatment of prisoners, nor did they tolerate them being left in pain; in such instances they were immediately anaesthetized. Gebhardt was especially concerned about the sterility of the bandages. I never heard complaints about Dr Fischer. I was not in a position to judge the scientific worth of these tests. Neither was I present at the meeting in the Military Academy in Berlin when these tests were discussed . . . .'[16]

The meeting to which Oberheuser was alluding took place from 24 May till 26 May 1943 at the Academy of Military Science in Berlin. After a short introduction by Gebhardt, Fischer gave a lecture on the subject *Special Experiments on the Effect of Sulphonamides*. The lecture had originally had another title, '*Experiments on human beings with regard to sulphonamides*', but Professor Gruber and Reichsdoctor SS Ernst Grawitz, who had glanced through the lecture beforehand, had considered it more prudent to change the title. No need to be unduly provocative! Nevertheless there was no doubt that the tests had been carried out on prisoners in concentration camps. Not one of 200 doctors present raised a voice in protest or found any fault with the experiments, which led prosecutor McHaney to conclude that:

> 'Without a doubt the leading medical figures in Germany were aware of these criminal experiments. These people were in a position to clearly know their duty as doctors and to know that it could and should not happen ... .'[17]

Gebhardt gave the impression during his hearing of not having the remotest idea why he had ended up on trial. From the beginning to the end he claimed not to have sinned against medical ethics and to have experimented only on prisoners who had been condemned to death. He shifted all responsibility on to the man who was never there: Heinrich Himmler.

> 'What kind of agreement did you reach with the SS with respect to the fate of those who, let's put it this way, co-operated in the tests?'
> 'Most importantly, and this is what I told Himmler, that the test subjects would have a chance to survive. I believe that two or three were given pardons and set to work in German service. The others however, did not receive Himmler's permission to leave the camp. To be frank, I must confess that I did not know whether people who were experimented upon were volunteers or not; I was not engaged in the legal side of things, that was the concern of the authorities in charge ... .'
> 'Whom do you mean by that?'
> 'Himmler, of course!'
> 'So Himmler was simply empowered to decide whether a prisoner did not have to take part in a test.'
> 'Yes, but look here, you asked me to bear witness here as a skilled medic and now you want a judgement

on the legal details. I can only tell you that at that time I had no doubts at all about Himmler's omnipotence . . . . He could do with and within the concentration camps whatever he liked, though it be in Hitler's name. That was my opinion then and it is my opinion now . . . .'

'Dr Gebhardt, are you of the opinion that it is criminal to perform an experiment upon a prisoner whose right to refuse has been denied?'

'If no account is taken of attendant circumstances such as the reason for the experiment, responsibility, the intervention of the state and so on, it is impossible to answer this question . . . .'

'On the 17 October 1946, in response to exactly the same question, you replied: "No, not in principle".'

Gebhardt stuck to his point: 'Such observations are the inevitable result of long discussions. Since I understood that the experiments were legally entirely in order, I never asked whether the test subjects had been forced to co-operate.'

'Were you of the opinion that the test subjects were criminals?'

'I was given the facts by Himmler and I was responsible to him and to no one else!'

'So you set about your experiments without further ado? The test subject might well have been an ordinary prisoner who just happened to be present in the camp at that moment . . . .'

'While the experiments were being conducted, Himmler impressed on me that the tests were completely legal, he told me this repeatedly . . . .'

Despite Gebhardt's radical attitude towards the test subjects — according to him they were criminals — the prosecutor did not eschew a discussion to determine what 'criminals' were in order to emphasize the criminality of the experiments.

'Dr Gebhardt, was a distinction drawn between ordinary and political crimes?'

'No. Again, I was not involved in the legal details.

The German criminals were at Nebe's[18] disposal and in my opinion they were not convicted for political reasons . . . . '

'So the reasons for conviction had nothing to do with politics?'

'The reasons for conviction did not interest me.'

'However, I should like to define the concept of criminality. It is known that Jews who had sexual contact with Aryans were condemned to death. Did Nebe dispose of these too?'

'First of all: your assumption that in such instances Jews would have been sentenced to death is based on a misrepresentation of the facts. A person was not sentenced to death for *Rassenschande* but was sent to a concentration camp.'

'What provisions did you make for the women made ill for months, sometimes years by the operations? Let me cite just one instance, that of Mrs Kusmierczuk.' (She had been subjected to several experiments, and had been grossly neglected thereafter, as was attested by three witnesses (author).)

'It has been claimed that this woman was ill for years as a result of the experiments; I deny this. The majority of the test subjects recovered quickly. The girls were looked after by the camp doctor and we were always available in emergencies.'[19]

This version was too much for the prosecutor and he called witness after witness to attest the opposite. But Gebhardt stuck to his guns and continually stressed Himmler's responsibility in this kind of case:

'As far as these medical tests are concerned, I am simple enough to believe that if the authorities in a totalitarian state say: "We are the centre, we decide", then they should also carry the responsibilities. Himmler himself was always saying: "How can you be responsible? You are just an instrument. I give the orders and I assure you that no legal measures will be taken". The tests were entirely legal and took place, as Himmler always said, on Hitler's express orders.

I was in no position to doubt the correctness of such orders and Himmler had to carry them out. Himmler was my superior and I was bound to him by the SS oath of loyalty ... .'[20]

Herta Oberheuser, too, defended herself vehemently and was filled with indignation at the accusations levelled at her. She admitted that she had given patients fatal injections but 'only five or six in hopeless cases for which there was no cure.'[21] Her attitude during the entire interrogation was the same as Gebhardt's, i.e. one of systematic denial.

'Did you tell the young girls before the operation, that they would receive a pardon if they lent their co-operation?'

'No, I had nothing to say about that.'

'We have already established that after their operations a number of girls were shot dead. Had they been experimented on?'

'I suppose so.'

'Were the sulphonamide experiments painful?'

'No, I didn't think so. The test subjects were suffering mentally, but they already were suffering because they knew that they were going to be executed.'

'You were assigned the patients post-operative care. How long did they remain in your hands?'

'Until their recovery.'

'You have seen a few of the girls who were experimented on here. Some still looked ill, didn't they?'

'I can make no judgement on that, I am a dermatologist.'

'Did you give these girls medicines regularly to relieve their pain?'

'Yes, regularly.'

'But one of the girls has testified here that you refused her medicines because they would delay the healing of the leg, and that you withheld them not only from her but also from other girls ... .'

'I cannot recall anything about it ... it was four

years ago. For that matter, we had received instructions to go easy on the morphine.'

'During this hearing, you have attested several times that you meant well towards the prisoners. I should like to draw your attention the following testimony from Helena Piaska:

'In early 1942, there was an old woman, about eighty, in the camp hospital. She wore a yellow triangle on her sleeve (indicating her Jewishness) she was very ill and could hardly walk. She was in great pain and asked Dr Oberheuser for medicine. The latter asked why she was in the camp and when she did not reply, Dr Oberheuser gave her a kick, and she fell writhing to the ground. Oberheuser laughed and ordered her to get up and get lost. She would get no pills and that was that!

'Well now, Dr Oberheuser, is this not a typical example of your conduct in Ravensbrück?'

'That is a gross lie; I never did that. On the contrary, I tried with all my might to improve the situation.'

'Then I will ask you to hear another testimony, this time from Miss Baj, who begins, and I quote:

"I saw Dr Oberheuser hit women in the camp hospital ..." (...). How many women were murdered after they had been carried out?'

'I haven't the faintest idea, that this happened at all I hear here for the first time ... .'

'Do you regard those instances where your administration of injections resulted in their death, as euthanasia?'

'I administered injections solely to alleviate the pain.'

'And this medical help brought about death?'

'They were dying already ... .'

'So if I understand you rightly you administered injections in order to alleviate their pain and not in order to hasten their deaths?'

'Solely to alleviate their pain. Those patients whose circumstances were heart-rending and to whom I administered injections were dying. I know from personal experience, that in large hospitals injections are given at the patient's own request. Given my responsibility in the circumstances, I decided accordingly. I usually went to the doctor on duty and, with his permission, increased the dose of painkillers. In a few cases, maybe four or five, I sat at the patient's bedside and gave a substance handed to me by the duty doctor . . . .'

'If I understand you rightly, you did not know precisely what this ''substance'' was?'

'In two or three cases morphine but in the other cases, no, I didn't.'

'What was the result when you used this fluid?'

'The same as with the morphine . . . the patient fell asleep.'

'Would the patient wake up or did death follow?'

'*Es war dann der Tod* . . . .'[22]

The tribunal sentenced her to twenty years imprisonment, in contrast to Gebhardt who was condemned to death. Herta Oberheuser was however released before her term was up and opened a practice in Stocksee. On 20 July 1958 the British Medical Association brought their indignation to the attention of the German authorities. Once more an investigation was instigated and, after a long and protracted trial, on 20 November 1960 her authority to practice was withdrawn.

Finally, the man charged with actually conducting all the experiments: Fritz Ernst Fischer.

A procession of witnesses pointed accusing fingers at the dock from which Fischer gazed back seemingly unmoved. But, in fact, his apparent indifference masked a remarkable capacity for self-dramatization. He was able to whip up a passionate defence of his innocence with regard to incorrect behaviour of any kind. He dismissed the accusations against him, and it is still a question whether he ever understood them fully. He was sincerely indignant about the ignorance and indifference of the prosecutor with regard to the holy National Socialist rule '*Befehl ist Befehl*'. The calling into doubt of his claims annoyed him intensely but did not unsettle him at all. Skilfully, he employed intellectual conversation and logical analysis in order to exploit his feelings. He pushed his devotion to Gebhardt to an absurd degree. During

National Archives

Fritz Fischer

the course of his hearing he sealed himself off hermetically from the reality of how he had lived and worked. However paradoxical this sounds, he dimly realized that his past was less than spotless but held that the pressure from his superiors was more than 'Private' Fischer was able to withstand. During the hearing he opposed the idea that the tests on prisoners could not in any way be justified by the war situation. The war had, indeed, been the reason for his change of heart:

> 'Mr Prosecutor, at that time I had but one idea: I had to adapt to the situation and that situation was one of war!'[23]

He added that under normal circumstances he would never have performed such experiments. He repeatedly referred to Gebhardt's responsibility and to the great influence which Gebhardt had exerted on him. This attitude elicited the following question:

> 'Dr Fischer, suppose for a moment that Gebhardt had given you, a young obedient soldier, the order to amputate Dr Oberheuser's leg as part of an experiment. What would you have done?'

Fischer, after long reflection, eventually replied:

> 'I cannot answer that.'

How obedient Private Fischer held himself to be became clear in the following part of the hearing.

> 'You have attested that the girls upon whom you experimented had been convicted. Did you know the nature of their crimes?'
> 'I can't answer that exactly but I understand that most of them had been resistance members.'
> 'Is it correct that the girls were shot down after the operations?'
> 'I know nothing about it.'
> 'We have proved that the girls were not given pardons, as had originally been the intention. In her

testimony on 22 January, witness Szulpluska said that
two Polish girls were murdered in cold blood after their
operations. And do you remember the witness
Magzka who asserted that six girls were shot dead after
their operations? It seems to me that there was never
any intention to pardon them at all. They had to
disappear; that was much safer for you . . . .'

'I was entirely dependent on Gebhardt. I put my
fate into his hands; he was the highest authority. I
consciously put my personal initiative aside in order
to serve him.'

'Do you mean by that, that if at that time Gebhardt
had ordered you to jump in the lake, that you would
have done so without further ado?'

'Mr Prosecutor, I am an obedient soldier!'

'After the experiments, the girls were generally
entrusted to the camp doctor's care, and as we have
already demonstrated, that care did not amount to
much. Could you not have done something about it?'

'Mr Hardy, if that's how you see it, you have
accorded me too much responsibility . . . .'[24]

Prosecutor Hardy went on to expand on the testimony of Dr
Magzka who had attested that Fischer had amputated a whole
arm complete with shoulder blade. As later became clear, the
shoulder blade was used in an operation of one of Gebhardt's
private patients in Hohenlychen. Fischer:

'A student of Lexer, Gebhardt had long planned
a free hetero-plastic bone-graft (transplanting a bone
from one person to another). Although some of his
associates were in disagreement, he was determined
to perform such an operation on the patient Ladisch,
whose shoulder joint (scapula, clavicle and the head
of the humerus) had been removed because of
sarcoma. I and my colleagues raised medical
humanitarian objections until the evening the
operation was performed. But Gebhardt ordered us
to carry out the operation. Dr Stumpfegger, in whose
special field of research the operation lay, was to
remove the shoulder blade (scapula) at Ravensbrück

and had already made special preparations. But since Professor Gebhardt needed Dr Stumpfegger for the final transplant of the shoulder to the patient Ladisch, I was ordered to go to Ravensbrück that same night to perform the removal operation. I begged Drs Gebhardt and Schulze to describe the precise technique they desired me to follow.

The next morning, I went to Ravensbrück. The camp physician who assisted me in the operation finished it, while I returned to Hohenlychen as quickly as possible with the bone to be transplanted. In this way the interval between removal and graft was shortened. The bone was handed to Professor Gebhardt in Hohenlychen, and he, together with Dr Schulze and Dr Stumpfegger, transplanted it.'[25]

The application of inadequate legal ideas to the reality of the complex of offences with which the doctor's trial was concerned was clearly demonstrated when the accused played tricks with the magic '*Befehl ist befehl*'. Fischer, especially, turned out to be a gifted juggler. In his final appeal he once again exemplified the opinion of the experimental doctors.

'It is regrettable that fate forced me, as a physician, to violate the '*nihil nocere*'. People have been called to bear witness against me and have claimed that I did not help them, but ill-treated them. However, I have learned that if one desires to judge a particular kind of behaviour, one has to consider the aims which underlie it. I hoped by means of these experiments to obtain certain results by which many wounded people might be helped. There were millions of wounded and it was of primary importance that help be offered to them. I committed these acts as an obedient member of the military forces. The law, the Führer, and the Government, so I perceived it then, ensured me of legal protection. My personal responsibility played no role in this at all. At that time, when the German people were engaged in a life or death struggle, when their fate was being decided, I was of the opinion that the state had the right to take measures from which a person detached himself as an individual. Obedience to the state appeared to me at that time, with 1,500 soldiers at the front and hundreds of civilians dying every day, to be the highest moral duty. The test subjects awaited certain death and co-operation in an experiment was their only chance of survival. I believe that if I had been in a similar situation, I would have grasped the opportunity with both hands. Moreover, you must not forget that all this took place in 1942: the war was at its height.

At that time I was hardly a civilian doctor, free to do as he pleased. No, I was a specialist, educated in medical affairs, expected to behave as an obedient soldier. If I received an order that I disliked, who was I to appeal against it? Facing me was Gebhardt's eminent authority. And this authority, Professor Gebhardt, whom I had come to know during my work as a sincere doctor, was someone who also inspired considerable confidence in me. If he decided that these experiments were necessary, then I was the last to doubt it. He pointed out that in a person's life, in the life of a people, a moment could arise when it became necessary that the individual abandon his reservations if the general good were thereby served. And that was what counted: the general good.

A soldier at the front does things he would normally never do. He has to switch off his personal feelings at that moment. I found myself in the same situation as a soldier who had to fire a torpedo at a ship, or a pilot who had to bomb a city. I do not believe that these people would have performed such acts had they followed their instincts. They also acted because the situation was that bad. In doing so, they were legally protected and that was, for them of the highest importance. Moreover, I am of the opinion that one cannot expect, from a subordinate, a discussion of what is and what is not permissible. I learned during the war that this sort of obedience is not typically German, but was also found in the states with which we were at war; however to what extent I cannot judge. I learned during the war that my choice lay between obedience and disobedience, and besides, I have always regarded disobedience as the greatest error . . . .'[26]

Cohen's thesis is in general agreement:

'Thus, the authoritarian view of life was already present with the German people as a matter of course before Nazi Government; the Nazi dictatorial system fitted into this perfectly. Within the family, at school, in the attitudes of the young, and still later, in military service and at work, the authoritarian system held sway. In Nazi-Germany the Germans learnt obedience, they learnt to follow every order from above mechanically. This entirely accounts for their concept "*Befehl ist Befehl*"; such conduct is simply German and already existed before the Nazi era.'[27]

This attitude was prevalent in every layer of society and as we shall see, it found expression in many ways.

Fischer was found guilty on three of the four charges against him and was condemned to death, a sentence which shocked him deeply and which in all probability he understood as little as he did the indictments . . . .

3

Conti and Brandt

In 1929 the National Socialists set up their own Medical League which, until the end of the war, carried out a veritable witch hunt against all dissenting doctors. The origin and the rise of this organization is closely linked with the figure of Leonard Phillippo Conti. He was born in Lugano on 24 August 1900; his father was Swiss and his mother Prussian. He passed through primary and secondary school with no trouble; his exam results promised a bright future. In 1918 he enrolled in the medical faculty at the University of Berlin, but after two years he considered himself finished with Berlin and moved to Erlangen where he continued his studies. At the same time he developed a considerable political interest in everything to do with the Weimar republic. Little is known of his undergraduate years, but in 1923 he suddenly popped up as a president in the National Socialist Student Society of the University of Erlangen and at the end of the same year he held a high position in Ernst Röhm's SA. In 1927 he joined the NSDAP, receiving registration No. 71.225. From that year onwards he relinquished anonymity and revealed himself to be a gifted and passionate National Socialist orator.

In 1930 he enrolled in the SS where he quickly reached the rank of colonel, but to what extent he was active at this level in the SS remains open to question. It had always been one of Himmler's tactics to ally himself with people by offering them a high position in the SS.

Besides this post, Conti attained many others, including the post of delegate to the Prussian National Assembly and that of medical advisor to the Ministry of Home Affairs.

National Archives

Leonardo Conti

Whoever follows his career will note that cunning, purposeful diligence and ruthlessness, as well as duplicity and deceit were the pillars upon which he built his success. Nevertheless, it cannot be denied that, however important the help was that he received from others, the foundations of Conti's success were laid by his own energy and skill as a political leader. His success in the latter capacity lay in the unequalled insight into the potential of propaganda and his flair for its utilization. When Hitler came to power in 1933, all but a few of the National

Socialist élite were already known to him, a factor which was to prove a decisive influence in the course of his career.

Conti was entirely convinced of his potential and perhaps even more of his own qualities. Every step he took was deliberate and purposeful. He would reward the renderer of a service by tying that person even more strongly to him and he did not know what real gratitude meant. Heavy was the hand that helped his colleagues forward, in which respect he had much in common with the man in whose shadow he would remain throughout his career: Martin Bormann.

In 1939 Conti achieved what was without doubt the high point of his career. In March of that year, he succeeded Dr Wagner as 'Reichsgesundheitsführer', and by that summer, he had been appointed Secretary of State for Public Health. In this way, he became the most powerful medical figure in the Third Reich. However, the appointment had not come out of the blue and its procedure had by no means been irreproachable. Only after Himmler and the Minister of Propaganda, Goebbels, had both given their support to his nomination did Hitler see his appeal. Not everyone was pleased with Conti's nomination; certainly not the German medical community itself. In their opinion, he was too politically oriented and too willing an instrument of the ruling élite. But nothing could prevent his appointment. Scarcely had he taken office as Secretary of State for Public Health when the doctors got a taste of what was to come. With a stroke of his pen, Conti destroyed what little was left of the independence that the medical organizations had enjoyed.

At the same time, he launched a plan whereby the Third Reich would rid itself, within the foreseeable future, of Jewish physicians. Even Jewish war veterans were in for it this time and were forbidden to practise. Conti also wrote a number of 'scientific' and racist essays on subjects such as race, peoples, hygiene and vitamins, making a name for himself as one of the most influential military biologists.

The only brake on his radical and racist reformatory zeal was the Minister of Internal Affairs, under whose responsibility Conti's office eventually fell. Germany had no Ministry of Public Health and all affairs to do with public health were handled by Internal Affairs. Until he was succeeded by Himmler in 1943, Dr Wilhelm Frick wielded the sceptre in this office; and as for a number of reasons, Conti was on bad terms with Frick, he was obliged to resort to his protective contacts such as Himmler, Goebbels or Bormann.

This search for support made his authority deficient but his opponents did not dare to make use of this yet.

At the end of the thirties, a figure appeared in the Nazi-élite who would slowly but surely put Conti on the sidelines: Karl Brandt. He had a decisive advantage over Conti: the absolute trust of both Hitler and the German medical organizations. Hitler conferred many qualifications on Brandt, making Conti's position practically untenable; and from the very beginning, Conti waged a fierce campaign against Hitler's prima-donna protégé. In this long and protracted war, he was supported by powerful friends: Himmler, who decorated him with the highest SS rank *i.e.* that of SS Oberstgruppenführer; Reich Marshal Goering, the arch-plotter; Goebbels; and lastly, Hitler's shadow, Martin Bormann. The support of the latter would prove to be decisive.

At first, however, even this powerful combination did not seem able to prevent Brandt from gradually becoming the new leading man in the medical world. Hitler was not unaware of his unusual qualities and acknowledged them by conferring many responsibilities on to Brandt. The fact that by doing so he made Conti's position more insecure did not bother him. In any case, Hitler was indifferent to doctors, or rather, had an ingrained aversion to them. He had always considered trust in his own opinions as one of his greatest gifts, and that Brandt eventually achieved a privileged position through having had an influence on those opinions, may be considered unique. He stood far above Hitler's other favourites; many had striven to attain the far reaching powers that he enjoyed, but few had succeeded in extraordinary circumstances.

Dr Brandt, was according to Speer, a sound man. 'He was modest; and during the entire time that he was important to Hitler, he did not change. He remained the same person, which you cannot say for the most people in Hitler's vicinity.'[1]

Hitler's insights affected and influenced him, but did not control him; perhaps this was just what made him so culpable in the eyes of the others, for in Nuremberg he was considered one of the worst SS doctors. It would be true to say that it was not his intention to obey Hitler's commands to the letter, but rather to manipulate them carefully. He turned away from extremist Nazi ideologues such as Himmler and Rosenberg, and due to his too close relationship with Speer, he and Bormann were at daggers drawn. When a person's life goes astray this nearly always has demonstrable causes. Conflicting motives have as their usual cause genuine psychic disturbances. Intuitive behaviour can, in the large majority of instances, be reduced to the appearance of primitive motives; a disproportionately inflated desire for riches, a superiority complex, exaggerated aggressiveness as the result of an inferiority complex, the tendency to achieve the legally impracticable by crossing the line of acceptable behaviour. The pure lust for power alone is hardly a sufficient motive. However, in Karl Brandt's case, it is impossible to specify either a single motive or a complex of associated motives. The most varied impulses traverse each other.

The shadowy picture that emerges from the recollections of the few people who knew him in the early thirties, is of a man who divided his passion between politics and medical science. Who was this Karl Brandt about whom opinions were so divided after the war?

Brandt was born in Mulhouse, in the Alsace-Lorraine province of France on 8 January 1904. He was born into a renowned medical family, and, strongly influenced by this, he decided to carry on in the family tradition. Having studied under the best professors in the country, Sauer, Magnus and Bier, he graduated with honours at the age of twenty-four and moved to Berlin, where, under the tutelage of Professor George Magnus, he specialized in surgery. In the university clinic in the Ziegelstrasse, he demonstrated a considerable gift for skull and spinal operations. Trevor-Roper assumes that the physicians in the Ziegelstrasse were out-and-out National Socialists, but there is no evidence for this.[2]

The doctors at work there were regarded as patriotic but certainly not as fervent Hitler supporters. The senior physician at the clinic, Professor Magnus, though a regular consultant to prominent Nazis, was certainly known as someone who was quite neutral. It is therefore highly unlikely that Brandt became entangled in the National Socialist nets during this period. All the more so since he had no intention of staying in Germany. In his heart, he cherished a deep admiration for a fellow-Alsacian, Professor Albert Schweitzer. Their profession had

National Archives

Karl Brandt

brought them together several times already, and it was not long before Brandt decided to exchange the comfortable life in Berlin for an adventurous one in the Congo. He was determined to spend the rest of his life together with Schweitzer serving mankind in this underdeveloped part of Africa. However, a few weeks before his departure, a problem arose which effectively put the whole affair aside.

Brandt's official domicile was the Alsace, which in those days was in French hands. The French authorities demanded that he do his military service, implying that they considered him to be French. He refused and chose to make his permanent home in Germany, moving house to Bochnum where he accepted the post of surgeon in a local hospital. At this time, the early thirties, he showed no great interest in politics, but the social situation — Germany was still reeling under the effects of the crisis of 1929 — lead him to enrol as a party member in 1932. He was working in the Ruhr area and was daily confronted with social misery and the promises of the National Socialists. Undoubtedly, there were also other reasons for his decision to apply in that same year, for membership of the SA and of the National Socialist's Medical league.

Time passed by and the young Brandt became acquainted with the new swimming champion Annie Rebhorn, a personal friend of the Führer. Within a few months they were engaged. Annie Rebhorn introduced her fiancé to Hitler who, in due course, came to be quite fond of the young congenial surgeon.

The new Reichschancellor invited the pair regularly to private parties and was struck by their friendly and unobtrusive manner, a rarity in those days.

On 6 June 1933, Hitler left his private residence on a trip to Berlin. One of the cars, carrying his secretary Wilhelm Brückner, burst a tyre and crashed. Brandt, who was travelling in the convoy, gave first aid and, in a nearby hospital saved the life of Hitler's first secretary. Brückner rapidly recovered to full health. In this way, Brandt had indirectly demonstrated his skill to Hitler for the first time, but as yet, this did not lead to anything. Life went on as usual and the incident seemed to have been forgotten. At this time Brandt, in conjunction with Professor Magnus, wrote a number of articles on skull disorders which found recognition all over Europe. His fame as a medical theoretician increased and led to highly interesting job offers which he resolutely refused. He was pleased with his work in Bochnum; furthermore, it enabled him, in addition to his practical activities, to go more deeply into theory.

In 1934 he received the first official request. Hitler was to pay a state visit to Mussolini, and every detail had been organized except one: a first aid doctor. Hitler had forgotten Brandt, Brückner had not.[3] Brückner asked Brandt to consider the proposition; this he did, and soon after he expressed his willingness. After Hitler had given his consent, Brandt was officially appointed '*Begleitarzt*', a post that should not be confused with that of personal physician. This position was already held by Dr Theodore Morell, whose aversion to flying meant that Hitler did not wish him to accompany them on the journey.

In this way, Brandt came to occupy the post of *ad hoc* personal physician, a duty he discharged admirably. The journey passed without incident and afterwards Brandt returned to Bochnum. He maintained informal contact with Hitler and from 1936, the latter made more frequent appeals to Brandt's skills, from advice in medical matters to practical instructions. The expertise and élan with which Brandt carried out these tasks was a source of great satisfaction to the Führer. Apart from being congenial company, Brandt also appeared to be an exceedingly able worker.

His popularity with Hitler grew, but so did the hostility of Brandt's opponents. This nonentity seemed to have earned Hitler's absolute confidence. Suspicion was reinforced by the fact that Brandt was frequently in Hitler's private company, an exclusive privilege enjoyed only by few. This loyal coterie comprised among others, Speer, Bormann, Goering and Goebbels; Himmler was seldom to be seen.

In 1934 Brandt was transferred from the SA to the SS where he found himself under Himmler's authority. He had, however, no intention of dancing to the Reichsführer's tune and meant to establish a position in which he could regard Hitler as his direct superior. Luck was on his side, for Hitler tacitly accepted this. This was a real thorn in Himmler's flesh; he could not bear the idea that one of his subordinates was on such amicable footing with his Führer!

Brandt and Himmler therefore despised each other, and it was clear to both that one of them would have to suffer the consequences. Albert Speer:

> 'On the relationship between Brandt and Himmler,
> I cannot really give you my opinion for the simple
> reason that I know too little about it. Still, I would
> like to draw your attention to the fact that Brandt was
> not allowed, unlike others, to make a career for himself
> as an officer. This was most unusual for anyone closely
> associated with Hitler. Later, after the trials, I asked
> myself whether the very rapid promotions to high SS
> ranks he received suddenly and in great haste, were
> really the direct result of these activities; they could
> mean that Himmler had initially held to principles
> that led him to preclude Brandt's promotions .... .
> At a certain moment, something must have happened
> to make Himmler drop his objections .... .'[4]

Whether these promotions had anything to do with Brandt's
eventual approval of the medical experiments, Speer leaves open
to question. He himself considered it to be quite possible that
Brandt knew nothing of them:

> 'You must take care not to underestimate the
> secrecy principle; this was also applied to contacts
> between SS chiefs. The whole system by which people
> told each other nothing was characteristic of the Hitler
> regime and is typical for an authoritarian state. It was
> enough that each should know what he had to do
> concerning his own activities. Nobody spoke of his
> work to others and, generally, people liked it that way.
> A brief example: Brandt never spoke a word to me
> about the execution of the euthanasia-programme. I,
> in my turn told him nothing of my plans concerning
> the production of rockets with which London was to
> be destroyed.'[5]

Speer had always enjoyed a special relationship with Hitler,
who as a failed draftsmen had an ineffable admiration for Speer's
artistic talents. In Speer, Hitler found the personification of ideas
and qualities that he did not himself possess. Often, after his
daily cares, he would turn to Speer to talk about architecture,

and shortly after the assumption of power, he even appointed him State Architect. Speer thereby attained the privileged position of having been admitted to Hitler's private company, and thus he made friends with Brandt; their work would also bring them together.

There was considerably chaos in the medical world during the war. The cause for this lay primarily in the fact that the health services of the State, the Party, the Army and the SS all operated independently of one another; there was no co-ordination at all. Hitler therefore gave Brandt instructions to create some sort of co-operation between the services.

The first to turn against Brandt's growing power was Hess' successor Martin Bormann, 'A miserable creature', according to Hans Frank.

> 'This man having risen unobtrusively to even greater power, shared with his predecessor a distaste for pose, publicity and for discussions at a high level. Like Hess, he felt himself no match for experts. But that was all they had in common. Bormann was no dreamer. He had both feet on the ground; plotted to his heart's content, so much in fact, that it was thought unusual even in these circles, where plots were rife. The kind of aggressiveness he displayed was only matched by that of Himmler, with whom he also shared a great contempt for human life. His scorn for truth was so unscrupulous that even Goebbels had to envy it. He was made of coarser material than Hess. No lenient Party administrator, he kept the district leaders well in hand, and they mostly resigned themselves to this, though they were grinding their teeth.'[6]

And the then Minister of Finance, Lutz Graf von Krosigk, had this to say about him:

> 'Purposefully, and using great stealth, Bormann extended his powers — a process that went almost undiscerned by those around him. He set to work with such skill that he succeeded in misleading practically everybody. As the Third Reich grew, so grew the

influence of the Party and thereby Bormann's power.'[7]

In actual practice, all power in the Third Reich was concentrated in two organizations: the Party and the SS. When, after the invasion of Poland, the SS began to widen its powers, Bormann took hold of the opportunity to lay down the necessary duties for the party. When Rudolf Hess, Hitler's secretary, fled to England in May 1941, Bormann reached the height of his career; he became the Führer's secretary. Brandt's relationship with Bormann was ill-fated as his relationship with Himmler. Speer:

> 'Brandt and Bormann didn't get on well. Bormann was not too delighted to see that people in Hitler's circle had a good relationship with me. For some obscure reason, it seemed to undermine his special position . . . .'[8]

There were many areas where Bormann could use his authority to crush resistance. However, his authority in the medical field was limited since Brandt was in charge there. The Reichsleiter therefore allied himself firmly with Conti; they were resolved to dethrone Brandt. Gradually Bormann gained ground, with well-laid plans, careful statements, cunning methods and ruthless resolve; for Hitler's trust in Brandt was as yet unlimited.

Still on 28 July 1942, Hitler invested Brandt with a large part of the responsibility for State medical affairs; despite tentative pressure from Bormann, Hitler had ignored Conti.

Brandt denied that he had ever been informed of the medical experiments performed in the German concentration camps. He argued that he had been extended no authority over the SS, and that since it had been primarily SS doctors who had performed the tests, only Himmler was to be held responsible.

In the course of lengthy dialogues with the prosecutor, Brandt gave the impression of being the typical product of a totalitarian state. The State, not the individual, had been responsible for the experiments carried out by doctors. He admitted that many of the tests bordered on the criminal but at the same time thought it conceivable that in certain situations it was morally justifiable to perform tests on prisoners:

'In my opinion, the question of consent plays an important part in judging the experiments as a whole . . . a serious part if the experiments are qualified as criminal.'

'Well, Herr Brandt, why do you make a distinction between the types of experiments? What difference does it make what type of experiment it is, if the experimental subject has not consented to undergo the experiment?

'You may well call it an experiment even when it is only a matter of testing some newly introduced drug. There is the conviction that it will be helpful, but there is, as yet, no guarantee. I should therefore like a distinction in the matters the questions refer to. In addition, the question of voluntary and involuntary experiments is of psychological significance in the case of a prisoner, as it may be with a mental patient. If the overall answer to the question is that it is a criminal, it must be made clear what kind of experiment is involved. There are three aggravating factors with respect to the question of the criminal element in experiments; their involuntary character, the lack of necessity for them and the danger involved . . . .

'In other words, you find situations where it is possible, although the experimental subjects does not volunteer, that nonetheless the experiment is permissible, both by way of law and morals? Is that right?'

'Both are possible, yes.'

'You are a doctor. I should think that you are probably fairly familiar with malpractice cases and statutes in Germany. Suppose, Dr Brandt, you tried out a new drug on one of your patients in pre-war Germany, without telling the subject about it or asking his consent in any way, and as a result the person was injured by this drug, would you not be subject to a charge of malpractice?'

'I should certainly have risked such a charge.'

'Well, then, I don't quite understand the situation in which you say it is permissible to do something to a person without his consent?'

'That is why I made the distinction just now, because it is essentially a question of the degree of the danger. And what you have said implies an even greater danger, because lack of consent is added. To my mind, the case would be then twice as bad, and if the experiments should also be non-essential, then the ultimate degree of aggravation would be reached.'

'Assuming the experiment was carried out in the manner that the prosecution's proof has tended to show, in your opinion, was that a criminal experiment?'

'I cannot answer the question in this form. For I am here presented with a complex of what constitutes criminal behaviour and a legal evaluation of this concept. I can only make a statement on the whole complex of the freezing experiments, or the necessity for freezing experiments, when the entire situation that led to the experiments in the first place has been made clear.

'Thus, I can only tell you something about the ethical side. This ethical side is partially influenced, decisively influenced, by the whole manner in the first place. The critical factor in proposing an experiment is the question whether the experiment is important or unimportant. When this is applied to the freezing experiments, the importance of such experiments can be affirmed under wartime conditions which added official interest to general medicine and human factors. Indeed, one can reach the point when orders to carry out the freezing experiments must be given. It is then beyond a certain point, a question of how the experiments are to be conducted. The conducting of such experiments must again be specified according to their voluntary or involuntary nature. I make further reference to their risks or lack of risks that they involve.

'If the experiment is not dangerous, it may possibly, in my opinion, be carried out by a physician taking into account general, medical and human considerations; I wish to express myself carefully. If there is any danger, the physician must be relieved of all responsibility for the danger that is involved. This is possible only by way of an official order on the part of some superior authority, or of some government dispensation, the interest of the state allowing for various interpretations in time of war. . . .'

'Herr Brandt, for the sake of clarification, let us assume that it would have been highly important to the German armed forces to ascertain, as a matter of fact, how long a human being could withstand exposure to cold before succumbing to the effects of it. Do you understand that? Let's assume, secondly that human subjects were selected for such freezing experiments without their consent. Let's assume, thirdly, that such involuntary human subjects were subjected to the experiments and died as a result or indirect thereof. Now, would you be good enough to inform the tribunal what your view of such an experiment is — either from the legal or ethical point of view?'

'May I first of all repeat, so that I am sure I have understood correctly. In conducting the experiments, it is assumed that they are of the highest military importance, that the test subjects have not given their consent, and that the experiments are dangerous, with death as a possible consequence. In such cases, I am of the opinion, considering the war situation, that the individual or the government institution determining their importance must also undertake to relieve the physician of responsibility in the event of a fatal outcome of the experiment.'

'Now, in your view, does it take away that responsibility from the physician, or does it share that responsibility jointly with the physician?'

'In my opinion, it removes it from the physician, for from this moment on the physician is only an instrument, in about the same way as an officer in the field who is ordered to take a group of three or five soldiers, without fail to a position where they will fall and perish. When I apply this situation to our German conditions during the war, it is basically the same. I do not believe that the physician on his own would or could agree to conduct such an experiment by considering his medical ethics or his moral sense, unless he had been given this immunity by the authoritarian state, which would give him, on the one hand, security under formal law, and on the other hand, a direct order to carry out. Of course, in this case, such considerations are rather theoretical, since they refer to a specially formulated case, the freezing experiments, on which I do not have complete information. I do not know in what forms this order and this general dispensation were given. I want to make a fundamental distinction between an experimental set-up that is primarily based on medical needs as such, with the state under certain circumstances taking a secondary part on the basis of medical initiative; and the converse case, where the demands of the state make use of the work of the physician . . . .'

'In your view, would an order which authorized or directed a subordinate medical officer, or subordinate medical group, to carry on a certain medical experiment, let us assume for the moment this freezing experiment, we have then a general order, let us assume, directing a certain institute to carry on freezing experiments without delineating or specifying in detail the exact course of those experiments. Would you conceive that such an order would authorize the medical officer to whom the order was addressed to select subjects involuntarily and subject them to experiments, the execution of which that officer knew or should have known would likely result in the death of the subject?'

'This is a very difficult question to answer, for it depends on the nature of the clear chain of command that would apply in such a case. I may perhaps reply with an example. If Himmler ordered a Dr X to conduct a certain experiment, it is quite possible that such a Dr X may have been unwilling to carry out that order. In such a case, however, this Dr X may quite likely have been incapable of appraising the importance of the experiment in question. Just like the lieutenant who has received a certain military order, and we are dealing with military orders, who cannot understand why he with his group of eight men must hold out and perish on a bridge head. Nevertheless, this officer and his eight men, to whom he has passed on the command, will perish on this spot. Dr X too, who received the order from Himmler, may under certain circumstances, have to conduct an experiment without grasping all the fundamental factors entering into it and causing it to be ordered by a central agency. Had this physician refused to carry out the experiment, he would surely have been called to account for his failure to do so. In such a case, and here the authoritarian character of our system of government must be taken into account, personal response to a code of ethics peculiar to a specific profession had to give way to the total character of this war. I must state once again that I am giving expression to a set of suppositions rather theoretical in nature. I want to show at the same time how difficult such decisions are . . . .'[9]

As has already been described, Brandt stood head and shoulders above the rest of Hitler's favourites; his power and prestige grew by the day, and with it the enmity of his opponents. In 1943, in the military research centre in Peenemünde, Wernher von Braun put the finishing touches to the development of his rocket, the V-2. At its first demonstration, Hitler went into ecstasies, immediately promoting the twenty-eight-year-old Von Braun to professor and giving orders for mass production.

Albert Speer, however, who had been made Minister of Armament in 1942, did not have sufficient manpower at his disposal to put the V-2 into mass production. Himmler offered a helping hand. He proposed using concentration camp prisoners to work on the production line; a proposal for which Hitler gave his approval. In December 1943, Speer, went on an inspection tour around several arms factories in which concentration camp prisoners were working and was confronted with an appalling state of affairs; malnourishment, poor hygiene, lack of medical facilities, bad housing etc.[10] At the end of his tour he asked Brandt to take measures, in order to improve conditions which indeed Brandt did;[11] he appointed a number of civilian doctors to posts in the factories. This turned out to be the straw that broke the camel's back. Brandt appointed these people without consulting either Himmler or Conti. Himmler was furious because doctors had been removed from his (nominal) authority without his knowledge. Both protested to Hitler who, however, protected Brandt. This time the Nazi clique buried the hatchet. Conti, Himmler and Bormann sealed an alliance whose aim was the overthrow of Brandt — and of Speer, who had now definitely become their target too.

In mid-May 1944, the storm broke. Himmler had Von Braun arrested on suspicion of treason. Von Braun had made a few sketches of future bombs for a weekly paper. Himmler hoped that by arresting Von Braun he could get indirectly at Speer. Though Von Braun was set free after Speer's intercession, the latter did get a severe telling off from Hitler. He ought, as Minister of Armament, to prevent such excesses on the part of his subordinates. Furthermore, he would do well to take care that he did not undertake work which was in Himmler's domain . . . .

In fact, Karl Brandt's eventual downfall was brought about via an entirely different route. Theodore Morell, Hitler's private physician, seems to have been the hidden link in a mysterious chain of events leading to Brandt's dismissal; and to this day, it is still a mystery how this obscure character Morell, whose medical skills were called in question by every physician in Hitler's company, could nevertheless retain the complete responsibility for the Führer's health for nine long years.

Morell, originally a ship's doctor and later healer to Berlin's *beau monde* was often described after the war as a charlatan but this does no justice to the truth.[12] Not at least according to Speer:

> 'One of Morell's talents was his ability to exaggerate immoderately any illness he cured, in order to place his skill in the proper light. He alleged to have studied under the famous bacteriologist Illya Mechnikov (1845-1916), Nobel Prize winner and professor at the

Pasteur Institute. Mechnikov, he claimed, had taught him the art of combatting bacterial diseases. Undoubtedly, he was not an out-and-out quack — rather a bit of a screwball obsessed with making money.'[13]

In 1936 Hitler's health was failing; he was continually plagued by stomach cramps and insomnia, for which he was unsuccessfully treated by several physicians. Through his official photographer, Heinrich Hoffmann, Hitler met Morell who cured him of his troubles within nine months. Hitler's gratitude knew no bounds. At the next Party Day in September 1937, the Morell couple had seats in the box of honour. News of his successful treatment of the Führer spread like wildfire and soon a large part of the Nazi-élite was under his ministration. He tackled infections with large doses of sulpha-preparations and no one left his consultations without having had a shot. Goering referred mockingly to Morell as the 'Reichsinjektionsmeister'.[14]

Morell led a busy life and divided his attention between patients and the development of new medicines. Since he suffered from fear of flying, and Hitler always wanted a doctor in his entourage, the post of 'accompanying physician' was created. In practise, this meant little more than escorting Hitler on plane trips and, when Morell was too busy in the medical industry, acting as a substitute personal physician. The 'accompanying physicians' Hitler most prized were Brandt, and in his absence, Von Hasselbach, according to Speer 'a friendly, intelligent and congenial man'.[15] These two repeatedly warned Morell of the danger of continued use of sulphanilamides, but he shrugged these remarks off;

> 'Don't worry. The Führer takes the Ultraseptyl excellently. They make him feel better . . . .'[16]

This reply contains the essence of his therapeutic technique. His injections and pills resulted in a temporarily improved condition but were fatal in the long run. Neither did Hitler wish him to be ill-spoken of: 'Morell once saved my life.' End of the discussion. Imputations to the effect that Morell did not seem to take such special care of his own personal hygiene were dismissed with:

'Morell is not there to be sniffed at but to keep me healthy!'[17]

This situation became gradually less tenable. Brandt and Von Hasselbach could not but passively observe how Hitler was gradually being poisoned. In 1944, matters finally came to a head. An attack was made on Hitler's headquarters from which he emerged unscathed. But shortly after the explosion, he began to complain of buzzing in his ears, and the hastily summoned ear specialist, Dr Erwin Giesing, discovered that Morell gave Hitler ten to sixteen tablets to take per day, tablets whose origin was unknown. He took one away and had it analysed by the toxological department of the University of Königsberg. The tablet turned out to have a high strychnine content, deadly if regularly taken over a long period. Together with Von Hasselbach, he informed Brandt of the fact, who in turn told Hitler.

The Führer, furious showed him the door; but the affair was not closed. On the contrary! Von Hasselbach could not ignore the fact that Hitler was being poisoned by a charlatan and, in an unguarded moment, he gave Bormann the details, adding a request to deal with it quickly. Dr Von Hasselbach never suspected what a calamity he had caused. Bormann was Morell's ally and decided to strike back. He led Hitler to believe that Brandt and Von Hasselbach were gossiping about his health and were thereby causing uneasiness among the ranks; and the condition of the ranks was a concern close to Hitler's heart. Von Hasselbach was fired and on 4 October 1944 Karl Brandt met the same fate.

Only Giesing remained an obstacle to Morell's supremacy but Bormann came to his aid. Amicably, politely and with a cheque for DM 100.000 he was requested to leave and never appear again. Now the problem was to find a suitable replacement for Brandt, someone who would not take too independent a line. After long deliberation, one of Gebhardt's assistants was chosen, Dr Ludwig Stumpfegger. In this way, Bormann gained his first triumph, but he was not content. Brandt was no longer 'accompanying physician', but he retained his other posts and Bormann considered every living opponent as a potentially dangerous one; only Brandt's elimination could give him satisfaction and, determined to make his contribution towards it, he lay in wait.

By the end of March 1945, the end of the Third Reich was in sight and in Berlin, the exodus of the ministries began. Brandt also received orders to leave his post. For safety's sake, he moved his wife to the — as yet — unravaged city of Thüringen. Near despair, Hitler gave orders to proceed to a 'scorched earth' policy: everything that might reasonably be expected to be used for the rebuilding of Germany had to be destroyed. Speer spoke out strongly against this order and wrote directly to Hitler in an attempt to make him change his mind. Hitler remained inexorable and persisted in his demands: total destruction.

On 2 April Karl Brandt paid his last visit to Hitler to report on the medical situation. In a thick document, he advised an end to hostilities and a ceasefire. At the same time, he sharply criticized the 'scorched earth' policy. Bormann accused him of defeatism and Hitler supported this accusation. He wished never to see Speer or Brandt at General Headquarters again since their arrival was invariably accompanied by negative reports.

When the Americans took Thüringen, Brandt's wife and child found themselves in the occupied zone. Bormann struck a final blow. He openly accused Brandt of treason. Hitler was infuriated:

> 'I told Brandt that he should bring his wife and child to the Obersalzberg and he agreed. And now he sends them to the Americans! Bormann, find out if they took any secret documents with them. If they have, there is only one solution; a court martial!'[18]

On 16 April 1945 Brandt was arrested by the Gestapo. The next day a show trial took place in the ruins of Berlin. The president of the tribunal was the youth leader Arthur Axmann, and Goebbels took the prosecutor's part. Brandt was not allowed to have a barrister and, his own defence notwithstanding, the case was settled within the hour. The death sentence, with Hitler's signature, lay ready. The execution was set for 19 April but nothing happened.

When Speer heard of it all he decided to do something about it quickly. Incredibly enough, it was not that much trouble; his orders still had authority and at his command, Brandt was released. Bormann was furious and ordered a search operation.

But the bird had long flown; Brandt popped up in Flensburg on 2 May where, on 13 May he was arrested by the Americans. After a short hearing, he was transferred to Nuremberg where he would stand trial with twenty-two colleagues in the largest medical trial in history: United States of America v. Karl Brandt et al, Case 1, or 'doctors' trial' for short.

On 21 November 1946, the president of the tribunal, Walter B. Beals, opened this giant trial and the fight could begin. The battle ended on 21 August 1947; seven death sentences were passed, and one of them was for Brandt. The tribunal had judged him for his part in the euthanasia programme, 'One of the greatest crimes in human history . . . .'[19]

4

Euthanasia

On 8 August 1939 Hitler's *aide de camp* Engel made the following entry in his diary:

'Today we went through something horrible. Bouhler and Karl Brandt showed Hitler a film about "unworthy lives"; it showed the behaviour of incurable mentally deficient people in several institutions. It is truly shocking what takes place there! Impossible to understand the poor nursing staff, together with these unhappy creatures every day, you must have an idealistic and a Christian attitude to be able to keep going.

At the end of the evening, a most remarkable thing happened: Bormann suggested to Hitler that the film, which had been made on Conti's orders, should be shown as the first part of the programme in every cinema. Dr Brandt opposed this strongly; he asked Bormann what would he think if one of his own children should find himself amongst them . . . thank God, the Führer joined the conversation and it quickly took another turn . . . .'[1]

As early as 1924 Hitler had already stated in 'Mein Kampf':

'The demand that it be made impossible for mentally deficient people to beget equally deficient offspring is the demand of a healthy understanding, and a purposeful campaign to this end would signify the most humane act imaginable.'[2]

In 1933 Dr Franz Gürtner, Reich minister of Justice who then rejected the legal sanction of euthanasia introduced a law enforcing the compulsory sterilization of men and women suffering from hereditary diseases. On 8 October 1935, this law was followed by the '*Erbgesundheitsgesetz*' — a law 'to safeguard' the hereditary health of the German people. This expanded the original law by allowing for abortion in cases of pregnancy in which either of the partners suffered from a hereditary disease.[3]

At Nuremberg Brandt testified that euthanasia had long been on Hitler's mind. In 1935 he had told the then Minister of Health, Gerhard Wagner, a notorious advocate of euthanasia, that

> 'If war came, he would take up and resolve this question, because it would be easier to do so in wartime when the church would not be able to put up the expected resistance.'[4]

However, before things had gone this far, a campaign of propaganda and mis-information both paved and pointed the way. On 28 July 1933, the Minister of the Interior, Dr Wilhelm Frick, gave a lecture concerning national and racial politics. According to Frick, from the standpoint of genetics, twenty percent of the German population was inferior and he also stated that these people's children were undesirable members of the Third Reich. He demonstrated that the cost to the state of

> 'all the insane, the mentally retarded, the ill and the criminal was, to his reckoning, an average of four and a half marks a day per person. However, uneducated workers and petty officials could, in most cases, command only two and a half marks a day.'[5]

From this fact, Frick concluded that Germany had to spend too much time looking after the social welfare of the individual, and that no account had been taken of the insights provided by genetics and studies of 'racial hygiene' and improvement.

Less than a year later, Dr Gustav Franke, in his book *Vererbung und Rasse* came to the same conclusion *i.e.* that genetically inferior people formed too great a financial burden for Germany, particularly since it was they who produced a number of children higher than the average. He frequently quoted professor Fetcher from the University of Dresden who had calculated, for example, that educationally subnormal children (!) cost the state three times as much as the education of normal children at primary schools. According to Fetcher's figures, the state spent DM 350,000,000 on people deemed genetically inferior. An epileptic, for instance, cost around DM 23,885 over twenty years, and a mentally deficient criminal cost DM 6.576 over four years.[6]

Even children were not spared these racist mathematics; a maths textbook for primary schools printed in 1935 contained the following problem:

> 'Lunatic asylums cost the State DM 6,000,000 per year to maintain. How many working-class cottages costing DM 15,000 each could be built with this money?'[7]

By means of this kinds of veiled propaganda, the German people were primed for euthanasia. According to Dr Menges in his excellent thesis on German euthanasia:

> 'Euthanasia presupposes a kind of treatment in which relief or prevention of the suffering is of primary importance. The alleviation of fear and pain at a deathbed, true euthanasia, is part of the daily work of a practising physician and poses no problem at all. But other forms of euthanasia (the withholding of drugs should complications arise during an incurable illness, passive euthanasia; and the curtailment of a prolonged illness, active euthanasia) require that the doctor concerned has a love for his patient and that he is honest towards the patient or towards his family

With "Nazi euthanasia", none of this mattered. The patient's wishes did not count, only those of the State. There was no question of openness; bogus organization, the use of false names, disgustingly hypocritical letters of condolence and even the misleading of the doctors concerned, ensured from the very beginning that a veil of deceit was drawn over the whole affair. The facts alone condemn "Nazi euthanasia" and demonstrate that this was not so much salvation but murder.'[8]

Hitler's chancellery had a department that handled several petitions for mercy killings. In February 1939 a request was received from the father of a deformed child, asking for the child to be killed. Hitler turned the matter over to Karl Brandt, instructing him to investigate. If the father's statement was true, Brandt was authorized to tell them that, should they become involved in legal procedures as a consequence, these would be stopped on Hitler's orders. In fact, the Führer expressly stated to the parents that he alone, not they, bore the responsibility for this action.[9]

The undisputed highpoint in the advertising campaign for euthanasia was the film *I accuse*, made on the orders of SS Oberführer Viktor Brack, who served in Hitler's chancellery as a liaison with the Health Department in the Ministry of Interior. The plot was a simple one: a doctor's wife appeared to be incurably ill and her husband diagnosed a painful and protracted period of suffering ending in death. To spare her this, he proposed euthanasia and the climax of the film is a scene in which he gives her the final injection and, kissing him, she died in his arms.

After six years of such preparatory work, in October 1939, Hitler drew up, on private notepaper, a decree, the so-called '*Erlasz*', in which he empowered Bouhler and Brandt

'with the responsibility of enlarging the authority of certain physicians to be designated by name in such a manner that persons who, according to human judgement, are incurably ill, may, upon the most serious evaluation of their medical condition, be accorded a mercy death.'[10]

Hitler had originally appointed Conti as head of the euthanasia programme but after having learnt that Conti had asked the Secretary of the Reich Chancellery, Lammers, for some sort of official legitimation, Hitler, enraged, replaced Conti with Bouhler who willingly accepted verbal orders.

Menges:

'It is strange that such a radical decision, a state-

organized mass murder, should be set in writing on
Hitler's private notepaper. Hitler decided, not as
Head of State but as ''father'' of the German people;
he wanted full responsibility for this rather than share
it with the state authorities.'[11]

It is extremely important to bear this fact in mind because
it meant the absence of a legal basis for the euthanasia
programme. Hitler had always rejected one. His greatest fear
— and as we shall see, he was mistaken — lay abroad; he did
not want to give his enemies a single chance to issue counter-
propaganda. This was why the euthanasia programme was
administered, not by the Ministry of Justice but by Hitler's
private secretary, the '*Kanzlei des Führers*'.

Philipp Bouhler, head of Hitler's private chancellery, and
according to Brandt 'an honourable man who was concerned
about the euthanasia programme because he feared that, in
wartime conditions, the various district commanders would take
such matters in to their own hands',[12] was given administrative
control of the programme. Brandt was made responsible for its
medical direction. A large number of problems had to be solved:
the selection of medical and nursing staff, the criteria by which
patients would be selected, the method by which euthanasia
would be effected, and so on.

The greatest problem was considered to be the selection of
doctors and nurses; the first requirement was that they embraced
Nazi doctrine, at least, those who were to be fully appraised
for the purpose of the programme. For it must be remembered
that a large proportion of the doctors found themselves
unwittingly involved in the programme. If a doctor discovered
the real purposes of this 'euthanasia', he was at once faced with
considerable problems. He could choose to break his rule of
confidentially, but this could have dire consequences. To resign
in disgust meant to abandon the patients to the arbitrary care
of the Berlin-appointed successors.

Menges divided the German doctors, as far as their co-
operation with and attitude to the euthanasia is concerned, into
three groups: i) those who, by requesting early retirement or
by enlisting in the army, decided to leave their posts; ii) those
who remained at their posts but who endeavoured to sabotage
the campaign from the beginning; iii) those who extended their

full co-operation.[13]

To return to the organization of the 'euthanasia': once the medical candidates had been selected in Berlin, they were invited to a meeting and informed about the secret nature of the euthanasia programme. Dr Walter Schmidt, later to be condemned to life imprisonment, referring to one such meeting in February 1940:

> 'Some ten or twelve physicians unknown to me had been asked to attend this conference, in addition to myself. We were told by Drs Hevelmann and Bohne and by Herr Brack that the National Socialist Government had decreed laws under which socially unfit lives (*lebensunwertes Leben*) could be extinguished.
>
> The assembled physicians were asked whether they cared to function as medical consultants. We were urgently enjoined not to discuss these matters, since they were classified "top secret". During the conference Herr Brack read out a communiqué, the exact contents of which I do not recall. To my recollection, it gave assurances that the physicians co-operating in the programme would be immune from penalties.
>
> The discussion then turned to the work we were expected to do — submitting medical opinions on institutional patients, that is, mental patients. The other physicians assembled were all gentlemen of mature years, including some eminent figures, as I learned later. Since all these gentlemen consented without hesitation, I joined in this decision and offered my services as a consultant ... .'[14]

And Dr Fritz Meinecke, medical director of the Eichberg Institute, said of the same meeting:

> 'The legal gentlemen in Berlin told us that this was a legitimate matter, that it was a law of Hitler's, a decree having full legal force. The question as to whether Hitler was empowered to issue such decrees was likewise discussed by the lawyers and answered in the affirmative. (...) The question of secrecy was

also discussed at length. It was stated that this was
a new type of law, that for this reason, patients must
not have prior knowledge of the measure otherwise
they might become too agitated, and that this was
probably the crucial reason why the law had not been
made public. Besides, we were at war at the time, and
such matters on the home front had to be kept secret.
We were told that only incurable patients were
involved who were suffering severely, though it was
not quite clear as to where the line was to be
drawn . . . .'[15]

Not all the doctors who had been approached promised their
co-operation. Dr Ferdinand Hölzel declined the offer in writing:

'I must honestly confess that I do not deem myself
suitable for the assignment you have offered me. As
a doctor, I feel emotionally bound to the patients and
I cannot imagine that this is a shortcoming, at least,
from a national socialist viewpoint (. . .) I realize
that your offer is an indication of your confidence in
me, to which I can only respond with absolute
sincerity.'[16]

Despite his refusal, no steps were taken against Hölzel and
he remained at his post which did not, however, mean that the
institution where he worked was safeguarded from the euthanasia
actions.

The second problem that remained was the method by which
the euthanasia was to be effected. On the advice of Professor
Werner Heyde, one of the doyens of the euthanasia movement,
it was decided to use morphine-scopolamine injections to kill
the subjects, but gassing was another usual method.

In January 1940 an experiment took place in the Brandenburg
Institute for the benefit of the cream of the euthanasia
programme; Bouhler, Brack, Dr Conti, Professor Nitsche,
Professor Heyde and Karl Brandt were all present. Brandt and
Conti gave mentally ill people injections which consequently
resulted in their deaths. Professor Heyde considered that the
initiative for this experiment came from Karl Brandt:

'He was a conscientious man who took his

responsibilities very seriously. Since Hitler had made him responsible, together with Bouhler, for putting the euthanasia programme into practice, he clearly wanted to see with his own eyes which method of killing the patient was the most suitable. At that time, it was repeatedly stressed that Brandt and Conti were to administer the injections in order to demonstrate that even the most authoritive physicians in the country did not shy from the Führer's orders . . . .'[17]

As soon as the preparations were completed the *Erlasz* was put into practice without delay. The Reich Operative Team of Asylums and Nursing Homes (*Reichsarbeitsgemeinschaft Heil — und Pflegeanstalten*) sent questionnaires, the so-called *Meldebögen*,[18] to every institute for the mentally handicapped in Germany. These were to be filled in by the institute's doctor, who was asked to supply details of patients such as name, date of birth, civilian status, race (!), nature of the illness, the type of medicines being used, the degree of unsuitability for work, whether the patient received visitors regularly (!) and so on.

The reasons for which this information was required was unknown, and the doctors supplied answers to the best of their ability. The *Meldebögen* were to be sent by return post to Berlin where they were copied in triplicate and passed on to three medical experts (*Gutachters*), whose independent judgement of the patients based on the information supplied in the *Meldebögen*, took the form of a plus or a minus sign within a black-lined rectangle. A plus sign meant the patient could go on living, a minus sign meant death.

For a final decision, the questionnaires were submitted to two senior experts (*Obergutachters*), Professor Heyde and Professor Nitsche. If these experts also decided on a patient's death, then the institute concerned would, in due course, receive a list of 'euthanasia candidates' who were to be taken away.

This *Meldebögen* system inundated the institutes with work. Most had only one or two doctors on the staff and, for this reason, Berlin prepared doctors' committees which were to assist the institutes' doctors in the completion of the questionnaires. The physicians on these committees had considerable authority: they could come and go as they pleased and could demand any information. These committees were therefore the terror of those institutes where the staff did not agree with the euthanasia campaign; though to be exact, it should be pointed out that in the beginning, before suspicions arose that the information thus supplied was being used in the euthanasia campaign, these committees themselves aroused suspicion within the institutes by their methods, which were both careless and extreme.

The next step in the system was taken by the Public-Benefit Patient Transportation Society (*Gemeinnützige Krankentransportgesellschaft*), which came to collect those patients Berlin had decided should die. They were taken, not directly to a 'euthanasia institution'. This was done to confuse the family of the patient; to begin with, they were not informed of the patient's transfer and should they decide to search for him or her, they often got no further than this transit point. By the time they had traced the relative this far, he or she had already been gassed.

In the observation institution and the subsequent installation, a summary medical examination was made, on which grounds a patient might still eventually be returned to the institution from which he was taken; however this seldom occurred.

There were six euthanasia installations on German and Austrian soil, officially designated by code-letters: at Bernburg near Dessau, Grafeneck near Würtemburg, Hartheim near Linz, Hadamar in Hessen, Sonnenstein near Dresden and Brandenburg near Berlin. When the patient had died, the General foundation for Affairs of Insane Asylums (*Allgemeine Stiftung für Anstaltswesen*) looked after the remaining and financial business. The deceit reached its peak in the way in which the families of the dead were informed of the news. Each 'euthanasia' installation had its 'letter of condolence department' which used a number of standard letters;

> 'Dear . . . . . ., It is with deep regret that we must inform you that . . . . . ., a patient in our institute, following a sudden . . . . . . has passed away. Medical attention proved, alas, of no avail. It may be of some reassurance to you, however that . . . . . . died quickly and painlessly in his/her sleep. Considering the grave and incurable illness, death came as a relief . . . . . . Heil Hitler, (false name of the doctor).'[20]

Another version:

> 'We sincerely regret the need for advising you
> that ...... who had to be transferred to this
> institution on ......, in the course of measures taken
> by the Reich Commissioner for Defence, died here
> suddenly and unexpectedly on ......, of a brain
> oedema. Because of her grave mental illness, life was
> a torment for the deceased. You must therefore look
> on the death as a release. Because danger of epidemic
> currently threatens this institution, the police
> authorities ordered the body to be cremated
> immediately. We request notification of which
> cemetery we should advise the police authorities to
> ship the urn to with the mortal remains of the
> deceased. It is required that any inquiries be made
> in writing to this address, since visits are at present
> prohibited for public health reasons.'[21]

It did not take long before people learned what was actually
going on because in such a large and ambitious programme
mistakes were made. In fact, huge blunders did occur. The most
extraordinary example is of a patient who was supposed to have
died from an inflammation of the appendix — which had in
fact been removed ten years previously. In another instance,
the family of a patient received two urns of ashes and two letters
of condolence, detailing two different causes of death, signed
by the same doctor!

There were cases in which the next of kin, suspicious of the
whole affair, entered into lengthy correspondence with the
institution doctors.[22] Instances where the next of kin went to
court were exceptions because the lack of evidence meant that
the case was lost from the outset. The Press obituaries also
aroused suspicion; the deathrate in certain institutions rose
suspiciously high!

After more than a year of rising public clamour in Germany,
Hitler, reluctant to legalize the operation, instructed Brandt
in August 1941 to cease this killing of mental patients. It had
been estimated that between 75,000 and 95,000 people were
murdered under the auspices of T-4.[23] A period of so-called
'wild euthanasia' began: the institution doctors could behave

according to their own discretion and the pressure from Berlin was dropped until it became insignificant.

Under the code name 14 F 13, the euthanasia programme spread to the concentration camps. The official designation here was *'Sonderbehandlung* 14 F 13', a term introduced, in all probability, by Heydrich. Formally, the same system was employed as in the civilian programme but as time passed, the formalities were diluted until the whole thing eventually gave way to, or rather became a part of the Final Solution.[24] At regular intervals, medical committees visited concentration camps to select patients; the most important criterion was reluctance or incapacity to work. Health played a subordinate role, Oskar Schiedlausky's evidence as camp doctor at Mauthausen notwithstanding:

'In June 1941 the Reichsführer, accompanied by Oswald Pohl, made a tour of inspection around the Mauthausen concentration camp. Shortly before he left, the Reichsführer was presented with a prisoner who had been shot while attempting to escape. The man's liver was hit and it was clear that he would die within a few hours. Nevertheless, the Reichsführer made the following remark: "I want this man dead by nightfall!" After his departure, the camp commander Ziereis, called the camp physicians together and asked us, referring to a previous camp doctor whose name I can't remember, to prepare lethal injections for prisoners. We refused. Later, during a conversation with Enno Lolling,[25] several doctors raised the question as to what extent it was permissible to give lethal injections to seriously ill patients, especially in connection with the danger of epidemics.

They described the situation in the camp as grave and asked for further instructions. Lolling replied that he could not give binding orders but promised to talk with each of the doctors privately after the meeting. As to the question of to what extent a doctor would be held personally responsible for the administration of the lethal injection, he gave no explicit answer. But he did respond with something to the effect: "I'm one hundred percent behind you.''

When I visited Oranienburg in October I met Lolling again. At that moment I was in a very difficult position. A few weeks beforehand I had received a telex from the Dortmund Gestapo with the message that there was a Polish prisoner in the camp with TB and that the local doctor was to ''euthanise'' him. I summoned the prisoner and examined him; the man was in good health and there was no need to give him medical treatment at all, let alone practise euthanasia on him. However, the Dortmund Gestapo remained insistent and I eventually went for advice to the camp commander, who told me that this was a medical matter. I decided to refer the whole affair to Lolling. He stated that I was allowed to effect euthanasia, but could not be compelled to do so. Naturally, I never practised such a form of euthanasia ... .'[26]

And Dr Muthig, his colleague in Dachau remembered:

'In the autumn of 1941, on the occasion of a duty inspection of my Revier (camp hospital) by Dr Lolling, he told me that a commission of four doctors led by Professor Heyde would shortly be visiting Dachau camp. The commissions duty was selecting prisoners unfit for work and therefore candidates for euthanasia and then transfer them to Mauthausen concentration camp to be gassed. Shortly after my conversation with Dr Lolling, the commission duly arrived. It consisted of four psychiatrists and was led by Professor Heyde, who was also present.

Neither myself nor the other camp doctors had anything to do with the commission or its work. But I saw that the doctors sat down between two huts and that hundreds of prisoners were being paraded before them. The prisoners political records and their unfitness for work were being examined and then selected accordingly. I know that this commission spent only a few days in Dachau and that it was impossible to give so many prisoners a medical examination in such a short space of time. The examination consisted of simply checking documents in the presence of the prisoner concerned.

I can categorically state the Professor Heyde directed the operation and that he was present in person, but I have forgotten the names of the other doctors.

A few weeks after the commission had left Dachau in December 1941, the first trainload of several hundred prisoners selected by the commission left for Mauthausen to be gassed. The operation for selecting those unfit for work and for euthanasia was known in Dachau camp as *"Aktion Heyde"*.'[27]

Dr Fritz Mennecke was one of the doctors who regularly visited concentration camps in order to select prisoners for 'euthanasia.' This correspondence with his wife reveals how the euthanasia campaign actually took effect. On 20 November 1941, he wrote from Ravensbrück concentration camp:

'Work is going smoothly since the names have been already typed in and only the diagnosis has to be filled in. Dr Sonntag sits beside me chatting about the situation in the camp while an officer brings the patients up. It goes like clockwork. We still have 2,000 forms to complete, and in fact that's just a formality, as it's open to question if there really are so many who are eligible for euthanasia ... .'[28]

On 12 January 1942, he wrote from Buchenwald concentration camp:

'At last! All the questionnaires finished. Soon we start with a set of new forms. 16.45: so darling, that's all, job's finished at last. Still a bunch of Jewish women but if all goes well, I should be finished with them in a short time ... .'[29]

That the selection criteria were observed less than scrupulously is amply evidenced in his first letter from Buchenwald concentration camp, dated 25 November 1941:

'The first day's work is done. We were up and about from half past eight because we first had to complete forty questionnaires from yesterday, a group of forty people, on which two colleagues had already worked. When we had got through them (I took fifteen myself) (Dr) Schmalenbach threw in the towel and disappeared. There immediately followed the examination of 1,200 Jewish patients; that is to say, the grounds for arrest, frequently rather general and comprehensive, were taken verbatim from the act. Therefore, the patients were, in fact, not even examined; so my work is often only theoretical ... .'[30]

A brief example of this work:

'Isador Israel, born 25 April 1902, builder, stateless citizen, reasons for euthanasia: hostile towards Germany. Hans R. Jew, has already had more convictions (*Pfahlbinden*), reasons for euthanasia: hostile towards Germany. Ottile Sara, born 6 December 1879, official within the Marxist party, reasons for euthanasia: bitter hatred towards Germany, relations with the British embassy.'[31]

During his trial in Frankfurt, Mennecke admitted that 'Jews were judged not on the basis of their state of health but on the reasons for their arrest.'[32]

He even went so far as to admit that his work had nothing to do with euthanasia and everything to do with the fact that 'exclusively political and racist standards were in force.'[33] This candour must be seen in the light of his own health. During his trial Mennecke was a broken man; he suffered an incurable lung disease and knew he had not long to live. Apart from his (dubious) honour, therefore, he did not have much to lose.

'You stated that questionnaires were also filled out for prisoners in the concentration camps.'
'Yes.'
'What were the criteria applied?'
'That has already been discussed, Counsellor. The

Jews were not evaluated by health factors, but from the viewpoint of the reasons for arrest.'

'It was political and racial considerations?'

'Yes.'

'Who ordered you to proceed along these lines?'

'I mentioned that too, a little while ago. It all depended. Sometimes the procedure was set by Professor Nitsche, sometimes by Professor Heyde or even Herr Brack.'

'Wasn't this a complete break with what was stated at the outset?'

'Yes. At least, it had nothing to do with the euthanasia for mental patients.'

'When was the first time that this procedure for racial and political reasons was followed? Was that early as your visit to a concentration camp?'

'No.'

'When was it?'

'In my opinion, it may have started at Buchenwald or even Dachau.'

'What methods were used before? What was your job then in the concentration camps?'

'The examination of selected prisoners to establish the presence of psychosis or psychopathic symptoms.'

'It was first a question of mental illness?'

'A medical question.'

'And later it grew into a political and racial question?'

'Yes, that is, even later, apart from the political and racial question, I had to make purely medical judgements.'

'At the later period you thus had two types of cases — mental patients to be judged from the medical viewpoint, and those who were to be judged by political and racial criteria?'

'That can't be separated Counsellor. It was not subdivided and sharply distinguished.'

'When you examined a large number of Jews, do you mean to say that they were all mentally ill at the same time?'

'I have already given my position on that, to the

effect that, in my view, they were not sick at all, either mentally or otherwise.'

'But you filled out the questionnaires?'

'Yes, that was the way Berlin had ordered it.'

'Were you warned against sabotage?'

'Yes, repeatedly, and this pressure followed me during my activities; sabotage would be punished with concentration camp internment or by death.'[34]

According to the *Erlasz* of 1939, Karl Brandt had been given authority to appoint these doctors who were to perform euthanasia. In Nuremberg, however he strongly denied that he had anything to do with the euthanasia, claiming to have been only indirectly involved.

'Was the decree meant exclusively for the mentally ill, or did other illnesses fall within the programme?'

'First of all, there was no programme. The word "illness" was understood in very broad terms. I acknowledge that there were cases in which non-weak-minded persons were put forward for euthanasia. But, in principle, these did not form part of the framework for euthanasia that Hitler had intended.'

'But Dr Brandt, there are a large number of people who are weak-minded but nonetheless very happy.'

'I do not believe that it is possible to suppose that a weak-minded person can be happy, nor that the life of a weak-minded person holds anything of any human worth. The deciding factor was the suitability of continued life.'

'The declarations of all the witnesses have shown that this euthanasia was in no way restricted to those whose death might be considered imminent.'

'That is so, but it was not the intention.'[35]

According to the *Erlasz*, Hitler empowered Brandt with authority to extend the powers of certain doctors in connection with the euthanasia. Did Brandt designate these doctors? Again Brandt:

'No everything was arranged by officials within the
Ministry of Internal Affairs, where the euthanasia
headquarters were situated. I delegated this order, so
the selection and the responsibility for it devolve not
to me . . . .'

'And what if mistakes were made and doubtful
characters were appointed?'

'That seems to me to be out of the question. But
again, in such instances, the responsibility would not
be mine.'

'Could you tell me the names of a few doctors that
were appointed?'

'No, I cannot!'

'Dr Brandt, I must say that I am intrigued that it
is possible that a man in your position, responsible
for the appointment of doctors carrying out the
euthanasia programme in practice, cannot remember
ten or fifteen names. You do seem to be able to
remember that two to four percent of those deported
to euthanasia-institutes were not killed . . . .'

Brandt remained silent, whereupon MacHaney turned to the
court:

'I'm beginning to get the impression that the charge
against Brandt has to be based on a mistake!'

How could Brandt keep Hitler informed if he never received
any reports himself? Brandt:

'I discussed the matter with Bouhler and with Hitler
but as far as the practical administration of the
euthanasia was concerned, I did not inform the
Führer. Only in special instances, after Bouhler had
consulted me, did I go to Hitler.'

'What sort of instances were these?'

'For example, the question whether children of
seven or eight years of age also fell within the terms
of the programme. They were nearly all cases arising
from complaints from the church . . . .'

'So you were there to shoot trouble?'

'That would be a mis-supposition. I was asked to deal with those problems that I was considered capable of handling.'

The infamous questionnaires formed a chapter in themselves. Brandt claimed to have had little or nothing to do with this either. The *Meldebögen* were prepared by medical experts from the Ministry of Internal Affairs. He exposed the roles played by two men in particular: Heyde and Nitsche. A pity, but this was already well known; moreover Heyde was in hiding and Nitsche had committed suicide.

'Dr Brandt, now suppose two patients had been in an institution for a month, one German, the other not; was a questionnaire filled in for each one, or just for one, and in the latter instance, for which one?'

'It depended on the length of time that the person had stayed in the institution .... .'

'Now listen, I am in no hurry. If I consider it necessary, I shall keep you here three days in the witness box in order to get an answer to my question. Was a questionnaire filled in for both people?'

'In my opinion, no!'

'Very good, Dr Brandt. Euthanasia was therefore not practised on foreigners?'

'No.'

'On whose orders had they been excluded?'

'The Führer.'

'If foreigners were excluded from the programme, why was there still a question in the questionnaire concerning nationality?'

'The question whether someone was or was not a foreigner was not decided at the institution in which the questionnaire was filled in, but by the headquarters in Berlin. Measures were taken there to ensure the foreigners would not be transported to euthanasia centres.'

'You realize, of course, that had foreigners been drawn in to the programme, this would be criminal?'

'The elimination of foreigners was entirely against the Führer's orders.'

At this point, the prosecutor gave vent to his incredulity:

> 'Why then were questionnaires filled in for people
> who had been excluded on principle from the
> euthanasia programme?'

Brandt's feeble defence:

> 'For general information.'

MacHaney then alluded to Dr Mennecke's statement in which
he admitted that foreigners also had received the euthanasia
decree, but Brandt could 'no longer remember the details of
this statement'.

> 'Dr Brandt, the patient's race also had to be entered
> into the questionnaire. Why?'
> 'In my opinion, for statistical reasons only. I cannot
> see any other reason.'

Did Brandt know anything of the persecution of the Jews?

> 'No, I knew nothing at the time of the measures
> taken against the Jews. I did know that Jews had to
> wear identification badges and that, later, they had
> to live in certain areas. It was here that I first heard
> of their systematic extermination . . . .'
> 'But how can you declare that the extermination
> of 60,000 Germans, to confine myself for the moment
> to your own estimate, was general knowledge, and
> that a man in your position had no inkling of the
> wholesale extermination of the Jews, of a seven-figure
> number?'
> 'I think that the seven-figure number was not
> generally known!'[36]

Brandt claimed to know absolutely nothing of the euthanasia
practised in the concentration camps and not to understand for
whom Dr Mennecke, one of the great euthanasia experts, was
working. MacHaney:

'The psychiatrist's report tells us that you are a very intelligent man, that you have an IQ high above the average. I am confident that you can still remember Dr Mennecke's testimony. He was called to Berlin in 1940 and received instructions for the euthanasia programme. His job was to select candidates for euthanasia from concentration camp prisoners. He was one of those working on a programme that you had organized ... .'

'I have never heard that mentally deficient people were held in concentration camps, and such a scheme is entirely unknown to me ... .'

At the end of his trial, the doctor in him revealed itself by giving a warm appeal for euthanasia:

'It is possible, as has here been frequently claimed, that euthanasia has something inhuman about it. But this is merely an outward appearance and lies mostly in the application. Euthanasia was there to help the sufferer, alleviate the pain. These considerations can hardly be called inhuman, and personally, I do not find this unethical or amoral. I recognize that things went amiss; I am now thinking of the family who received two urns of ash and also of the incorrect diagnosis that were entered. These things are deeply regrettable but do not threaten the principle of euthanasia.

Professor Leibrandt, who gave evidence here, referred to Hippocrates, and particularly to that part of the oath in which the doctor is forbidden to give a sick person any poison even if the person asks for it himself. I am convinced that if Hippocrates had lived in our age, his oath would have been cast in a different mould. When the typhoid fever raged in old Athens around 439 BC, people came to him for help. He advised that the sick be left to die, since they could not be helped anyway, and that a wall be built in the valley so that the wind should not reach the city. He purposely let these people lie, not because he understood the danger of infection, but because he

knew from experience what health was and what
sickness was.

If Hippocrates is quoted today, one hears that
poison may not be given to a sick person, but at this
moment, there is not one doctor who would not
administer a narcotic to someone suffering terribly in
illness or on their deathbed in order to alleviate the
pain. One could say: this is not euthanasia. In any
case, it is against Hippocrates' oath. If one wishes to
make a judgement on euthanasia, one must first spend
a few days in an institute for the mentally ill. Rest
assured that life behind these grey walls is the most
worthless that a human-being can have. After this
visit, one must ask oneself two questions: the first,
whether one could ever live like that — the second,
whether one could ever see a member of one's family
live like that.

I have just read a book in which it was stated that
it had been possible to keep a child, who was
congenitally insane and brain-damaged alive for three
and a half years. The child had certainly cried for three
and a half years, anyway I am sorry, but I cannot
detect anything humane in this. Furthermore, I must
confess, that despite everything, I have no guilty
conscience. What I did, I felt was justifiable, and was
supported by the most human concern. My only
interest was to shorten the life, the painful existence,
of these miserable creatures ... .'[37]

During his hearing, Brandt had already mentioned the
reactions from the church, which had reached a high point when
the Catholic bishop of Münster, Count Clemens von Galen
accused the German government of murder while he was
preaching from the pulpit:

'Why must these poor defenceless people suffer?
Woe betide those, woe betide the German people if
God's commandment "Thou shalt not kill", engraved
in Man's conscience by our creator in the beginning
of time, is not simply broken, but violated with
patience and impunity ... .'[38]

Menges, speaking on the resistance of the church:

> 'There can be no doubt about it; the reactions in
> Catholic circles, culminating in Von Galen's
> celebrated sermon, were an essential factor in the
> Nazi's calling a provisional halt to the first stage of
> the organized implementation of the euthanasia
> programme. There can be no doubt either that the
> clergy found themselves protesting against attacks on
> the dogmatism of Catholicism and against attempts
> made on the material possessions of the Church. In
> other respects, we see the bishops applauding Hitler's
> political and military successes; strongly evoking —
> more often than not — rather the champions of an
> extremely nationalist Germany, than the
> representatives of Rome.'[39]

It was after the euthanasia programme had been officially
established, that is to say, working at full speed but still in secret,
that the first protest came from the church on 1 August 1940.

Archbishop Conrad von Freiburg wrote to the head of the
Reichskanzlei and referred to the rising unrest amongst the
population, an argument that appears frequently, and seems
to have been particularly effective. He made a generous offer,
and had the state's interest in the carrying through of the
euthanasia programme been primarily economic, it might
possibly have been accepted. The church declared itself prepared
to take on the cost of the maintenance of the mentally retarded.[40]
Naturally, the offer was ignored. The protests began to pile up,
until Graf Von Galen crowned the edifice: first the mentally
retarded, then the war victims, then the pensioners and *'dann
ist der Mord an uns frei gegeben'* (then murder will be offered to
us all).[41]

His sermon was printed up and sold in large numbers
everywhere, even as far as the soldiers at the front. A wave of
indignation swept across Germany. The soldiers were the most
deeply affected; while they fought for their fatherland, their
families were being massacred. They ran an accordingly higher
risk of mental collapse and of consequent consideration for
euthanasia!

Von Galen had predicted it: first the feeble-minded, then the

war veterans . . . . Results were not long in coming and on 23
August 1941 Hitler gave orders for the euthanasia to stop.[42]
The gas chambers were dismantled and, together with a
contingent of the personnel, transferred to the environs of Lublin
in Poland. Here, activities were resumed within the framework
of the *Endlösung* (Final Solution).

As has already been noted, Hitler had no wish to legalize the
euthanasia process; this would have placed a valuable
opportunity for counter-propaganda into his enemy's hands but
then, the enemy hardly reacted at all!

Opposition to the euthanasia programme came then, from
an entirely different quarter. Von Galen led the opposition and,
to begin with, the authorities were at a loss for a solution.
Himmler suggested that the bishop should be arrested but this
was blocked by Dr Goebbels. Arrest would only succeed in
arousing still more vehement protests and at that moment the
government enjoyed domestic peace. Hitler decided to send
Brandt to Münster to tame the turbulent bishop. There, they
had two long and candid discussions, but their principles were
manifestly incompatible. Hitler's adjutant, Engel, wrote in his
diary on 4 October 1940:

> 'When I asked Brandt whether he would tell the
> Führer everything he had discussed with Von Galen,
> he answered dismissively, saying: "If I told the Führer
> exactly what Von Galen told me, he would lock us
> both up in a concentration camp!" '[43]

State and Church were in a kind of stalemate. To arrest Von
Galen was to risk public opinion, and would, moreover, involve
a trial during which the sordid details of the euthanasia
programme would come to light. It was decided to keep an eye
on him, but nothing more. Nevertheless, it was Von Galen's
sermon which prompted Hitler to stop the euthanasia
programme.

Finally, it must not be overlooked that the programme —
according to Brandt's estimate, 60,000 mentally retarded people
having already been killed — was largely completed. And
Menges concludes:

> 'By "Action T-4" about 60,000 mentally ill people

met their death in the gas chambers. (...) In the
occupied territories too, mentally ill people had to pay
the price for their condition.

Especially in Russia and Poland, they fell victim
to the manner in which patients were treated in these
countries in accordance with the disdain which
Germans displayed for the Slavonic race. (...)

Abroad, people knew about the annihilation of the
mentally ill. However, there was no talk about
protestation, appropriate protestation. As a matter of
fact, the Pope expressed his abhorrence in a *decretum*
and the RAF threw lampoons over Germany, the
contents of which were aimed against "euthanasia".
But the reactions are pale when compared with the
committed crime ... .'[44]

5

The Buchenwald and Natzweiler Experiments

In the summer of 1937 near Weimar, one of the repositories of German culture, a concentration camp was built on a wooded hill: Buchenwald. For almost eight years this camp was the stage for barbarism and inhumanity where hundreds of prisoners were subjected to medical experiments. '*Jedem das Seine*' (To each one his own) was fixed in heavy bronze letters above the iron entrance gate of the camp. According to the ex-prisoner Jan Hemelrijk, 'Buchenwald was a hell on earth'.[1] And Buchenwald was also the residence of Dr Erwin Ding Schuler, the unrivalled medical experimenter. Before turning to his activities, first a note on the medical situation within the concentration camps.

The physician of the SS garrison (SS *Standortarzt*) stood at the head of the so-called Medical Service of the concentration camp and he was directly subordinate to the camp commandant. He was responsible for the state of health of the SS men, for the care of the prisoners and for all sanitary and hygienic installations. His most important duty was to prevent the outbreak and spreading of all kinds of epidemics and pestilence. The Standortarzt received orders and instructions directly from the head of Office D-3[2] in Berlin, who, at the same time, informed the camp commandant about all more important matters connected with sanitary conditions. Medical reports and those confirming the execution of orders were sent by the Standortarzt to the Head of Office D-3, while the camp commandant received copies for his information.

The subordinates of the Standortarzt were: physicians of the SS detachments (SS *Truppenärzte*) responsible for the medical care of the SS personnel, SS camp physicians (SS *Lagerärzte*), responsible for the medical care of camp prisoners, SS dental surgeons (SS *Zahnärtze*) responsible for the dental care of both

Buchenwald Museum

Buchenwald Camp hospital

the SS personnel and the prisoners and the SS apothecary (SS *Lagerapotheker*), who was in charge of the camp pharmacy.

Trained sanitary orderlies (*Sanitätsdienstgrade-SGD*), SS non-commissioned officers or privates, were subordinated to the Lagerärzte, whom they were detailed to assist.

The SS physicians in the camps were just décor, since it was not their task to extend medical help to 'inferior races'. The medical care of the prisoners, was in fact, entrusted to selected physician-prisoners. The SS doctor's job was simply the division of the incoming transportation of prisoners and he had the final decision in all health issues concerning the prisoners. It was the physician-prisoner who decided whether the prisoner was ill enough to attend the camp hospital (Revier), but he was always dependent on the whims of the Lagerärzt. If the latter considered that the physician-prisoner was too solicitous in sending prisoners to the camp hospital, he could relieve him of his responsibilities. In general, the Lagerärzt would make his diagnosis in a glance, without troubling himself to actually examine the prisoner. An SS physician who did not wish to work in this way was demonstrating in advance his unsuitability for camp service. However, the exception proves the rule. At the beginning of the war the Buchenwald camp physician, Dr Hofer, had an interview, with SS Standartenführer Dr Enno Lolling, head of all the SS physicians working in the concentration camps. Hofer would be pleased to work as 'No. 1 Lagerärzt in the camp'. He assured Lolling that — 'the number of deaths would fall in no time. It's improving even now!'

Lolling's answer was short, acid and characteristic: 'That's why you'll never be No. 1 Lagerärzt'.[3]

Hofer did, indeed, prove unsuitable for the job. He was too kind to the prisoners and was ostracized by his colleagues. He solved the problem himself by requesting a post at the front, which was arranged in a few days.

The atrocities committed by the physicians at Buchenwald concentration camp tax one's credulity severely. Eugen Kogon, erstwhile secretary-prisoner to Dr Ding wrote of the arbitrary behaviour of such doctors:

> 'The camp hospital was not the only place in which prisoners were cared for and cured, but also the place in which vivi-section was performed on them. Dr Neumann, attached to the Hygiene Institute of the Waffen SS, removed pieces of the liver from prisoners without employing anaesthetics. The victims died in the most terrible pain.'[4]

Of all the SS physicians at Buchenwald, Dr Hans Kurt Eisele was, without doubt, the worst of his kind. Between 1940 and 1943, during his frequent strolls through the camp streets, indiscriminately selecting prisoners and having an ambulance take them away was a familiar sight. Often he injected them with morphine and simply watched his victim's terrible end. He performed amputations which had not the slightest justification. One of the few survivors of his operations is the Dutch Jew, Max Nebig, upon whom Eisele performed an

Buchenwald Museum

Concentration Camp Buchenwald

unnecessary stomach operation. Usually, such patients were killed with an injection immediately afterwards, but in this case, the nurse gave Nebig a harmless injection of water and took the 'dying' Nebig from under Eisele's nose. He took Nebig to the TB block, which Eisele, for fear of infection, never entered. Nebig remained hidden there until the end of the war. [5]

A general strike was held in Holland in February 1941 as a protest against the persecution of the Jews. 389 Jews from Amsterdam and Rotterdam were deported as a reprisal measure. When Eisele heard of the strike, he ordered '*Reviersperre*' on the Dutch Jews; *i.e.* all the Dutch Jews who happened to be in hospital at that moment were to remain there until further orders. Then he began to give lethal injections to all these prisoners

Buchenwald Museum

Hans Eisele

In the summer of the same year he became of the opinion that the camp had too many patients with TB. His ready solution: lethal injections did away with all of them. The last two years of the war brought Eisele to Dachau, where he continued to leave a bloody trail and horrible memories behind him. He was condemned to death during both the Buchenwald and the Dachau trials. However, on 24 January 1946, his sentence was commuted to life imprisonment. Six years later, the German authorities quietly released him and financed his purchase of a practice in München-Pasing. No one suspected the charming Dr Eisele in the least — and those who did, kept quiet. Germany was licking her wounds and everyone took care to turn their backs on the past. However, in 1958, the tide turned against him. Ex-prisoners got wind of the Eisele affair and made preparations for a violent confrontation. Eisele wisely decided to leave Germany; such interest in his past might well have unpleasant consequences.

In the summer of 1958, he arrived in Cairo where he opened a practice under his own name. The local Egyptian aristocracy was not interested in his past; Buchenwald was a hazy notion to them. The Egyptian authorities regarded Eisele's exploits during the war as political crimes and refused to extradite him. German attempts to get him extradited for a new trial were therefore not frequent.

On 3 May 1967, at the age of fifty-five, Eisele died in the Egyptian capital[6] and his dossier disappeared for good into the archives of the German Ministry of Justice.

Besides the perverse experiments which have already been mentioned, official experiments also took place in Buchenwald, whose necessity no one doubted. That the tests were carried out was, in fact, encouraged by all the German authorities.

A few weeks after Hitler had declared war on Russia, serious problems came to light. At least 10,000 German soldiers were suffering from typhus. This illness was turning out to be deadlier than Russian barrages. Consequently, there was considerable uneasiness amongst the troops, and some regiments refused to advance while there was insufficient protective vaccination. The military staff was in serious difficulties; such disobedience was at odds with their idea of rigid discipline.

The existing typhus vaccine, Weigl's vaccine, was effective but so expensive and time-consuming to prepare that not enough was available. Only physicians and officers were being vaccinated with it. The newly developed vaccines by Cox, Gildemeister and Haagen could be produced in large quantities but their actual effectiveness had yet to be satisfactorily demonstrated. The results of experiments upon animals were too inconsistent for the vaccines to be designated 'efficious'.

On 29 December 1941, a conference was held in Berlin which was attended by Professor Handloser, Professor Gildemeister and Dr Conti, amongst others.

The typhus problems were brought up for discussion and, in the report prepared after the conference, it was concluded that: 'since tests upon animals have not had satisfactory results, such tests must be made upon human subjects.'[7]

Professor Rose, director of the Robert Koch Institute, an institution concerned with the campaign against tropical diseases and epidemics, testified at Nuremberg:

> 'During one of my visits to Professor Gildemeister, it must have been in May 1942, he told me that on Dr Conti's orders, the effectiveness of various vaccines was being tested on prisoners in a concentration camp in Weimar. I was astonished, and my initial reaction, impulsively enough, was to flatly reject the principle. Gildemeister became mildly irritated and suggested that I first pay a visit to Buchenwald concentration camp before expressing such an opinion. After some hesitation, I agreed.
>
> A few days later, I left for Weimar by train with Gildemeister. From there we drove to Buchenwald. There, we were introduced to various doctors and officers whose names I can no longer recall — but I am certain that Dr Ding was not there. He appeared to have been confined to bed with an infection. The doctor who showed us round explained how certain groups of prisoners were given test-vaccine injections and then infected with typhus to test the effectiveness of the vaccine. There was also a control-group who had received no vaccine but who were still infected with typhus. This group was used to test the effectiveness of drugs against the disease. The patients from this group appeared to be extremely ill. When, later in the laboratory, we received the fever statistics, it appeared that there was, indeed, a great difference between the vaccinated group and the rest.
>
> We spent the night in a cabin outside the camp and resumed the tour inspection the following day. We saw the patients again and this time the doctor presented two prisoners who had been given typhus injections but had not become ill. For the physicians working on these experiments, this was a great surprise since 118 of the remaining 120 patients had all become ill. The matter was investigated further

and it turned out that these two prisoners had already contracted typhus in a Berlin prison. The doctor added that there was considerable annoyance in Buchenwald with respect to the test subjects. They were obliged to use German criminals because prisoners from the east had often already had typhus . . . .'[8]

The experiments, which began in January 1942, took place in blocks forty-six and fifty. Both blocks were enclaves in the camp which no one could enter without the express permission of Dr Ding or of his deputy Dr Waldemar Hoven. Dr Hoven's practices at Buchenwald were as capricious as, indeed, his whole career had been capricious.

In 1930, after a sojourn in the USA, he enrolled with the SS and began to study medicine. He found it very taxing. With great difficulty and after several set-backs — due more to his laziness than nescience — he graduated in 1939. In the same year, he enrolled in the Waffen SS who directed him to Buchenwald as camp doctor. There, he could realize his ambition; gradually, he rose in the ranks until he became doctor-in-charge and deputy to Dr Ding. Within a short time he had succeeded in rising high on the social scale but one wish was still unfulfilled: to receive a doctor's degree from the University. Block forty-six offered unlimited possibilities and Hoven made grateful use of them.

During Dr Ding's absences, he independently selected a number of prisoners upon whom he performed a series of experiments with carbon-monoxide. He subsequently prepared a thesis within a short time with which he obtained a doctorate from the University of Freiburg.

Dr Hoven hereby dispelled any remaining doubts about his medical skills! He was a match for Eisele's brutality. Dr Kogon:

'Assisted by SS Hauptsturmführer, Dr Plaza, who was later transferred to Nordhausen concentration camp, Dr Hoven injected and killed hundreds of prisoners. On the one hand, he perpetrated these atrocious crimes while smoking and whistling, on the other, he made a vigorous effort to improve the medical provisions in the camp. Hoven was the great torturer during arrests, interrogations and punishments; sometimes he would torment someone out of pure relish! Even the SS began to fear him since he was capable of bumping off anyone who stood remotely in his way . . . .'[9]

For three years Hoven abused his medical power. However, in 1943 he was arrested, a remarkable phenomenon in a concentration camp. Together with camp commander Koch, he became involved in a camp finances swindle. When SS Oberscharführer Köhler discovered this and threatened to expose the fraud, Hoven decided to get him out of the way. His opportunity came when Köhler became ill and he attended to his medical needs. Hoven gave him a lethal injection. Afterwards, Koch and Hoven both claimed that Köhler had committed suicide, but at Berlin's mistrustful insistence, a post-mortem was performed. The pathologist established poisoning, probably alkaloid. Was it alkaloid? Was a large dose of alkaloid fatal? The SS needed proof, so a test was made on four unsuspecting Russian prisoners of war. The substance was added to their soup, with the result that all four died. Koch and Hoven were thereupon indictable — but the trial had to wait another two years.

The affair was eventually settled by Himmler himself when he gave the order for Koch's execution by firing squad. Hoven got off with a twenty-month prison sentence.[10] Hoven was very soon released because the Russians were advancing and Hoven's help was needed to destroy the evidence of Buchenwald's criminal activities.

However strange it sounds, Hoven's arrest resulted in a deterioration in the prisoners' situation. His successor, Oskar Schiedlausky, avoided any contact with the resistance movement at Buchenwald of which Hoven saved several members from certain death during the preceding years while he held a position at Buchenwald. Why he did this at all is unclear, but he must have gone through a period of crisis with his conscience. During his trial at Nuremberg, the help he had extended to the resistance was his trump card. The defence called on witness after witness to attest to Hoven's lenience and charitableness, an idea the prosecutor was unwilling to accept.

'We have established that between 1942 and 1943,

you gave fatal injections to a number of prisoners. Did you do this at random?'

'I personally killed a number of prisoners who had close connections with the SS and were therefore a danger to their fellow prisoners. I also killed prisoners who had murdered fellow prisoners.'

'With what right did you kill Gestapo and SS informers?'

'One can not compare those times with today. The prisoners I killed betrayed and murdered their comrades. These prisoners were miserable creatures who gave full rein to their murderous instincts. I was in the same position as the leaders of resistance groups considered to be heroes in their own countries . . . .'

'But here I have a declaration from a Dutch prisoner that you killed not only Gestapo informers but also other prisoners. Were there no other means for disposing of informers?'

'Had you been in a concentration camp, you would probably not have asked that question. What should I have done? Should I have gone to the SS administration, to Koch, Lolling, Himmler or Morgen and tell them: prisoner Kuschnarev has killed hundreds of fellow prisoners? They would have had me shot . . . .'

Gregor Kushnir Kuschnarev was a former Russian general sent by the Germans to Buchenwald were he was soon on good terms with the Gestapo and the camp SS, and became their willing servant. In exchange for the betrayal of other prisoners, mostly Russian prisoners-of-war, he was given extra rations and favours. But the prosecutor returned to the point:

'Why did you kill prisoners yourself instead of leaving it to the illegality of Buchenwald?'

'You could ask the same question to an officer after a battle at the front: Why did you not shoot at the enemy yourself, instead of leaving it to your soldiers?'

'The Kuschnarev case is clear. He had been sentenced to death by the illegality of Buchenwald a year beforehand, but no one dared to carry out the sentence as he enjoyed special protection from the SS. So it was only with my help that the sentence could be carried out. The leaders of the resistance were present when I decided he should die. I gave him an injection and later stated that he died of typhus . . . .'

'How did you bring this into accord with your medical ethics?'

'Medical ethics had nothing to do with this. I should have behaved in the same way if I had not been a doctor . . . .'

'When the camp commander gave you orders to kill prisoners with injections, what did you do then? Do you still maintain that you did everything to help them?'

'We (Hoven and the resistance members of the camp) did all sorts of things. We passed these prisoners off as sick, or hid them in the outlying camps. This took place in consultation with the resistance members.'

'Dr Hoven, you take responsibility for a large number of deaths, but how could you know whether all the people you killed had earned their sentence?'

'I was absolutely certain about it . . . as it happens, I did not kill all these prisoners myself; this was often done by members of the resistance, while I covered them by filling in a false cause of death on their death certificates . . . .'[11]

Despite a plea from ex-prisoners, the court sentenced Waldemar Hoven to death, a sentence which was carried out shortly afterwards in the courtyard of Landsberg prison.

* * *

'30 November 1942: to test the results of immunization, infection will be effected by means of typhus-bearing lice. The lice and their containers must be burned immediately afterwards. They might escape from the waste-disposal which would subject

Buchenwald to the risk of an epidemic.'

'3 December 1942: On Genzken's[12] orders, the research centre of Buchenwald will from now on be called: "*Abteilung für Fleckfieber — und Forschung des Hygiene-Institutes der Waffen SS*". Dr Hoven will take charge. In this case, he will take charge of the vaccine production . . . .'

'7 March 1943: water analysis and inspection of Vught concentration camp near Herzogenbosch.'

'8-10 March 1943: inspection of the Wehrmacht and SS accommodation in the Apeldoorn-Arnhem area. Gave head-surgeon and acting Chief in Holland advice on a diptheria epidemic in Apeldoorn.'

'24 March-20 April: large scale experiments on forty-five prisoners according to the directions of the Waffen SS Hygiene Institute. Directions originating in Professor Mrugrowsky. All sorts of vaccines administered: smallpox, cholera, parathyroid, typhus and diptheria . . . .'[13]

These are excerpts from Dr Ding's carefully kept diary. Thanks to the discovery of this diary, more is known about the typhus experiments than about all the others; however, as the above selections from the diary demonstrate, the experiments were by no means limited to typhus.

Erwin Ding-Schuler was an all-rounder. It is estimated that he used approximately 1,500 prisoners in his experiments. The number of these who died as a result is not precisely known, but the figures must lie at around 1,000. Kogon, Dr Dings prisoner-secretary during the war, put the figure even higher.

According to Walter Poller, Ding's first prisoner-secretary, Erwin Ding-Schuler was a remarkable man:

'I had been acting as a doctor's clerk in the prisoners' sick ward for a short time only and if questioned as to whether this man was capable of murdering a prisoner, I would have sworn an oath

Buchenwald Museum

Erwin Ding-Schuler

that such a deed was impossible for him to do. But I would have been mistaken. Dr Ding was a highly intelligent man, who was well-mannered, of an agreeable disposition, friendly and sometimes actually genial. His features were rather pleasant than stern, his eyes lively and observant. Above all, he was exceptionally self-assured and I was repeatedly surprised at the ease with which he always found a way out of the most complicated situations. He often sat before me at his writing desk, reading the papers that I had prepared, and my eyes would rest on his high, nobly-formed forehead, on the fine line of his nose, on the handsome, regular features, so full of character, and I often pondered over the bizarre,

incongruous aspects of his personality, his high
qualifications and abilities contrasting with
abominable crimes ... .'[14]

Erwin Ding-Schuler indeed emerges from the archives as a
remarkable man; besides his self-assurance, his unpredictability
was one of the most typical characteristics, and at the same time,
one of the most dangerous. He made the most profitable use
of his own capacities, and his egotistical side could be seen even
in insignificant dealings. In his relations with others he showed
a mutable character, playing the role of the enthusiastic orator
with the same perfection as that of the thoughtful man of a few
words. Both attitudes were, in fact, employed as the most
appropriate and timely means by which his abilities could be
put to use, whereby he enabled himself to leave a favourable
impression within a short time. This tactic of adjusting himself
to the views, the value-judgements and the disposition of his
companion developed into a fine art of influencing people. He
understood the art of agreement, without visible reserve, with
the opinions of his opponent; and his adaptability enabled him
to put his plans into action, and to allow the person to whom
he was talking to consider those plans as his own. The fact that
he could get the better of even powerful opponents and promote
his own opinions and plans affirms — besides his intellectual
and intuitive abilities — the presence of solid persuasive powers.

How else could it have been possible to perform unchecked
experiments, for years, on prisoners whose number was high
above the average — without seeming to achieve one single
tangible result?

Every medical student choosing the speciality of radiology
encountered the name of the Viennese scientist Professor
Kreuzfuchs. His name had spread far beyond the Austrian
borders and was found in every medical dictionary. When Hitler
occupied Austria in 1938, the Gestapo arrested him because he
was Jewish. On Himmler's orders he was deported to
Buchenwald where he was invited by Ding. Walter Poller;

'Kreuzfuchs stood before the doctor at last. There
on the one side was this shrivelled, emaciated man,
already destined to die; and on the other the all-
powerful SS Sturmführer, the personification of

exuberant health. They had nothing in common but their interest in the matter under discussion. On the one hand, the knowledge, on the other hand, the splendid possibility of mobilising this knowledge for the benefit of the whole of mankind. On the one side, the scientist whose knowledge was so great that it no longer had the effect of pedantic education so much as the power of the unobtrusive and unassuming instruction; on the other hand, the highly gifted SS officer who, possibly with the last dregs of decency still in him, could no doubt, sense how great a thing was spread before him, something which was apart from human personality and individualism.

Ding conversed, asked questions, expressed opinions and then dismissed the Jew without the usual malicious remarks, the gesture which might have indicated that he was no longer interested in him. I wanted to know more. I therefore pretended ignorance, as I asked: "What kind of fellow was that?"

"That was Kreuzfuchs", Ding replied. "The man knows something".

Some days later, Kreuzfuchs once more reported to the doctor. He had made a sketch and wanted to explain this to him. It dealt with the problem of aneurysma, a disease which caused enlargement of the aorta. Kreuzfuchs was completely absorbed in his explanation, while Ding himself could not at first take his eyes from the drawing. But then he looked at Kreuzfuchs and back to the drawing once more. There, what was causing Ding's eyes to flicker? I could see that he no longer followed the explanation, that something else stirred him. His chin moved forward, his lips tightened. Kreuzfuchs saw nothing of this change, his eyes constantly on the drawing, his words quiet and clear, his shaking hand continually following the blue and red lines, the crosses and dots he had drawn. Ding drew up his right hand slowly, like a tiger lifting his claws. Then he hit out, tearing the drawing from the completely staggered Kreuzfuchs, crumpled it in his fist and hit the Jew brutally in the face. At first, Kreuzfuchs was absolutely stupefied, not realizing what had happened; then, composing himself, he turned helplessly, and ran through the door, as if for his life. After Kreuzfuchs had left the room, Ding sneered in helpless rage, having lost all control over himself and devoid of shame. "What a swine! Such a Jew!" he muttered. It took me some time to appreciate what had taken place before my eyes . . . .'[15]

Undoubtedly Erwin Ding-Schuler had just those qualities one needs to become a respectable doctor. Still, he could conveniently make use of the Party to save him time. What others achieved only after years of effort, the party could arrange within a few months. Ding was impatient and he did not have the financial means to complete his study over the requisite number of years in the official curriculum. He also wanted to marry as soon as possible. Like Waldemar Hoven, the party enabled him to finish his studies early and the SS decided to send him to Buchenwald. Everyone who knew Ding was impressed by his intelligence and his astonishing textual knowledge, but as Poller stated: 'This was just a facade.'[16]

Ding enjoyed collecting facts with which to impress his audience, especially when the audience was the Health Department of the Waffen SS in Berlin, but he did not worry whether his facts were correct when it concerned his experiments. From the scientific point of view, indeed, his experiments had no results.[17] Professor Eugen Haagen, working like Ding on typhus research, called him a dilettante. Hoven added to this that Ding took all possible pains to build a myth around himself. Ding's practice was as efficient as it was simple. Maintaining order during the experiments was the duty of the Kapo Arthur Dietzsch. The Kapo was a prisoner who had command of a working party; the post had many privileges and was therefore given mainly to German criminals.

In most cases their cruelty and sadism exceeded that of the SS. In 1944, Arthur Dietzsch, serving a twenty-four year German prison sentence, was appointed Ding's assistant. In practice, this meant that he was responsible for the practical aspects of the tests. It was his job to bring unwilling prisoners to their senses. Armed with a large cudgel, he strutted through block forty-six and brought more trouble than Ding. He was not, however, allowed into block fifty. In this block, sera were developed which were then tested on the prisoners in block forty-six.

Here, the scientific cream of the German concentration camp world was at work. Within this wooden barrack, a deathly silence prevailed, and nothing could be heard above the moans coming from block forty-six. The walls were covered with research apparatus. In front of them were large tables upon which, dressed in spotless white coats, prisoners underwent experiments with vaccines.

In 1941 Ding had requested of Himmler whether all scientific researchers held prisoner in concentration camps might not be sent to Buchenwald, as he could really make good use of them. Himmler considered it to be an excellent idea and gave Sievers orders to extend all the help required.

While the Ahnenerbe chief had done the necessary detective work, several scientists were deported to Buchenwald, where they were given the choice: co-operation or a bullet. If they had family members in concentration camps, the case was even simpler: co-operate or your family gets it![18]

Despite renowned 'support' from men like Professor Fleck (Russia), Professor van Lingen (Holland), Professor Balachowsky (France) and Professor Ciepelowski (Poland), Ding did not succeed in his intentions. His experiments retained a pointless character. His reports to the Health Department of the Waffen SS were more convincing than his results. Nevertheless, his arguments having the desired impression, he was allowed to continue. In 1943, he was even promoted to Sturmbannführer which he regarded as encouragement for his research.

With renewed vigour, he threw himself into medical research, and this time, all fields were covered.

Not only in Buchenwald, but also in the French camp Natzweiler, typhus experiments were being carried out. Here, the tests were in the charge of Professor Eugen Haagen.

At the end of the war the Allies rushed to arrest scientific researchers who had offered their services to the Third Reich during the previous years.[19]

Many German scientists were only too pleased to be able to continue their research in the United States, or in the Soviet

Union — provided these powers were prepared to forget their Nazi past. Von Braun, father of the V-2 rocket, was seized by the Americans and ended up at the NASA (National Aeronautics and Space Administration), where be became the driving force behind the Apollo project. Haagen seemed to have a familiar future in store, but there was a large stain on his past. His career had been a long line of successes. In 1926 he passed his medical exams *summa cum laude*; two years later, he left for the United States, where he did research under Dr Rives in the world-famous Rockefeller Institute. In 1933 he succeeded in producing a vaccine against yellow fever which was rapidly employed all over the world. In 1936 he was nominated Professor of bacteriology and shortly thereafter he was appointed Director of the Robert Koch Institute.[20]

In 1945 he was arrested by Americans, but released after a few months internment camp. He appeared to have done nothing incriminating. After his release, he was approached by the Russians, who invited him to continue his research in the Russian sector of Berlin. Haagen leapt at the chance and spent three months working on a secret virus project. During this period, the first rumours about his activities at Natzweiler began to circulate. Eventually there was so much defamatory material that the French applied to the Russians for his extradition. It was refused, and the Russians allowed him to continue his project unhindered. When, in December 1946, Haagen entered the American sector in connection with his research, he was arrested by the military police and brought to the French authorities. Their research had revealed that, while at Natzweiler in 1943, he had tried out various vaccines on prisoners, and had grossly neglected medical norms and values. The accusations against him were serious but Haagen denied them completely. He had never tried out vaccines on prisoners at Natzweiler. The facts and the documents demonstrated otherwise, but he persistently rejected the accusation. He conceded that he had administered vaccines to prisoners but that these had been protective measures: at that time the camp had been threatened by an epidemic.

In that case, why had only a hundred prisoners been vaccinated while the camp contained thousands of people? Haagen: 'Because there was insufficient vaccine.'[21] Prisoners who had worked in the camp hospital testified that Haagen had infected guinea-pigs with typhus and then brought prisoner in contact with them in order to bring about their subsequent infection.

> 'Rubbish', Haagen retorted, 'these healthy little guinea-pigs had been brought in as a special diversion for the prisoners, so that their dull camp lives could be enlivened by looking after and playing with these pets. They took great pleasure in it .... .'[22]

This sort of defence took the prosecutor by surprise. Haagen handled the documents with subtlety and care; he shunned no discussion. For days he exchanged views with the prosecutor on the medical terminology he had employed in his reports, and was frank enough to admit that it might have led to 'misunderstanding'. Terms such as 'test' and 'experiment' should certainly not be taken too literally. But the prosecutor was not put off in the slightest by Haagen's pedagogical disputation. He demanded, and Haagen ultimately received twenty years imprisonment.[23]

The ex-Professor was furious and declared to all that he would have been in the line for a Nobel Prize had the French not sentenced him to such a lunatic punishment. Had he not so scandalously offended the ethics of his profession, he might have been right.

As has already been mentioned, Ding's research led nowhere, which nevertheless did nothing to diminish his confidence in the usefulness of it. The Waffen SS was actually very pleased and encouraged him to widen the scope of his research. In 1944, the Danish Sturmbannführer Vaernet was sent to him. The endocrinologist Carl Vaernet was famous for his experiments with homosexuals. Himmler had a special horror of homosexuals whom he was determined to exterminate. The historian Richard Plant:

> 'His raging homophobia, which was responsible for a vicious campaign against Germany's homosexuals, struck fear into the hearts of hundreds of thousands of gays, and resulted in the death of thousands of others.'[24]

Himmler considered homosexuals to be a catastrophe for Germany. If the spreading of this 'disease' continued, it would be the end of Germany. According to the Reichsführer:

> ' . . . a good race producing few children was destined to be extinct in two hundred years while nations with many children can gain supremacy and mastery of the world. All homosexuals are cowards; they lie like Jesuits and it leads to a state of mind that doesn't know what it's doing . . . . Homosexuality is a crime against nature and must be stamped out. An adolescent male must be encouraged to fall in love with a girl of good blood; then he will turn away from homosexuals, he will not participate in juvenile orgies of a homosexual nature. If we don't encourage this correct heterosexual behaviour, we will have sexually disturbed youngsters, not the right material for the élite SS, the new Holy Order . . . .'[25]

Dr Vaernet, who was assisted by Oskar Schiedlausky, was convinced that homosexuals could become heterosexuals by hormone treatments and in July 1944, he started his experiments. Kogon:

> 'In the spring of 1944, Ding told me that he had received a visit from Vaernet, who had requested his assistance in a number of experiments in connection with homosexuality. Ding did not want to be bothered with it as the matter was not in his field. Vaernet was to perform the experiments with Schiedlausky. I can still remember that the SS doctors had great fun at these sorts of experiments . . . .'[26]

After a few weeks, however, Vaernet was to stop the tests because the danger of a yellow fever epidemic in the camp. He went to Prague and then appeared again in the concentration camp Neuengamme where he attempted castration-hormone tests.

When Ding was arrested by the Americans in 1945, Vaernet disappeared and has not been found to this day. Although all the documents relating to Vaernet's experiments have been destroyed, it is almost certain that twenty to thirty prisoners fell victim to the Danish physician. At Nuremberg a witness declared that Vaernet had also performed tests at Mauthausen concentration camp.[27] Although the documents do not throw any light on Vaernet's activities in this camp, the fact still remains that he was there in June and July 1944 and performed experiments there.

Besides those experiments mentioned, Natzweiler was the backdrop for another medical disgrace in 1944. On 9 February 1942 Professor August Hirt, sent Himmler the following letter:

'Voluminous collections of skulls exist of almost all races and peoples. Only in the case of the Jews does science have so few skulls at its disposal that no valid results can be arrived at from their study. The war in the East now affords us a chance to make up for this deficiency. By securing the skulls of Jewish-Bolshevist commissars, representing a repulsive but typical species of subhumanity, we stand to acquire tangible scientific research material. The practical accomplishment of safe and smooth acquisition can be most suitably effected in the forms of a directive to the Armed Forces providing that, henceforth, all Jewish-Bolshevist commissars are to be immediately handed over to the Military Police alive. The Military Police, in turn, will receive special orders to make current reports of the number and location of these captured Jews to a designated office, and to guard them carefully until the arrival of a special commissioner.

This commissioner will be charged with safe guarding of the material. He should be a junior medical officer or student in the Armed Forces or even the Military Police, and should be provided with an armoured car and driver. It will be his job to prepare a previously determined series of photographs and anthropological measurements, and to establish in so far as possible, descent, birth dates, and other vital statistics. Subsequently, when the death of these has been effected — the head must not be injured — he severs the heads from the bodies and sends them on to their destination, immersed in specially constructed air-tight tin containers filled with preservatives. The photographs, measurements and other data concerning the head and finally the skull, will then form the point of departure for comparative anatomical research, research on racial characteristics, on pathological features in skull formation, on the shape and size of the brain, and on many other subjects.

To conduct this research and serve as depository for the skull material acquired in this fashion, the new Reich University of Strassburg would seem to be the most suitable place because of the responsibilities it has been given.'[28]

Himmler expressed his full interest and gave Sievers the job of contracting Hirt in order to develop a plan of action. Sievers immediately left for Strassburg where he and Hirt, who lay ill in bed, discussed the horrible operation. They agreed that it would be much more straightforward and efficient to deport the imprisoned Jewish-Bolshevist commissars directly to Strassburg, and they dropped the original plan of allowing the doctors to select the *Untermenschen*. The prisoners would be killed in Natzweiler concentration camp, which lay near Strassburg.

They also altered the original suggestion put forward for rounding up the subjects which originally involved the Wehrmacht and the Military Police. Hirt proposed that they begin with a collection of 150 skeletons and Sievers thought that there was but one place that could meet that demand: Auschwitz. He contacted the *Reichssicherheitshauptamt* (Reich Security Main Office) department 4 B-IV and requested SS Obersturmbannführer Adolf Eichmann to arrange the transportation from Auschwitz to Natzweiler. But before it got that far, a selection had, of course, to be made; and for this purpose, the philosopher-physician Dr Bruno Beger, working for the Ahnenerbe, made his way to Auschwitz. He was given the honour of selecting the least fortunate from this reservoir of 'Untermenschen': seventy-nine Jews, thirty Jewesses, two Poles and four Asians. These were the chosen few whose skulls might adorn the Aryan museum galleries of the University of Strassburg.

When the Auschwitz concentration camp was officially opened
on 16 June 1940, many of the architects of the Final Solution
were present. Moving within this eccentric circle of men was
a man whose career had paralleled the history of the German
concentration camp. Rising in the ranks from guard to
commandant, for thirteen years, this ex-offender drifted from
one concentration camp to the next. He left his traces
everywhere; Bergen-Belsen, Estervegen, Sachsenhausen,
Natzweiler, Mauthausen, Auschwitz, Dachau. Much of the
gruesome '*Grundlichkeit*' of the Endlösung's application can be
laid at the door of the 'Beast of Belsen', Josef Kramer, who had
once been the adjutant of Rudolph Höss, camp commander of
Auschwitz-Birkenau.

Few war criminals could claim to have seen so much human
suffering in so short a time. Gas chambers, mass executions,
medical experiments, hunger, typhus, atrocious torture, Kramer
had seen it all and furthermore, he had loyally co-operated with
it all. What he had done as a loyal soldier, he claimed, he had
done as his duty and had obeyed orders and the law. He too,
had a crisis of conscience, but one of a special kind. He confided
to his questioner, Colonel Draper, that when he came home he
assured his wife that he wouldn't want to stand in the shoes of
those who gave such dreadful orders!

Clearly, Kramer had a split personality: what he did had
nothing to do with what he thought. He was convinced that no
blame could be laid on him in any way whatsoever. Impassively,
he described his part in the extermination of Auschwitz inmates:

'I received orders from the Oranienburg camp —
or rather, from the SS High Command in Berlin
which forwarded them to me — to receive some eighty
inmates from Auschwitz. In a letter accompanying
this order, I was requested to communicate at once
with Professor Hirt of the Strassburg Medical Faculty.

I went to the Strassburg Anatomical Institute where
Hirt was. The latter told me that he knew about the
prisoner convoy en route from Auschwitz to Struthof.
He said these people were to be killed by poisonous
gas in the gas chamber of the Struthof camp, then their
bodies were to be taken to the Anatomical Institute
for his disposal.

At the end of the conversation he gave me a bottle containing about half a pint of salts, I think that they were cyanide salts. The Professor told me the approximate dosage I would have to use to poison the inmates arriving from Auschwitz, about whom I have told you already.

Early in August 1943, I received the eighty inmates who were to be killed with the gas Hirt had given me. One night I went to the gas chamber in a small car, it was about nine o'clock, with about fifteen women on this occasion. I told the women they had to go into the chamber to be disinfected. I did not tell them, however, that they were to be poisoned. With the help of a few SS men, I stripped them completely and shoved them into the gas chamber when they were stark naked. When the door was closed they began to scream. After the door had been closed, I introduced a certain amount of salt through a tube installed to the upper right of the peephole. I then closed the opening of the tube with a cork attached to the end of the tube. This cork had a metal pipe. This metal pipe projected the salt and water toward the inside of the room by means of a switch installed near the tube and I observed through the peephole what happened inside the room. I saw that these women breathed for about half a minute before they all fell to the ground. After I had turned on the ventilation inside the flue, I opened the doors and found the women lying lifeless on the floor, covered all over with excrement.

The next morning I told the SS hospital orderlies to place the bodies in a small car, it was about five-thirty am, so that they could be taken to the anatomical institute, as requested of me by Professor Hirt. A few days later, I again took a certain number of women to the gas chamber under the same circumstances, and they were gassed in this way. This same procedure was again repeated several days later about two or three times until fifty, or perhaps fifty-five inmates had been killed with the salts given to me by Hirt ... .'[29]

'Mr Kramer, did you know what Professor Hirt actually did with these bodies . . . ?'

'No, I did not take the trouble to find out what Hirt meant to do with the bodies of these inmates whom I had poisoned. On the basis of what he said at Struthof, I didn't think it was my business to ask him . . . .'

'You have spoken of the conditions in which you have executed the inmates with asphyxiating gas. In case these inmates would not have been killed following the introduction of the gas by yourself, would you have killed them with a bullet?'

'I would have tried once again to suffocate them with gas, by throwing another dose of gas into the chamber. I had no feelings in carrying out these things, because I already told you. That, incidentally, was the way, I was trained . . . .'[30]

Hirt received the bodies and put them into alcohol-filled basins, being too busy to begin work on them immediately. However, the longer the corpses lay there, the riskier it became, as the Allies were advancing rapidly on Strassburg. Hirt, aware of the impending danger, asked Sievers for instructions. It would be a delicate business indeed if the Allies came across such a bizarre find. Sievers turned to Himmler:

'In view of the time required for eighty specimens, Hirt requests instructions in case of a threat to Strassburg as to what to do with the collection, now stored in the morgue of the Anatomy Building. He can remove the flesh thus rendering identification impossible, but in that case, part of the work will have been in vain, with scientific loss to collection since Hominit casts would no longer be possible. A skeleton collection as such would not be conspicuous. Fleshy portions would be described as remnants from old bodies left behind by the French when the Anatomy Building was taken over, and would be disposed of by burning. Request decision on following proposals: 1. Collection is to be preserved. 2. Collection is to be partly dismantled. 3. Collection is to be completely dismantled.'[31]

When the prosecutor asked Sievers why he had wanted the flesh removed from the bodies and the blame passed on to French, he replied:

> 'As a layman I had no say in this affair. I took no part at all in the murder of these people and acted more as a kind of postman, simply passing on messages ... .'[32]

Himmler decided for the last option and had the entire collection cleared away. On 26 October 1944, Sievers reported that the orders had been carried about, but this turned out to be incorrect. Hirt's assistant and amanuensis Henry Henpierres:

> 'When the bodies had been embalmed, they were placed in containers. They remained there for a full year, without being touched by anyone. In the month of September 1944, the Allies made an advance on Belfort, and at this moment Professor Hirt ordered Bong and Herr Meier to cut up these bodies and have them burned in the crematory. When this work had been finished by Bong and Meier in the room where the containers were, I asked Herr Bong the next day whether he had cut up all the bodies but Herr Bong replied:
> "We couldn't cut up all the bodies, it was too much work. We left a few bodies in the store room." '[33]

This lugubrious discovery was made by an Allied Commando of the Second French Army. Army photographers immortalized the scene and according to the prosecutor:

> 'These photographs tell the terrible story of this mass murder more vividly than any document or testimony could.'[34]

Hirt also had a special place in the gamut of medical experiments; his research was closely connected with the possibility of chemical and bacteriological warfare.

In August 1944 Churchill had asked for a report on England's capacity to wage gas warfare. The survey revealed that about

32,000 tons of mustard and phosgene gas was available, enough to destroy more than 965 square miles of German territory. German production was much higher. In 1944, no less than 3,100 tons of mustard gas were being produced per month.[35] Albert Speer.

> 'Though Hitler had always spurned such a form of warfare, after the failure of Operation Barbarossa, he began to consider the possibilities of a gas-war.'[36]

Banking on the probability that America and England would not intervene against a German gas attack on the Soviet Union, he gave orders for the setting up of a commission to look into the possibilities and the consequences of such a method of warfare. This commission, '*Komitee Blitzableiter*', which consisted of a toxicologist, a zoologist and a botanist, concluded after extensive research that Germany stood to profit from a poison-gas war. However, the generals in Hitler's entourage resisted the idea. In their eyes Germany was too vulnerable to risk being given a taste of their own medicine.

Nevertheless, already in September 1939, at the behest of the Armed Forces High Command, experiments with mustard gas were being conducted at Sachsenhausen and Natzweiler-Struthof. The purpose of these tests was to find the best therapeutic measures to combat mustard gas lesions. Because there were not tangible results, Himmler intervened and asked Hirt, who had already been working with mustard gas for years, to continue his research in a concentration camp 'with the use of unique facilities.'[37]

As well as a promotion to SS Sturmbannführer, Himmler offered him the use of a well-equipped test laboratory in Natzweiler concentration camp. He was assigned Dr Wimmer, candidate for the doctor's degree and staff physician of the Luftwaffe as an assistant and, in the autumn of 1944, both doctors set to work. The ex-prisoner Ferdinand Holl, testifying to their activities:

> 'In mid-October, when the "Ahnenerbe" arrangements had been made, Professor Hirt selected a few prisoners who were still reasonably sturdy, that is, they at least looked healthy, and had them taken

to his ward. There were two rooms and fifteen men were quartered in each. The men were first fed on SS rations, for about two weeks, and then the experiments began. The men were taken to the pathology division, and there the first tests with liquid gas were conducted.

Before selecting the men, Professor Hirt had spoken to them and intimated that if any of them volunteered, he would intercede with Himmler about their discharge. But the men in the camp had already heard about experiments in other camps, and there were no volunteers. The men were then simply selected at random. In the first experiments, there was Professor Hirt and then this German Air Force officer who conducted the experiments. The prisoners were then stripped to the skin. They entered the laboratory one by one. There, I had to hold their arms while one drop of this liquid was smeared on, about four inches above the elbow. The patients then had to go to the adjoining room, and all the men thus treated had to remain standing for about an hour with their arms spread out.

After about ten hours, or it may have been a little more, burns began to appear, all over the body. There were burns wherever the vapour from this gas had reached. Some of the men went blind. The pains were so terrific that it was almost impossible to stay near these patients. The patients were then photographed every day on all of the injured or burned places.

On the fifth or sixth day, the first death occurred. At that time, the bodies were still shipped to Strassburg, since we had no crematorium in the camp. But this body was returned and dissected in the "Ahnenerbe" ward. The lungs and inner organs were completely eaten away. In the course of the next few days, another seven men died. This treatment lasted for about two months, until the men were in some kind of condition to travel. Then they were taken to other camps. Besides these test, there were also the experiments in the gas chamber. The gas was in small ampoules of one or two cc. The prisoners were taken to the gas chamber which was about a third of a mile from the camp, and there, two men at a time had to enter this gas chamber. The gas chamber was, of course, locked and then one of these prisoners had to break the ampoules and they had to breathe the gas that escaped. Afterwards, they were taken out again, some of them unconscious, and returned to the ''Ahnenerbe'' ward, where they were treated, or the course of the damaged was observed. The results were about the same as with liquid gas . . . .'[38]

Otto Bickenbach, professor on the medical faculty at the University of Strassburg, was considered the greatest 'gas-expert' of the Third Reich. He had published a great deal on the subject and his name was known well outside Germany. His most important discovery was considered to be the drug utropine, with which burns caused by phosgene gas could be treated.

In 1943 the Allies landed in North Africa, which caused great constellation in Berlin. In the area captured by the Allied forces, no less than 50,000 tons of phosgene gas was stored!

The chiefs of staff took the possibility of a phosgene gas attack very seriously and the phosgene gas experts of the Third Reich were summoned to Berlin with all speed. Hirt and Bickenbach were also invited. Himmler came straight to the point: would Bickenbach be prepared to perform phosgene research on humans? Bickenbach had reservations. He had already made utropine tests on animals and written up the results in a substantial report. He considered tests on humans pointless; furthermore, his conscience forbade such a method of research. When Hirt stressed that the tests would be performed on criminals condemned to death, but whose assistance gave them the chance of a reprive, Bickenbach eventually concurred after hesitating for quite a time.

Before he began experiments on prisoners, he performed a utropine test on himself in the gas chamber at Fort Ney in order to obtain some idea of what his subjects would shortly have to undergo. Bickenbach:

'Despite Himmler's express forbiddance, I made a test on myself in the gas chamber at Fort Ney. Then I performed two series of experiments, the first on forty people, the second on fourteen. In the first series, no one died, but one did become ill as a result of the experiment. In the second series four people died, which I do not impute to the test, but to the poor physical condition of these people. Those upon whom the tests were performed showed symptoms of oedema of the lungs. In the first series Dr Hirt was not present; in the second series, he took an active part. Dr Letzt was present for both series .... .'[39]

When the prosecutor asked him what he now thought of performing experiments on prisoners, he replied:

'Experiments on people conflict with medical ethics. However, I did it, because I knew what the results of a gas war would be. The German population, in the event of such a war, was inadequately protected. The fate of thousands, especially of women and children, was uppermost in my mind when I decided to add my efforts to the creation of this necessary protection. Of course, it was also Himmler's order. I had been assured that my assistance was of utmost importance. Only I was considered capable of developing an effective protection against phosgene gas .... .'[40]

Witnesses acknowledged to the court in Metz, where Bickenbach stood on trial, that however horrible the experiments had been, Bickenbach compared with Hirt, had not needlessly tortured his test subjects. He put them at ease and gave them an anaesthetic for each test.

Where necessary, victims whose nerves had failed them were given sedatives. The experiments he had carried out were a blemish in a spotless career. The court sentenced him to twenty years imprisonment, a sentence which was commuted — his case having been re-opened, since several witnesses by Bickenbach's counsel had not originally appeared — to twenty years hard labour. In 1956, he was given early release, and left Germany for an unknown destination.

6

The Dachau Experiments

Karl Gebhardt testified at Nuremberg that Hitler had approved of the principle of medical experiments on concentration camp prisoners. Logically, it was up to Himmler to put this principle into practice. However, the Reichsführer did not take this initiative himself but left it to his protégé Sigmund Rascher.

In 1937, aged twenty-eight, Rascher passed his medical exams and, with the intention of specializing in surgery, accepted a post at the municipal hospital in Munich. He had a great admiration for the professors in whose company he daily lingered. During the two years that he worked in Munich, he developed the desire to one day also become a professor. Rascher was ambitious, and what started as an innocently cherished desire quickly took the form of an obsession.

In 1939 he was called up for military service and incorporated into the Luftwaffe's Medical Research Centre in Munich. The young doctor stepped into a new world: measurements, pressure-experiments, chemical research and medical experiments upon animals. This latter form of research, especially, left an indelible impression on him. He saw that his best chances lay here: scientific research, revolutionary discoveries, and then the coveted university professorship. It was during this period that he met Nini Diehls, a not unattractive woman in her late thirties who could boast that she belonged to the most exclusive *'Freundenkreis'* around Heinrich Himmler.

Their engagement was soon announced and shortly thereafter they were married, at which ceremony Himmler himself put in an appearance. Although he was not actively interested in politics, Rascher understood that tremendous opportunities were offered by this relation with Himmler. His original reserve made way for deferential respect, and the Reichsführer, vain as he

150

was, was charmed by the young doctor. More than once he was impressed by Rascher's arguments on the Jewish question. If only all doctors took that view! However, the Reichsführer was an unpredictable man, and therefore a dangerous one. He had been known to end long-standing friendships without any reason.[1] Rascher was aware of this and feared that it might one day happen to him. For this reason he made a decision in 1941 which was to characterize the whole of his subsequent career. To demonstrate his love for the Fatherland, he betrayed his own father to the Gestapo for sabotage. Rascher was still attached to the research centre in Munich and not much had come of plans for the future.

In the spring of 1941, however, he saw his chance. During the Polish campaign the Luftwaffe had demonstrated enormous power; the Polish Air Force had hardly made an impression. However, in 1940 and 1941 Germany was dealing with another opponent: the British Royal Air Force. Goering had promised that within a few weeks he would have the English on their knees. But the 'Battle of Britain' was for the Germans an outright defeat. The British had one decisive advantage: their aircraft could reach higher altitudes. In addition to this, the Channel appeared to be an unbridgeable gulf. Dozens of German pilots met their death in its cold seas.

Professor Erich Hippke, staff physician of the Air Force, received instructions to solve the medical problems that were arising from the rapid development of air travel. He discussed the affair with two close colleagues, Dr Hubertus Strughold and Dr Siegfried Ruff. Under Hippke's directions, a range of experiments was begun in Munich in order to examine the effects of high-altitude flying. One of the doctors working on this project was Rascher who saw that success could mean his breakthrough.

In April 1941, however, he was confronted with the possibility of complete failure. The research was at an impasse since no human test material was available. Rascher was desperate. On 15 May 1941, he turned to his powerful patron, Himmler:

'My humble thanks for your warm congratulations and the flowers on the occasion of the birth of my second son! It is a lusty boy again this time, though he arrived three weeks prematurely. Perhaps you will permit me to send you a snapshot of the two children some time.

I would like to have a third child very soon, and I am very grateful to you, dear Mr Reich Leader, for your help in making the marriage possible. SS Colonel Sollman told me today that the 165 marks in question, lacking for a marriage, will be supplied by the ''R'' account and will be included in the ''Ahnenerbe'' check.

I thank you with all my heart! The Air Force has already seen my passport, but I still need a brief certificate confirming my Aryan descent. I shall dictate a draft to Nini D. before I leave tomorrow, and she will then send it to you, dear Mr Reich Leader.

I also wish to thank you warmly for the generous regular remittance, of special importance to mother and child this time . (. . .) I therefore ask this question in all seriousness: Could two or three professional criminals be made available for these experiments. The experiments will be conducted at the Air Force Ground-Level Testing Station for High-Altitude Research in Munich. The experiments, during which, of course, the test persons may die, will proceed with my collaboration. They are definitely of importance in high-altitude flight research, and cannot be conducted with monkeys, as has been tried, since monkeys react altogether differently. I have talked about this matter in strict confidence with the deputy air surgeon who will conduct these experiments, and he shares my views that the problems in question can be clarified only by way of experiments on human beings. (Feeble-minded persons might also be used as testing material).'[2]

Himmler, via his secretary Rudolf Brandt, gave his authorization and advised him to elaborate his plans. A research commission was set up, consisting of the doctors Romberg, Ruff and Rascher, and so the dubious honour of launching the first attack fell to this trio. When the prosecutor at Nuremberg asked Siegfried Ruff, chief of the Institute of Aviation Medicine of the German Experimental Institute for Aviation in Munich, if he had not been entirely amazed when approached and asked

National Archives

Siegfried Ruff

to perform medical experiments on prisoners he replied:

> 'No, because I knew that Himmler had given his
> consent to such experiments. I must admit, however,
> that the ethics of this situation were completely new
> to me. In the past, we had occasionally experimented
> on ourselves, but never on prisoners. The reason I
> agreed to it was in fact two-fold: in the first place there
> was the great need to perform experiments on people
> and in the second place, I knew, from the international
> scientific literature, that experiments upon prisoners
> were in generally accepted use.'[3]

Hans Wolfgang Romberg clearly had more difficulty with the
idea, and even more so when it became clear to him that
Rascher's experiments were of a criminal character. In contrast
with the original intention, the tests took place not in Munich
but in Dachau concentration camp. In the roadway between
block five and six, a decompression chamber was installed. It
must be stated clearly that Drs Ruff and Romberg wanted to
conduct the experiments at Dachau without the aid of Dr
Rascher. Mrs Rascher, however, who had established her
husband's connection with Himmler strongly objected in the
first instance.

When the experiments at Dachau had began, Himmler
expressly declared that permission had been granted only on
condition that Dr Rascher would participate. Rascher had asked
for two or three professional criminals, but Himmler gave him
carte blance to select prisoners from the camp at will. In total,
Rascher used 200 prisoners for his tests, of which sixty died in
the most dreadful circumstances. The prisoners who took part
had been offered the prospect of freedom, but in only one
instance was this promise kept. In the summer of 1942, Himmler
pardoned the Polish prisoner Ludwig Sobota.

The prisoner-nurse Anton Pacholegg testified to one of the
tests:

> 'I personally watched a prisoner through the screen
> of the low-pressure chamber who stood in the vacuum
> until his lungs burst. In the cabin, the prisoners went
> crazy, tearing their hair out in their attempts to relieve

National Archives

A victim of the high-altitude experiments

the pressure; some clawed their faces and heads open
with frenzied nails. They beat their heads and hands
on the walls and screamed for the pressure on the
eardrums to be released. These cases usually ended
in the death of the test subjects ... .'[4]

In his first interim report on the tests, dated 5 March 1942,
Rascher noted that the 13,000 m experiments were fatal. It is
an inconceivable document. In its second half, Rascher
concludes:

'The third test of this character proceeded along
such extraordinary lines that I went to get an SS camp
physician as a witness, since I was conducting the test
alone. It was a sustained test without oxygen at the
equivalent of 29,400 feet altitude, conducted on a
thirty-seven year-old Jew in good general condition.
Respiration continued for thirty minutes.

After four minutes, the test subject began to perspire
and roll his head. After five minutes, spasms
appeared; between the sixth and tenth minute,
respiration increased in frequency, the test subject
losing consciousness. From the eleventh to the thirtieth
minute, respiration slowed down to three inhalations
per minute, only to cease entirely at the end of that
period. Meanwhile, intense cyanosis was observed,
together with frothing at the mouth. At five-minute
intervals, electro-cardiographic tracings were recorded
in three sections. After respiration had ceased, such
records were made continuously until heart action had
ceased completely. Subsequently, about half an hour
after breathing had ceased, an autopsy was begun.
After opening the chest cavity, the pericardium was
found to be distended (pericardial tamponade). Upon
opening the pericardium, eighty cc of clear yellowish
fluid spurted out in a stream. The moment the
tamponade had ceased, the right auricle began to beat
vigorously, initially at a rate of sixty contractions per
minute and gradually growing slower ... .'[5]

Himmler was delighted and, on his orders, Rudolf Brandt
wrote:

'The Reich leader was very much interested in the experiments. I wish you continued success in your further experiments. Warm greetings to your wife as well ... .'[6]

After his second interim-report, Himmler wrote:

'I should like to request that this last experiment be repeated on prisoners condemned to death and that Dr Fahrenkamp be informed of the tests. Should such experiments be a success, then the death penalty would, of course, be changed to one of concentration camp internment for life ... .'[7]

This last remark caused Rascher especial alarm and he asked the Reichsführer if Poles, Russians and Jews also came into consideration for such reprieves. His mind was put at rest by the reply that arrived a few weeks later stating the Poles, Russians and Jews did not come into such consideration.

In addition to the detailed reports, the tests were filmed from time to time, and a few of these gruesome films were found in Rascher's apartment after the war .... These abominable high-altitude tests were discussed for days at Nuremberg, where Ruff and Romberg, among others, stood trial. Both claimed that Rascher had selected the test subjects and had confined himself to professional criminals. Ruff even had the persistent impression that the test persons had presented themselves voluntarily. When the prosecutor objected that this goodwill had been volunteered at the point of a gun, Ruff appealed:

'It would have been impossible to work with non-volunteers. The test subjects had to demonstrate interest and initiative in the experiment.'[8]

It became clear at Nuremberg that this series of experiments had fallen into two groups: one under Rascher's direction and one under Ruff's and Romberg's. During the latters' experiment no one died, but during Rascher's experiments, deaths occurred repeatedly. That no one died as a result of Ruff's and Romberg's experiments did not mean their acquittal, for both had assisted Rascher in his deadly experiments. However, establishing the degree of guilt proved less easy.

The prosecution alleged that both doctors were guilty of gross negligence, an accusation they both heatedly disputed. Ruff:

> 'I did do something. When one of the test persons died during an experiment of Rascher, I could, of course, take no action against Rascher himself. However, after his death, I had the decompression chamber towed out of Dachau to prevent Rascher from carrying out more tests . . . .'[9]

Why, then had he, despite these deaths, added his signature to the final report. Ruff:

> 'We had to prepare a final report on the tests, and it was entirely normal that the three doctors who had worked on the experiments should sign it. That Rascher had three deaths did not alter that fact . . . .'[10]

Despite his co-operation in these experiments which he regarded 'not as unethical, especially in wartime',[11] the charges against him could not be sustained and he was acquitted. The verdict caused a sensation but the prosecutor had not been able to prove that Ruff had been instrumental in the victim's death or in the medical offences committed. Wolfgang Romberg, who described himself as a 'non-boxer' denied, together with Ruff, any responsibility.

> 'Dr Romberg, when people died during the experiment in which you assisted Rascher, what were you doing? Were you looking through the window, or operating equipment?'
>
> 'It was my task to watch the cardiogram. Rascher operated the equipment. At a certain point I saw from the cardiogram that the situation was critical and I told Rascher that the experiment should be stopped . . . .'
>
> 'What could you have done to stop the experiment yourself? Could you have turned a handle, pushed a button or something?'
>
> 'Rascher held the handle which controlled the cabin

National Archives

Hans Wolfgang Romberg

pressure. Only he, by using this handle, could have
stopped the experiment. I would have stopped long
ago, and I said as much to Rascher ... .'

'Well, what exactly did you say? Did you say:
"Watch out Sigmund, you're going too high, or watch
out, you should stop"?'

'I don't know any more what I said exactly. In any
case, I brought the danger to Rascher's attention.
Furthermore, I never called him Sigmund, but Mr
Rascher ... .'

'Could Rascher see the cardiogram from where he
sat?'

'Yes.'

'Why did you not bend forward and turn the wheel
to change the pressure and save the life of the test
subject?'

'I told Rascher that he should go down ... .'

'That's not what I asked. Why did you not turn
the wheel. It was hardly miles away, was it?'

'That was impossible. If Rascher did not want to
change the pressure, then it didn't happen. I would
have had to knock him down, or shoot him ... .'

'I agree with you that scientists are no boxers, but
surely, Rascher was hardly a giant. Couldn't you have
simply turned the wheel and discussed it later with
Rascher?'

'No, I repeat, I warned Rascher several times, but
if it was his opinion that the experiment should go
on, that's what happened. I should have to go for him
at least ... .'

'You didn't have to go for him! You had only to
bend forward to turn the wheel. Very simple. He had
the handle in his hand ... .'

'Yes, he had the handle in his hand, and if he didn't
want to turn it back, that was that. He would have
done the experiment without me, if need be.'

'When the test subject died, why did you not go
to the police to lodge a charge of murder? That would
have seemed logical to me.'

Romberg rejected the idea completely:

'It was a medical experiment that proved fatal. Such experiments are done all over the world, and no one talks of "murder" if they prove fatal.'

'What I can not understand is that, despite this death, you remained present for the dissection of the victim . . . .'

'I admit that this doesn't sound so nice, but seeing that nothing could be done about it, I stuck around . . . .'

'You told Ruff all about it. Is that right? Did he call the police in?'

'I told Ruff all about it but he did not call in the police. The police would have been incompetent in this business; it was a case for the Air Force. I discussed it at length with Ruff and we came to the conclusion that it would be of little use to see Himmler. He would probably have told us that the dead person was not our problem. So we stayed at Dachau and decided to round off the experiments.'

'In 1942, you prepared a report with Rascher; I suppose you were still on good terms with him?'

'Well, that's putting it very strongly . . . .'

'Still, you worked with a murderer . . . .'

'I do not consider Rascher a murderer either from a legal or a moral point of view . . . .'

'But Mr Romberg, you testified yourself to having witnessed the death of a test subject. And in spite of it, were you not still proud to be Rascher's assistant?'

'No, that's not true. I wasn't proud to be Rascher's assistant. In fact, I managed to withdraw my co-operation with him.'

'But was it not Rascher who nominated you for a Cross of Merit?'

'He wanted to carry on with the experiments, and hoped that by nominating me he could get my help again. I received a Certificate of Merit for my high-altitude research, signed by Keitel . . . .'[12]

None of the physicians involved in the Dachau experiments wished to discuss this with the author. Dr Romberg was, after long insistence, prepared to answer 'questions of historical interest' via his lawyer and only in writing. He would rather avoid a direct confrontation since he could add nothing new to what he had already said at Nuremberg. He maintained that he had no further medical occupation during the Third Reich because he retracted himself 'as fast as possible after Dr Rascher's experiments and never saw him again ... .'[13]

Dr Hubertus Strughold was conspicuous by his absence from the medical trial. How did this happen?

In the summer of 1945 Strughold, Ruff and forty-nine other physicians of the Air Force were questioned by the Americans on their activities during the war. The Americans seemed to be more interested in the scientific results that the medics had established than in the means by which they had been obtained. Whether the doctors had or had not been fanatical Nazis left the Americans cold. On the contrary, in preparation for their continued scientific work in the United States, every doctor wrote a report on his activities during the war and Hubertus Strughold edited their manuscripts, carefully excising every reference to experiments performed upon prisoners in concentration camps. This became the authoritive work on German Air Force medical skills, 'German Aviation Medicine — World War 2.'

The Americans were well aware that some of the doctors had performed experiments in concentration camps upon prisoners but agreed to publication notwithstanding. Why? Dr Ullrich Luft, one of the Luftwaffe specialists who, after the war was enabled to continue his research for the Americans, was in no doubt;

> 'Let sleeping dogs lie. What is the use of bringing that up ... you can only run into trouble. The less said, the better ... .'[14]

Shortly before Strughold and his colleagues were due to leave for the United States, the Americans arrested four doctors on suspicion of war crimes, amongst whom were Siegfried Ruff and Hans Wolfgang Romberg. Strughold was left alone, and for discernible reasons. Once Ruff had been released, nothing prevented the Americans from bringing Strughold to the United States. He was put to work in San Antonio, Texas, and at the Randolph Air Force Base he founded the first Aeromedical School in America. His own name was later given to it:

Strughold Aeromedical. He became the great pioneer of American space medicine and was, amongst other inventions, responsible for the spacesuit in which John Herschel Glenn orbited the earth in 1962, the first American to do so.

That Strughold knew of the medical experiments at Dachau is beyond the slightest doubt. Together with Ruff and Luft, in 1942 he watched a film about the experiments practised in Dachau and not a word of protest passed his lips. He worked closely with Ruff and Hippke, which led Dr Luft to conclude 'that he must have been aware of the operations that were going on in the concentration camps ... .'[15]

As it later became clear, Strughold was one of the so-called 'paper-clip boys',[16] scholars whose dossiers were purposely altered, against the directives of the American Ministry of Justice, the Ministry of External Affairs and the order of President Harry Truman, in order to facilitate their entry into the United States.

* * *

In July 1942, Rascher and Romberg went to Berlin to give Himmler an account of the experiments, and the subject of the experiments with low temperature was raised for the first time. Romberg:

> 'We had to report to the SS headquarters and here Rascher introduced me to Himmler. Himmler was very friendly to Rascher, who had given me instructions as how to behave beforehand. When Rascher had delivered his report, Himmler told him to present himself to Goering and inform him of the results of the Dachau experiments.
>
> He also gave orders to effect preparations for cold-experiments and talked about popular methods of warming up near-drowned and frozen people. In particular, the story of a fisherwoman, who warmed her half-frozen husband up in bed seemed to please him. I entered into the conversation and said that it was not so much the method by which a person was

warmed up, as the speed in which this was done.

A painful silence ensued and I realized that this was not the moment to speak to Himmler. Afterwards Rascher asked me whether I did not have a screw loose, talking like that to Himmler, his "Reichs-Heini!" Himmler also took this opportunity to explain again that in this all-out war, concentration camp prisoners had to be used for medical experiments. He added that those who did not understand this, failed to understand the whole war; for it meant life or death for Germany.

Then the film made during the experiments was shown and Himmler appeared to be pleased. He asked me if I wanted to assist in the cold-experiments but I tried to get out of this by saying that I was attached to the Air Force Research Centre whereupon he immediately offered his mediation, and there the matter rested. I had actually decided long ago to back out of the Dachau experiments. I was lucky enough to succeed . . . .'[17]

Having begun the offensive against Great Britain and with the Russian campaign in sight, it was high time the Luftwaffe addressed the problem of freezing and its consequences. It had become clear that Goering's pilots, despite their warm clothing and pills, died like rats if they ended up in the Channel. Even pilots fished out alive after having made use of their parachutes, died despite intensive medical care.

As early as 24 February 1942 Dr Holzlöhner, professor of physiology at the University of Kiel, received a research assignment from Professor Hippke to investigate the effect of chilling on warm-blooded organisms. At Rascher's suggestion, investigations were extended to human beings, and the approval of Himmler was obtained in making suitable testing facilities available through the SS. To carry out the experiments, a research group was assembled with the code name of '*Seenot*' (Marine Emergency) consisting of Professor Holzlöhner as director, Dr Rascher and Dr Finke.

Holzlöhner was a familiar face in Air Force circles. As a scientist with an impressive research background and reputation, he was responsible for several inventions considered to be revolutionary at the time. For example, the German pilots wore boots and gloves impregnated with a gas that generated heat when brought into contact with water. The German navy used lifebelts that had also been designated by Holzlöhner. Once again, Dachau concentration camp was the chosen test area. In Block five, a tank was built measuring 2m X 2m X 2m. Around its edges was an impressive array of measuring equipment. The tank was filled to the brim with ice-cold water. To simulate the real situation as closely as possible, the prisoners who were forced to co-operate, were dressed in full air pilot's kit. They were forced to jump into the water and the experiment began. All sorts of methods were employed to warm the prisoners up after they had slowly frozen. Witnesses' reports showed that Holzlöhner and Finke anaesthetised the test subjects before sending them into the icy water to prevent their unnecessary suffering. Rascher, however, wanted nothing to do with anaesthetics, as they would influence the test results!

In his first intermediate report on the freezing experiments, dated 10 September 1942, Rascher wrote:

'The test subjects were immersed in water in full-flying uniform, winter and summer combination, with flying hood. A life-jacket of rubber or kapok prevented sinking. The experiments were conducted at water temperature 36.5 and 53.5°F. In the first test series, the back of the head and the brain stem were above water. In another series, the back of the neck (brain stem) and cerebellum were submerged. Temperatures as low as 79.5° in the stomach and 79.7° in the rectum were recorded electrically.

Fatalities occurred only when the medulla and the cerebellum were chilled. In autopsies of such fatalities, large quantities of free blood, up to a pint, were always found in the cranial cavity. The heart regularly showed extreme distension of the right chamber. The test subjects in such situations inevitably died when the body temperature had dropped to 82.5°, despite all rescue attempts. These autopsy findings plainly prove the importance of a heated neck protector for the foam suit now in the process of development. Experiments in the restoration of chilled people showed that quick warming is, in every instance, to be preferred above slow warming, since body temperature continues to drop after removal from the cold water. Warming by animal heat — the bodies of animals or women — is much too slow. The only available aids to prevent chilling are improvements in flying clothes. Chief importance must be assigned to the foam suit developed by the German Textile Research Institute at München-Gladbach, together with suitable neck protection.

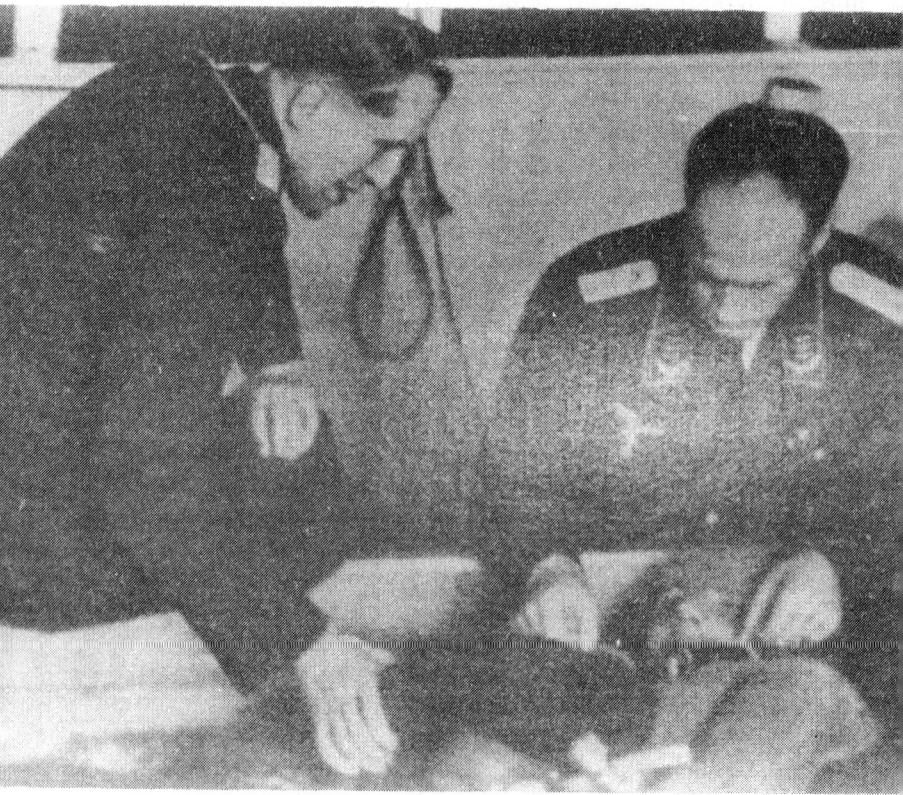

National Archives

Dr Rascher (right) and Dr Holzlöhner during an experiment at Dachau

The tests show that medication is probably unnecessary if the aviator is at all recovered alive . . . .'[18]

A few days later Himmler responded:

'I would nevertheless arrange the experiments in
such a way that all the possibilities — rapid warming
and warming by medication or animal heat — can
be tried in turn . . . .'[19]

In October, Holzlöhner considered the research completed
and any further experimenting to be pointless. Together with
Rascher and Finke, he prepared a thirty-two page report,
classified 'top-secret', entitled 'Freezing Experiments With
Human Beings', which was discussed during a medical
conference at Nuremberg in October 1942. An audience of
ninety-five scientists heard Holzlöhner's report on the Dachau
experiments. A few conclusions:

'When the back of the neck is involved in the
chilling, the temperature-drop is accelerated. This
must be attributed to the failure of the regulatory
centres governing body warmth and blood vessels. In
addition, brain oedema sets in.
Blood sugar rises during the temperature drop and
does not sink as long as the chill is maintained. There
are indications of a temporary disturbance in
metabolism. After emergence from the cold water, a
further temperature drop may ensue for fifteen
minutes or longer. This offers a possible explanation
for fatalities occurring after a person has been rescued
from the sea. Strong external heat application never
does any harm to the badly chilled person. Active and
massive heat treatment was shown to be the most
effective therapeutical measure. The best method is
immersion in a hot bath. Tests with cold protective
clothing showed that the time of survival can be more
than doubled . . . .'[20]

When the congress was over, Rascher heaved a sigh of relief.
Holzlöhner's criticizing gaze had disappeared and he could now

do just as he pleased without any hindrance. A witness to this was the prisoner-nurse Walter Neff who estimated that, during the Holzlöhner-Finke period, sixty prisoners were used of whom eighteen died as a direct result of the tests, and that in the following Rascher period, another 220-240 prisoners were used. The death toll amongst these latter is no longer discernible with any accuracy but must be approximately 200.[21]

Neff described one of these experiments as one of the worst ever carried out:

> 'Two Russian officers were brought from the prison barracks (Bunker). They arrived at about four o'clock in the afternoon. Rascher had them stripped, and they had to go in the vat naked.
>
> Hour after hour went by, and whereas usually unconsciousness from the cold which set in after sixty minutes at the latest, the two men in this case still responded fully after two and a half hours. All appeals to Rascher to put them into sleep by injection were fruitless. About the third hour one of the Russians said to the other: "Comrade, please tell the officer to shoot us." The other replied that he expected no mercy from this fascist dog. Then they shook hands with each other and uttered the words "Farewell, Comrade".
>
> These words were translated for Rascher's benefit by a young Pole, though in a somewhat modified form. Rascher went to his office. The young Pole at once tried to chloroform the two victims. But Rascher came back at once, threatening us with his gun and the direst consequences if we dared to touch the victims again. The experiment lasted at least five hours before death supervened. The two bodies were taken to the Schwabing Hospital in Munich for post-mortem examination . . . .'[22]

When Romberg was asked for his opinion of this account, he replied:

> 'While I am no specialist in this field, I do consider this story to be exaggerated, and to be honest, I can

not believe that it happened as has been described. I read through the experimental reports (at the beginning of the trial) and they lead to the conclusion that a person becomes frozen stiff in only ten or twenty minutes. Speech or movement becomes impossible. Moreover, it is well known that, after one hour, unconsciousness sets in, while Neff claims here that the two Russian officers were still talking after three hours ... .'[23]

According to Neff, in January 1943, Rascher began a new series of tests, the so-called 'dry-freezing.' In this, prisoners were bound naked to a stretcher and left in the cold overnight. A number of problems arose which led Rascher to give Himmler hints that he would like to transfer his test-grounds to Auschwitz. Winters there were much more severe and there would also be more opportunities to carry out experiments in outlying areas where the other prisoners would not hear the victim's screams at night. Why this did not go ahead is unknown. Again Neff:

'A prisoner was placed naked on a stretcher outside the barracks. This was in the evening. He was covered with a sheet, and every hour a bucket of cold water was poured over him. The test subject lay out in the open like this until the morning. The temperature of these test subjects was taken with a thermometer. Later, Dr Rascher said it was a mistake to cover the subject with a sheet and to drench him with water. This caused the wrong effect since the air could not reach the test subject.

In future, the test subjects must not be covered (...) I do not recall precisely, however, whether, there were fatalities during these experiments and how many. I would like to state, with reservation, that about three victims lost their lives at this time ... .'[24]

Himmler followed his protégé's experiments with special interest and he was particularly interested in the re-warming of hypothermics. Romberg:

'During the conversation in July 1942, Himmler

spent some time on this sort of experiment and how it should be carried out. For example, he gave Rascher orders to find out how coastal dwellers dealt with such situations. As I have already said, the Reichsführer could well imagine that a fisherwoman had warmed up her frozen husband by cuddling up to him. He especially urged Rascher to try out these kinds of folk remedies ... .'[25]

As a consequence of Himmler's wish, four women were collected from the camp brothel in Ravensbrück and taken to block five at Dachau where, naked, they were to clasp the survivors of Rascher's ice-tank. Rascher took one look at the girls and burst into a fury. He wrote an angry letter to Rudolph Brandt to complain about the poor selection in Ravensbrück:

'Four women were assigned to me from the women's concentration camp at Ravensbrück, for purposes of testing the warming of chilled people by animal heat, as directed by the Reichsführer SS. One of the women assigned showed impeccably nordic racial characteristics, fair hair, blue eyes, corresponding skull shape and physical build and aged twenty-one years.

I asked the girl why she had volunteered for brothel service. This was her reply; "To get out of the concentration camp. All who volunteered for half a year's brothel service were promised that they would be discharged from the concentration camp in return."

When I objected that it was shameful to volunteer as a brothel girl, I was told; "Better half a year in a brothel than half a year in a concentration camp."

An enumeration of a series of very curious conditions in the Ravensbrück ensued. The conditions described were for the most part confirmed by the three other brothel girls and the women overseer who had accompanied them from Ravensbrück. My racial conscience is outraged by the prospect of exposing a girl to racially inferior concentration camp elements who is outwardly pure nordic and who might be led on the right path by proper employment. For this reason, I decline to use this girl for my experimental purposes, and I have rendered an appropriate report to the commandant of the camp and to the adjutant of the Reichsführer SS . . . .'[26]

As time went by Rascher gradually lost the need for any feelings at all, and any vague idea that he was engaged in criminal activities wore off. Not only was he fulfilling his supposed duty as a responsible doctor, but he was also acting on Himmler's orders. Every action that brought him a step closer to the professorship, his deepest desire, was performed with great care and no scruples. The following account will illustrate this once more.

One of the prisoners at Dachau was the eminent chemist Dr Robert Feix, sent there for having attempted to conceal his Jewish ancestry by bribing SS officers. In the trial that followed his arrest, Feix was carrying out important research into blood-clotting. The Germans, keen to obtain the fruits of his research enabled him, in Dachau itself, to put the finishing touches to the drug he had developed, Polygall ten, a drug which delayed bleeding by six hours.

When Rascher was informed of Feix's activities, his malignant imagination went to work at once. He would invite Feix to work together with him, and, at the end of the ride, he would claim the discovery of this vitally important drug as his own. However, despite handsome promises, Feix refused to work with the SS Sturmbannführer. He was aware of Rascher's experiments in Block five and did not consider him the most appropriate person with whom to conclude his study. He could allow himself the luxury of refusal, thanks to his great fame in the German scientific community, where many efforts were being made to secure his release from Dachau. For this reason, Rascher's original intention of liquidating Feix after the research was completed was also too risky.

Nevertheless, Rascher did not give up, eventually going so far as to plead Feix's case with Himmler. In a letter to the Reichsführer he wrote that

'. . . in the interest of the research, it is naturally desirable that the patent holder of the drug, Feix, is given back his former status of half Aryan. To my knowledge, the Gestapo reports are not of such a nature that a research project such as this can be turned down . . . .'[27]

This was asking too much and Himmler let it be known, via Sievers, that this request could not be fulfilled. He may well have wished otherwise, but there would have been immediate problems with Bormann, which was the last thing the Reichsführer wanted!

Rascher, however, pressed the matter further with Feix, who eventually succumbed to temptation. Rascher had promised him that he would be freed immediately after the research was completed. Feix took on the chemical side of the research, Rascher the medical side. Rascher's uncle, the physician Dr Fritz Rascher (who had nothing to do with the behaviour and the experiments of his nephew), testified as to the nature of the experiments at Nuremberg:

'During my nephew's absence, I came across a number of documents on his desk. They concerned the testing of a drug, Polygall ten, for which purpose four people had been shot. As far as I can remember, one was a Russian officer, and another, a Cretan woman, the other two escape my memory. According to the report, the Russian was shot high in the right shoulder by an SS soldier standing on a chair (. . .). It had been noted that the Russian collapsed from the pain, and died after about twenty minutes. I was so dismayed that I could not read the other reports. I took a tablet of Polygall ten and had it analysed in a laboratory . , . .'[28]

The uncle decided to call his nephew to account for his activities. Rascher was furious when he understood that an outsider had discovered his criminal activities. A long talk followed in which Rascher confided to his uncle that it was all too much for him:

'I can't go on, I can't think clearly any more. I know I am wrong but it's too late to change now . . . .'[29]

In May 1944, Himmler gave Freiherr von Eberstein orders to arrest his protégé. What was the reason for this? His children's births were a deception, something the Gestapo had long suspected. In fact, Rascher's wife was infertile, and the children she 'bore' came from an orphanage. A pillow under her dress had concealed the truth. Himmler was known to admire large families and Rascher had not wanted to disappoint him. This alone might well have been forgiven, were it not for the fact that the Gestapo had also discovered that Rascher had been in touch with Swiss pharmaceutical companies concerning the sale of the rights of Polygall ten. This was an unforgivable mistake and the Raschers were arrested. Sigmund was locked up in the Dachau bunkers and Nini was deported to Ravensbrück.

Rascher maintained his innocence and insisted that it must all be due to some mistake. When, in May 1945, Captain Payne Best found him in the Dachau bunker, Rascher declared that he was related to the British Prime Minister Chamberlain.[30] He admitted in so many words that he had developed the gas chambers![31]

His imprisonment was all a terrible mistake. He had wanted to publish the result of his work in a Swiss periodical whereupon the Gestapo had made him their prisoner. Such publication of his brilliant research would have reached the British too, and what a waste of work that would have been![32]

Rascher was ultimately murdered in the SS bunker by the SS officer Bongartz, who having brought him supper, shot him through the head. Professor Holzlöhner committed suicide after the war and Dr Finke vanished.

In closing, we return to Romberg's hearing:

> 'Dr Romberg, it strikes me as being very odd that a doctor did not acquire information about the patients he used for the tests. Even Dr Ding in Buchenwald knew something of the prisoners on whom he experimented. You have testified that the selections were made at roll-call. Was that roll-call just for the professional criminals condemned to death, or were all sorts mixed together.'
>
> 'I must confess that I do not know exactly how the roll-call worked.'
>
> 'Did you offer a future pardon to those prisoners

who co-operated with you?'

'No, I was not in a position to do that!'

'Well, did you inform the prisoners of the danger that the experiments involved?'

'I told them what would happen, as well as the possible risks, although these were, of course, not known accurately. However, I did guarantee the prisoners that they would come to no harm.'

'You have heard what the original intention was, to extend a pardon to the prisoners who took part. Was this the pardon that Himmler suggested in his letter of 13 April 1943? The death penalty would be commuted to concentration camp for life, but Jews, Poles and Russians did not come into consideration ... .'

'I didn't know. I never read that particular order of Himmler.'

'Why did you not prevent Rascher's tests, whose nature and intent were clearly criminal ... .'

'The upbringing and education of a scientist make it difficult for him to indulge in brute force. I am no boxer .... I had no desire to promote my ideas with violence. Furthermore, given my subordinate position in Dachau, I could do nothing to prevent the experiments taking place. I was, shall we say, "a visitor". Had I attacked Rascher, he would have undoubtedly shot me. He always carried a revolver. If I look back on it all now, and if I were in the same situation again, after the first death, I would go to Berlin to make a report — and then stay ill ... .'[33]

* * *

For centuries scientists have attempted to find a means by which sea water might be de-salted, and the military operations of the Second World War compelled the scientific researchers of the Waffen SS to pursue the task with renewed intensity. There were two methods in existence in Germany by which sea water could be made drinkable. One, devised by the Air Force engineer,

Dr Berka, consisted of the substance Berkatit which was added to the sea water, changing its taste but not its composition. The other method, developed by the Viennese doctor and chemist Schäfer, used the substance Wofatit, which, when added to the sea water genuinely removed the salt. This last method was undoubtedly the best, but also by far the most expensive. Its manufacture required a great deal of silver, and, more important, the construction of enormous factories. A more efficient means was needed, and with this as its aim, a research committee was set up whose task it was to establish guidelines for experiments with various desalination methods upon people.

On 7 June 1944, the chairman of the commission, Professor Konrad Schröder, Medical Inspector of the Air Force, approached Himmler with a request to make the experimental laboratory at Dachau available for experiments:

'On a previous occasion you gave the Air Force an opportunity to clarify medical questions in experiments on human beings. As a result of numerous animal experiments and also tests on human volunteers, I am today faced with a problem calling for a final solution. The Air Force has simultaneously developed two processes for making sea water drinkable. One of the methods, developed by a medical officer, actually removes the salt from the sea water, turning it into real drinking water. The other, reported by an engineer, leaves the salt content unchanged, merely removing the unpleasant taste of sea water.

The latter process, in contrast to the former, requires no bottleneck raw materials. From the medical point of view, and from our present knowledge, this process must be regarded as doubtful, since the intake of concentrated salt solutions may give rise to serious symptoms of poisoning. Since it has been possible, up to now, to conduct human experiments only up to four days, whereas actual practice requires a margin up to twelve days for people adrift at sea, appropriate experiments are necessary. Forty healthy test subjects are required to be permanently available for four weeks.

As it is known from previous experiments that the Dachau concentration camp has the necessary laboratories, this camp would be eminently suitable.

The experiments are to be headed by Captain Beiglböck of the Vienna Medical University Clinic (Professor Eppinger). I shall send you the names of the other participating physicians on receipt of your general authorization.

In view of the great importance of clarifying this problem, affecting personnel of the Air Force and the Navy caught in emergencies, I should be greatly indebted to you Mr Reich Minister, if you could see your way clear to granting my request . . . .'[34]

Wilhelm Beiglböck was no stranger to the Austrian medical community. As assistant to Professor Eppinger, in his time considered the most talented and revolutionary medic in the German-speaking world, he had shown exemplary research ability. Together with Eppinger, he prepared a number of medical articles covering the most diverse subjects. In 1944, the year in which he received a professorship from the University of Vienna, he was summoned by the medical department of the Luftwaffe to Berlin, where Dr Becker-Freysing informed him of the sea water experiments.

Beiglböck was shocked when told that the tests had to be carried out on prisoners condemned to death but when Becker-Freysing added that the co-operating prisoners were to be pardoned, the thirty-nine year old professor gave his consent. According to Becker-Freysing, it was absolutely necessary that the experiments take place in a concentration camp, a position he later again defended at Nuremberg:

'It was obvious that the tests should take place in a concentration camp. A reformatory or prison fell considerably short of providing the possibilities and facilities available at Dachau. The chairman of the research committee, Professor Schröder, felt that the supply of prisoners might pose a problem, but I pointed out that, under his predecessor, Hippke and Professor Holzlöhner had also carried out experiments for which prisoners had been made available.

National Archives

Wilhelm Beiglböck

Schröder still had reservations, and only after I had pointed out to him the international literature on tests using prisoners did he put these reservations aside. He then asked me whether I knew how Holzlöhner had obtained his test subjects at the time. This I did not know. The only thing I did know was that Rascher had said that his test subjects were made available through the Chief of Police. Schröder thereupon replied that he would get in touch with Grawitz (Chief of the Health Service of the SS and director of the German Red Cross). I have already told you that, for these tests, forty healthy young men between the ages of twenty and thirty could indeed be found, but not forty healthy people who could choose to have four weeks free time in order to take part in the experiment. No, anyone would confirm that, in Berlin in 1944, this was out of the question ... .'[36]

Schröder did indeed get in touch with Ernst Grawitz who wrote to Himmler about the subject:

'The Chief of the Air Force Medical Service, in the enclosed letter, requests that experiments be made on prisoners to check two evidently promising and simple methods for making sea water drinkable. In accordance with your order of 15 May 1944, Reich Leader, I have obtained the comments of SS Major General Gebhardt, and SS Major Nebe, which are as follows:
1. Gebhardt: "I think it entirely appropriate to support the Air Force approach and to make a supervising internist available for the experiments of the Waffen SS."
2. Glücks: "With reference to the above letter, it is stated that this office offers no objection to carrying out the experimental series requested by the Chief of the Air Force Medical Service in the Rascher experimental laboratory in the Dachau concentration camp.
Jews or other prisoners to be take from quarantine are to be used as far as possible."

3. Nebe: "I agree to the proposal to test a process on prisoners in concentration camps for making sea water drinkable. I suggest that the anti-social gypsy half-breeds in the Auschwitz concentration camp be used for this purpose. Among them are men in good health who can not be used in general work. I expect to offer special recommendations shortly concerning these gypsies to the Reich Leader, but believe it would be appropriate even now to select the required number of test subjects from this group. If the Reich Leader would approve, I will pick the names of the test subjects."

With reference to the suggestion by Major General Nebe to use gypsies in the conduct of the experiments, I take the liberty of pointing out that with their somewhat different racial make-up gypsies may produce test results that can not be directly applied to our men. For this reason, it would be desirable if prisoners racially comparable to the European population could be made available for the tests . . . .'[37]

Himmler accommodated both proposals, and noted with his green pencil in the margin 'Gypsies — for control three others.'[38]

Ultimately, the gypsies selected for the tests were chosen not from Auschwitz but from Buchenwald and opinions vary as to the degree of voluntary choice involved.

During a roll-call in Buchenwald, gypsies were asked whether they might not prefer better work at Dachau. It concerned work with a blitz clearance unit. Given that many gypsies entertained the assumption that nowhere in the world could be worse than in Buchenwald, and that such blitz clearance work would mean better housing, food and privileges, a number of them volunteered.

Dachau soon showed them that their assumptions were false. After they had arrived, the gypsies were examined by the camp physicians, amongst them Dr Plötner, and then sent on to Beiglböck.

The Viennese student Fritz Pillwein, a prisoner-nurse at that time, on the question of coercion:

'In my opinion, some of the gypsies had
volunteered. In the case of two German gypsies I was
certain of this because they had come out of Dachau.
They had volunteered in order to get out of the so-
called *Strafkompanie* (punishment corps). I gathered that
there might have been some voluntary involvement
when, after discovering that the test subjects had
secretly drunk (fresh) water during an experiment,
Beiglböck flew in to a rage and castigated them for
having first submitted themselves for an experiment
and then not keeping to the rules. I believe that
Beiglböck too, who was not familiar with
concentration camps, was of the opinion that he was
working with volunteers . . . .'[39]

Karl Hollenreiner however, who was one of the test subjects,
testified:

'During a roll-call in Buchenwald, I and forty mates
were designated to carry out work at Dachau. Once
there we were taken to the experimentation block
where an Air Force doctor undressed us and took X-
rays . . . .'[40]

And Beiglböck stated:

'I left the prisoners entirely free to choose whether
or not to take part. It has been suggested that I
exploited their simplicity. I must say that their level
of intelligence was rather low, but I would
immediately add that they were in no way mad or
backward. That I made misuse of their
underdevelopment is a proposition that I utterly
refute. Once a test subject entered the testing station,
it meant that he had agreed to — and was obliged
to subject himself to the rules . . . .'[41]

The sea water experiments took place in the autumn of 1944.
Pillwein:

'For the first three days the test subjects were given

emergency marine rations, consisting of one tablet koka-kola, some dextropur and a few pieces of rusk, about ten to twelve small pieces. In addition, from the first day to the last, the participants were issued salt water four to five times daily to the total quantity of a pint. The forty-four subjects were subdivided into five or six groups. Two groups received pure sea water, two others, pure sea water with an added salt preparation, the remaining group received distilled sea water without any additives.

From the outset, daily blood specimens were drawn from the participants. With certain patients, weakness and especially thirst took such extreme forms that after only a few days, they could no longer leave their beds. In one case, I remember that the patient broke out into paroxysms of screaming.

It happened frequently that these patients drank from the slop buckets of the orderlies, or in unobserved moments, drained water from the air-raid protection buckets in the hall. Some patients actually lapped up the water poured out on the floor for mopping. I had to weigh the men taking part in the test every day, and noted that the daily loss of weight was up to two pounds.

One day, when Dr Beiglböck had established that certain patients had taken additional fluid, the orderly in charge was transferred out of the hospital.'[42]

According to Ignaz Bauer, patients often begged Beiglböck to give them water but —

'Dr Beiglböck was inexorable. A young fellow who had succeeded in obtaining some drinking water was tied to his bed in punishment. Added to all these physical torments was the constant fear of death . . . .'[43]

Beiglböck:

'I conscientiously informed the test subjects about the nature of the experiments but naturally, I could not predict exactly what would happen. I gave them my word, and this was really the most important, that they would not come to any harm. I told them truthfully that for a few days, but not for longer than was strictly necessary, they would be intensely thirsty. I promised that if someone could no longer bear it, I would consider (!) stopping the test.

Thirst is one of the most horrible sensations we can imagine. But the fact remains that thirst was one of the results of the experiment for which the test subjects had applied, it was part of the agreement ... .'[44]

'Which agreement?'' the prosecutor wanted to know.

'I had told the test subjects that after the experiments, they could made their wishes known to me, and I promised to help fulfil them. And that's what actually happened. For that matter, I have to say that I had no idea why the gypsies were in a concentration camp. I decided, for safety's sake, to keep this thought to myself ... .'[45]

The court sentenced Becker-Freysing to twenty years imprisonment, and Beiglböck to fifteen. The latter did not even serve a third of his sentence. Released early on good behaviour, in 1952, he was appointed Medical Superintendent of the City Hospital in Buxtehude; a position he held for a few years before leaving for an unspecified destination.

7

The Auschwitz-Birkenau Experiments

In April 1940 Heinrich Himmler made an inspection of the area around Oswięcim, in the cold, marshy, infertile region of Poland known as Silesia. He gave orders for the building of a concentration camp next to the former cavalry barracks of the Austrian Army to accommodate the growing number of Polish officers and resistance fighters. On 20 May 1940, thirty professional criminals arrived from Sachsenhausen concentration camp and, led by fifteen SS officers and supported by 300 Jews, the foundations were laid for the complex of buildings which would go down in history as the 'death factory': Auschwitz-Birkenau. The first prisoners were given leading positions in the internal management of the camp, and were to form a camp aristocracy which took over when the SS left at night.

On 14 June 1940, the camp was officially opened, and on the same day, the first transportation arrived — the first victims being 720 Polish political prisoners. On the occasion of the opening, a reception was held at which several prominent patrons of the Endlösung were present, including several whose careers would become closely bound up with that of Auschwitz itself: camp commandant Rudolf Höss and his adjutants Josef Kramer and Robert Mulka.

Under the inspired leadership of Höss, once destined for the priesthood, and 'a real pioneer of the Endlösung, thanks to new ideas and methods of upbringing',[1] as his 1944 dossier reveals, the camp was erected with great speed. When Himmler made a tour of inspection on 1 March 1941, he gave orders to expand the capacity of the camp to 30,000 prisoners — and to build a second camp at Birkenau, three kilometres away from the Stammlager, designed to hold 100,000 prisoners of war.

At the same time, an enormous industrial complex arose, to

which the camp offered cheap labour; German industry and the SS worked closely together. In October 1941, work was started on the building of Auschwitz-Birkenau, where the execution camp was set up; the existing *Bauerngehöft* (small farm) was converted into a gas chamber. In the course of 1942, the gassing capacity was expanded, and at the end of that year, Auschwitz was prepared to receive daily transports from all over occupied Europe.

In July 1942, Himmler demonstrated his appreciation to Höss:

> 'Eichmann's programme is expanding — every month it grows more. Make sure that you make progress with the enlargement of Birkenau. Gypsies are now in line for liquidation. You can press on with the liquidation of non-working Jews. I have seen your work and efforts, I am pleased and I thank you. I promote you to Sturmbannführer ... .'[2]

Höss talking about Auschwitz:

> 'The prisoners were prepared to work but could not summon the strength to do so, as a result of a general debility. They died like rats, and lacked the least resistance, so that their constitution could not withstand the most trivial illness. Even those amongst them who had some resistance against sickness grew smaller in number every day. Extra rations were useless. They consumed everything they could lay their hands on, but were never satisfied ... . This was how we explained to ourselves the mysterious disappearance of so many Russians ... .'[3]

The medical direction of the camp was in the hands of SS Hauptsturmführer Dr Eduard Wirths who succeeded Dr Kurt Uhlenbrock in September 1942. The latter had contracted typhus and was sent on convalescent leave and was afterwards detailed to the armoured SS division 'Viking'.

Former concentration camp prisoners and physicians describe Wirths as friendly, polite, charming, honest and decent. Hermann Langbein, his prisoner-secretary in both Dachau and

Auschwitz adjusted to this: 'He was completely different from the other SS doctors.'[4]

And Dr Hans Münch:

> 'As Standortarzt, he held ultimate responsibility for medical matters at Auschwitz. He was one of those who took the view that Auschwitz was an accepted fact, an actuality. The Endlösung had to be carried out properly, cleanly, efficiently, bloodlessly and without excess. He was certainly no raw SS world archetype . . . .'[5]

This same Wirths, however, was responsible for the camp's system of selections and medicalized killing. He supervised the overall process during the two years in which most of the mass murder was accomplished. During his study, he specialized in gynaecology and although he had shown talent as a surgeon, he settled into a general practice in the vicinity of Würzburg. In 1933, he joined the Nazi party and SA, and one year later, the SS. In 1940 he served in Norway and later in Russia.

In April 1942 he was declared medically unfit for combat duty because of a cardiac condition and was appointed camp physician at Neuengamme and later Dachau. At Auschwitz he showed a degree of medical humanity which became very important to many prisoners, and did a lot to improve medical conditions. Even Höss was positive:

> 'During my ten years of service in concentration camp affairs, I have never encountered a better physician.'[6]

Wirths extended the work of Polish prisoner-physicians who had been at Auschwitz for some time, and began to permit the large numbers of arriving Jewish doctors to do medical work and he accordingly protected them. Many survivors testified that he used his medical authority in many ways to save lives and that he took a stand against brutality and the random abuse of prisoners.

But Wirths was also an ardent and idealistic Nazi. According to Lifton:

'Wirths combined bureaucratic skill with a quality
of correctness and reliability within the SS. His
organisational loyalty was always clear to other SS
observers ... .'[7]

Again Höss:

'He was a man with a strong feeling of duty who
was extremely conscientious and obeyed all orders and
directions with painstaking care. His only fault was
frequently to be very soft and good natured with the
inmates and to treat prisoner-physicians as
colleagues ... .'[8]

Concerning his experimental research, the survivors are more
critical. His research concerned pre-cancerous growths of the
cervix. He undertook many tests with the cervix which was often
surgically removed and sent to his brother's laboratory in
Hamburg where the tissue was studied for pre-cancerous
growths. The experiments appeared relatively harmless but the
colposcopic examination (a new instrument at that time, the
colposcope, was inserted through the vagina so that the cervix
could be viewed before and after the application of certain
substances) was unreliable. Furthermore, it was unnecessary
to remove the whole cervix and the poor condition of the inmates
resulted in many complications, some of which either caused
deaths or else left patients sufficiently debilitated to be selected
for the gas chamber. Wirths ideological anti-semitism made him
accept Auschwitz as it was.

In the beginning he was strongly opposed to selections in
general and to doctors performing them. After a few months,
he saw how the camp commandant and his subordinates
conducted selections, many people fit for work were sent to the
gas chamber, he did all he could to bring selections under the
control of the physicians. And Lifton concludes that 'Nazi-
Germany committed him to loyal participation in the Auschwitz
project; his physician-humanitarian self rendered him a
prisoners' advocate.'[9]

Every day thousands of victims were transported into
Auschwitz, driven out of the cattle wagons on to the infamous
Rampe and subjected to selection. The prisoners had to file past

two SS physicians who decided, in a fraction of a second, between their life or death. Left meant a stay of execution, right the gas chamber.

The former prisoner Waitz:

> 'Slowly, the deported people approach the end of the platform. In the middle of platform are two SS soldiers, one is a doctor with an officer's rank. The deportees pass him by. With his thumb, or a stick, he points to the left or the right. Two lines are formed in this way. The left consists of those who look comparatively strong. The ages do vary somewhat; the youngest look sixteen or eighteen, the oldest fifty. The appearance and bearing affect the choice, for example, if he is not so well-shaven. . . . .
>
> In this line, a few young women can also be found. The right-hand line contains the older men, most of the women, the elderly, the children and the sick. Families do their best to stay together. Sometimes, the officer takes the useful youngsters out of such a large group; less often, he lets them stay with their parents in the right-hand line . . . .'[10]

People in the left-hand line were sent to the camp, where their martyrdom began: hard labour, inadequate food, miserable living conditions, lack of hygiene and continuous torture. The average life expectancy of this group amounted to no more than six weeks! The right-hand line was immediately gassed.

To begin with there were no clear selection criteria and the doctors selected at their own discretion. From 1943, with the death machine working at full capacity, it was 'survival of the fittest.'

With few exceptions, all the physicians at Auschwitz performed such selections. The former prisoner-doctor Elie Cohen about his selection:

> 'When we arrived at Auschwitz, I found myself in a line of old people. I later understood that this line was shortly to be gassed. An SS man came by and shouted; ''Doctors come forward'', and when I stepped up, I was moved to another line. Imagine,

if I had been talking with someone at the moment, or tying my shoelace, and had not heard the SS man .... I wouldn't be here ....'[11]

And Cohen became prisoner-physician. Cohen:

'The final decision about my appointment as prisoner-doctor was made by Dr Fischer. I had to walk naked before him and, on this basis, it was established that I was suitable. Not a single question on my professional medical knowledge was raised. No, the way I walked and the fact that I spoke German were the deciding factors ....'[12]

However, it was not only the SS physicians who did selections. Guards and even dentists like Frank and Schatz and the chemist Victor Capesius could be found regularly on the Rampe. And the other physicians? SS Untersturmführer Dr Hans Wilhelm König took an active part in selections of Jewish arrivals and on his orders, SS physicians terminated pregnancies after the fifth month, and these abortions were naturally made without the consent of women prisoners.[13] The inmate-physician Dr Lingens-Reiner:

'But apart from this, Dr König was in reality one of those National Socialists who should be of particular interest to the Anti-Fascists. He was the type of German whom foreign friends from pre-Hitler days would remember with sympathy and with the constant query: "How could this man degenerate in such a way? What possessed him? He can't be the same man!"

He was intelligent, saw through pretence, showed genuine medical knowledge, a rare thing among camp doctors, and he had the will to learn new things in his profession. In fact, he was deeply disgusted by the job he did at Auschwitz, but like Werner Rhode, who also hated his work, he had to get drunk before he appeared on the Rampe ....'[14]

One of the first people whom the new arrivals saw as they

stepped out from the squalid boxcars, was SS Untersturmführer Dr Fritz Klein, one of the few doctors who performed selections without stimulants of any kind. Klein, who was in charge of the women's camp at Auschwitz and later Bergen-Belsen, conducted pharmacological experiments and was one of the fervent zealots who ran the Nazi annihilation project.

> 'But', as the inmate-physician Dr Olga Lengyel stated, 'he was a correct assassin. To be just, I must say that he was less sadistic than his colleagues. I had the impression that whatever he did, he too was a victim of the circumstances. Perhaps he had a conscience. Anyway, he was the only SS butcher from whom I saw any human reactions toward the deportees. He did not hesitate to send thousands of sick to the "hospital" but I also saw him save few patients (...).
>
> A few months before the end of the war, he paid a surprise visit to our infirmary and expressed the desire to visit the hospital. I walked a few steps behind him as he had ordered me to do at our last meeting. He pointed to his bicycle and said: "My car has been taken away and we have no more gasoline .... Listen .... I am going to tell you something that will make you very happy. The war will be over shortly, and we shall be able to go home again. I have no more illusions. When the war is over, neither of you nor the others will have the slightest regard for me ... ."[15]

Although Klein might have had some 'human feelings', he was a virulent anti-Semite. Dr Lingens-Reiner:

> 'One day, I had a conversation with Dr Fritz Klein. Originally, he had shown some consideration to his non-Jewish patients, which made his unspeakable cruelties towards Jewish prisoners stand out all the more. I told him that I felt ashamed of being counted among the Germans. He asked naively: "Why?" I pointed to the chimney of the crematorium and answered: "How can you ask? You, a doctor! At this

Der Reichsführer-

Kommando ff und Polizei

Tgb.: 100 00-00 00 - 00 00 00 - 00 00 00

M.: 738/IV/42

Betr.: **Biochemische Behandlung von Sepsis etc. mit biochemischen**
Mitteln.

An den

Reichsführer-ff H. **H i m m l e r**

B e r l i n SW 11

Prinz Albrechtstrasse 8

Reichsführer !

Über die bisherigen Ergebnisse der biochemischen Behandlung
von Sepsis und anderen Krankheitsfällen erlaube ich mir nach-
folgenden Zwischenbericht vorzulegen.

1. Im ff-Lazarett **Dachau** wurden in der Berichtszeit folgende
40 Fälle mit biochemischen Mitteln behandelt. Ausser sep-
tischen Prozessen sind solche Krankheiten behandelt worden, bei denen mit Hilfe der Biochemie ebenfalls eine ent-
scheidende Wendung zur Besserung zu erreichen sein soll.

      Phlegmonös-eitrige Prozesse 17
      Sepsis 8
      Furunkulose u. Abscesse 2
      Infizierte Operationswunden 1
      Malaria 5
      Pleuraempyem 3
      Sept. Endocarditis 1
      Nephrose 1
      Chron. Ischias 1
      Gallensteine 1

Zur Anwendung kamen nach den Heilmittelanzeigen der Biochemie je nach Lage des Falles folgende Mittel:

      Kalium phosphoricum D 6
      Ferrum phosphoricum D 6 u. D 12

- 2 -

Nr. 000 Eberhart Verlagen 47 00 00

Auschwitz Museum

Report on medical experiments
performed at Dachau and Auschwitz

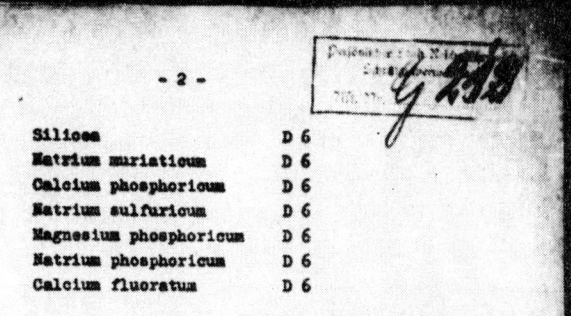

- 2 -

Silicea	D 6
Natrium muriaticum	D 6
Calcium phosphoricum	D 6
Natrium sulfuricum	D 6
Magnesium phosphoricum	D 6
Natrium phosphoricum	D 6
Calcium fluoratum	D 6

Die Sepsisfälle wurden zum grössten Teil künstlich gesetzt.

Als bisheriges Ergebnis ist zunächst festzustellen, dass der ungünstige Verlauf bei kaum einer der schweren Erkrankungen durch die biochemischen Mittel aufgehalten werden konnte. Sämtliche Sepsisfälle kamen ad exitum. Die Malariafälle blieben völlig unbeeinflusst.

Die Fälle mit ausgedehnteren phlegmonös-eitrigen Prozessen, mit Abscessbildungen, die Pleuraempyeme, die septische Endocarditis, die Nephrose, die chronische Ischias und die Gallensteine zeigten keinen auch nur einigermassen sicheren Einfluss der biochemischen Behandlung. Soweit sie günstig ausgingen, zeigten sie keinen anderen Verlauf, als sie nach ärztlicher Erfahrung bei absoluter Ruhigstellung im Bett auch ohne besondere Massnahmen zu nehmen pflegen.

Der Eindruck einer günstigen Wirkung auf Krankheitszustände durch die biochemischen Mittel bot sich nur bei 5 Fällen, von jenen 4 verhältnismässig leicht gelagert waren.

Bei dem 5. Fall handelte es sich um ein 17 Tage altes Kind mit schwerer Furunkulose. Hier setzte schon wenige Tage nach Beginn der Behandlung die Wendung zur Besserung ein. Allerdings ist hier in der Versuchsanordnung ein Fehler insofern unterlaufen, als zu Beginn der Behandlung gleichzeitig Albucid, also ein Sulfonamidpräparat, gegeben worden ist.

Auf Einwirkung der biochemischen Mittel ist vielleicht auch die stärkere Eiterbildung zu beziehen, die in einigen

- 3 -

Auschwitz Museum

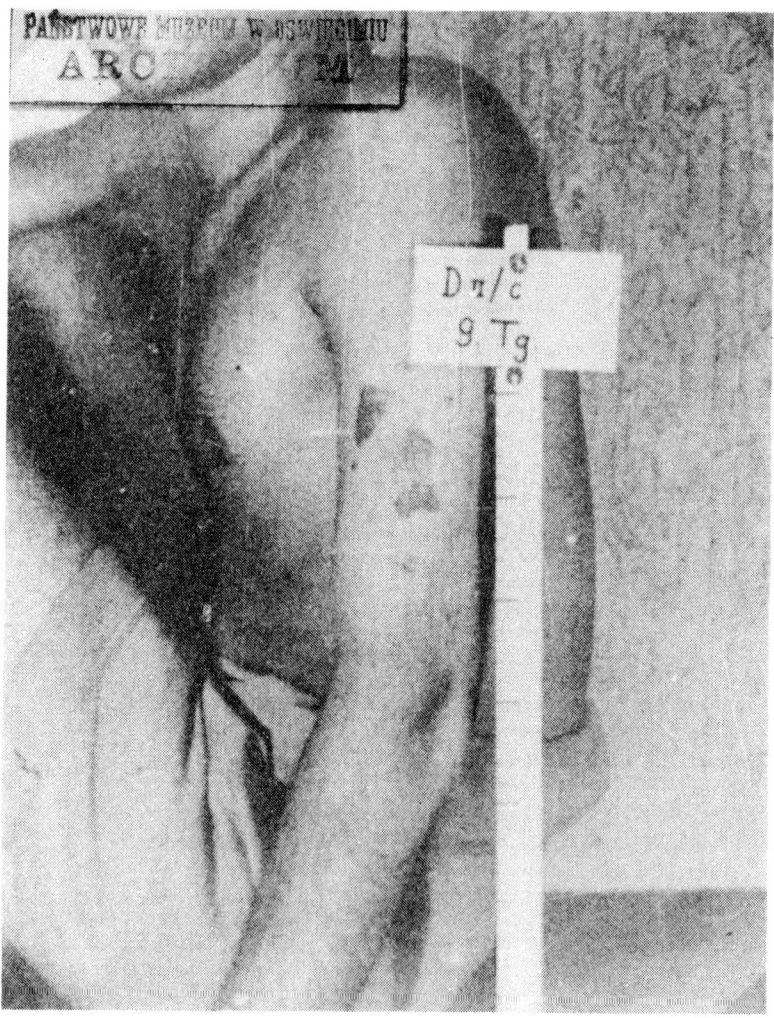

Auschwitz Museum

moment, I don't want to discuss the Jewish question
with you, neither the circumstances which might make
it difficult for Germans and Jews to live together, nor
the possibility or impossibility, desirability or
undesirability, of Jewish assimilation. It is not a
question of whether the Jews are nice and valuable
people, or the opposite. The only question here is:

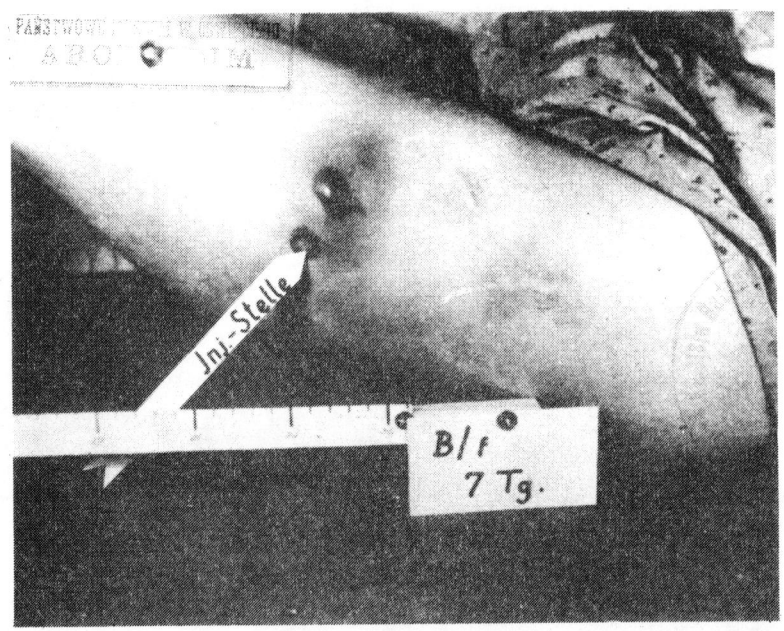

Auschwitz Museum

Photographs taken during
medical experiments at Block 10

'Have you, as a doctor, no respect for human life?'' '
  Dr Klein was in no way embarrassed. He only said:
''Out of respect for human life. I would remove a
purulent appendix from a diseased body. The Jews
are the purulent appendix in the body of
Europe ... .''[16]

And Dr Münch about Klein:

  'He was literally a little man (klein = little) with
  a distinctly inferior character. He was extremely
  authoritarian and concerned only with having
  everything his way. He was a terror to the prisoners.
  So far as I remember, he was a naturalized German,
  and in my experience, these were often not the best
  sort. Capesius was another ... .'[17]

SS Obersturmbannführer Dr Heinz Thilo was often at the Rampe to select arrivals and conducted pharmacological experiments. He visited the camp daily. At first he would make a general inspection, then he visited respective hospital blocks. The former prisoner Alfred Fiderkiewicz:

Auschwitz Museum

Dr Thilo (X) during a selection

'Neither the SS doctor, nor the SS men from the sanitary service came near the prisoners lying in bunks. An inspection of the blocks consisted solely in directing a glance right and left and in giving orders, mostly impossible to be carried out. The camp senior Schuster (political prisoner) was the only one who showed any interest in the typhus epidemic. He was not afraid of contagion but walked through the blocks and asked for details in order to transmit them to the camp physician.

Soon he came with Dr Thilo who turned to Dr Cohen (prisoner-physician) with the question:

"How many foreigners are ill with *fleckfieber?*"

"Eleven", Cohen answered. Then Thilo turned to me and asked: "How many have died?" I answered: "Three." "How many have died?" he asked again. When I told him that five had died he grew indignant and shouted "*Wieso?*" (Why, so many?)

I was flabbergasted and did not know what to say. The sick German patients relieved me of answering by saying: "*Herr Obersturmführer, wir sind hungrig, schwach und . . . .*" (Sir, we are hungry, weak and . . .). Thilo did not let them finish their complaints but shouted: "*Ich bin auch hungrig*" (I am hungry too).

He grew pale, frightened by his own outburst. After a while he scolded the prisoners, shouting that it was disgraceful of Germans to take such a stand: "You should be ashamed", he shouted. "The duty of Germans is to think of the needs of the army and the front and not to complain".'[18]

SS Hauptsturmführer Dr Helmuth Vetter was camp physician and at the same time associate of the IG Farbenindustrie. In 1941, he worked at Dachau and suggested to IG Farben that he test out new medicines in the camp hospital.[19] Towards the end of 1941, he came to Auschwitz and began experimenting with several drugs.[20] Although Vetter was interested whether any profit was drawn from his tests, it is clear that his pharmacological experiments were not merely a matter of private contract between him ad IG Farben.[21] The results were of interest to the highest SS authorities who also received current reports on conducted experiments both at Auschwitz and at Mauthausen. Vetter was a busy man because, in the spring of 1943, he conducted experiments both at Auschwitz and Mauthausen!

These tests were made using starving prisoners, weakened by exhausting work and by the stress of the camp life, in camp hospitals which, due to their unsatisfactory hygienic state and considerable overcrowding, did not ensure suitable conditions for conducting any medical test whatsoever. It must be added that the ultimate aim was not the wish to improve the state of

Auschwitz Museum

Block 10

health of the sick but solely the wish to test the reactions of the human organism to the preparations which were being tried out.

SS Untersturmführer Friedrich Entress conducted frequent selections among sick prisoners in the prisoners' hospitals and at the Rampe. In 1942, he received the MD degree without having submitted the required thesis!

It is clear that most of the physicians were present at selections at the Rampe or in the camp hospitals. Dr Cohen talking about such selections:

> 'When the camp physician came in to the barracks, in ours, it was mostly Dr Klein, an enormous silence fell over every one and you had the feeling that, as Klein arrived, death came in. Klein's most important question was always when we thought a patient would be *arbeitsfähig, ready to work again. The difficulty for*

us was that he was so unpredictable. We had noted the clinical picture, the diagnosis and the proposed treatment neatly on a chart. Just imagine what a farce this was ... even the unavailable medicines were mentioned on the chart.

During such selections, Klein was always quiet, friendly and always wore that smile ... sometimes I had the feeling that he wanted to treat me as a colleague, and address me as such, but that my Jewishness prevented him from doing so ... .'[22]

SS Obersturmführer Dr Werner Rhode emerges from the witnesses' testimonies as a friendly fellow who did his best for the prisoners. On the other hand however, Rhode, together with Dr Weber and Dr Capesius, performed mescaline experiments on prisoners in Block twenty-one. Like Dr König, it eventually seemed that he could only carry out his work under the influence of alcohol. Dr Münch:

'Rhode was a gigantic man who drank a great deal, and when under the influence of alcohol, he behaved unusually. He would declare to everybody that he found Auschwitz quite absurd — The "little Jews" were being gassed while the big boys kept out of the way. They had long since left for the United States ... .'[23]

The dentist Willi Frank was given charge of the dentists at Auschwitz in 1943. Later he was transferred to Dachau, and eventually moved to the Hungarian front. In Auschwitz his job had been not only the dental treatment of the SS personnel and their families, but also the supervision of the melting down of the gold teeth broken out of the mouths of the gassed.

During his trial, he denied every accusation:

'I did my best for everyone. In my parental home, Jews were often guests. I had a Jewish grandmother! I can only say that I found the events of that time to be unprecedented ... .'[24]

Auschwitz Museum
The "Black Wall" where many prisoners were shot.
(Left is Block 10).

In 1944 the dentist Willi Ludwig Schatz came to Auschwitz. The witnesses left no room for doubt concerning his activities: Schatz had made selections on the Rampe. The Polish witness Mikolajski added that both Frank and Schatz had assisted at the gassings in the crematoria. SS Sturmbannführer Dr Viktor Capesius, a Romanian and naturalized German, was a chemist who came to Auschwitz in 1943. Twenty-two years passed before he stood trial together with twenty-three other engineers of the death factory. The accusations against him were grave: liquidation of the gypsy camp, selections and gassings. The former head chemist at Auschwitz denied it all:

> 'Let's just wait and see what the witnesses have to tell the court'.[25]

What the witnesses had indeed to testify was serious, but many of the accusations were based on suspicions. Murder could not be proved, although his complicity in the deaths of 8,000 prisoners earned him a sentence of nine years.

In her authoritative work on Ravensbrück concentration

camp, Germaine Tillion devoted a long passage to Dr Lucas, who earns her outspoken praise for his courageous stand.[26] Dr Lucas was an exceptional case at Auschwitz. After leaving Ravensbrück, this gynaecologist came to Auschwitz in the summer of 1944 where he remained until its evacuation.

After the war, he settled down as a gynaecologist in the Elmshorn Town Hospital near Hamburg. At the end of March 1965, two years into the Auschwitz trial at Frankfurt, he was arrested on suspicion of having taken part in the selection of prisoners, a charge he vehemently disputed and, initially, with much success. None of the accused standing trial at Auschwitz were able to produce as many witnesses for the defence as Lucas.

Former prisoners came from all over the world to testify how they had Lucas to thank for their lives, and how he had treated them as real people. He was the only defendant prepared to talk openly of the horrible situation at the camp and the misconduct of the SS. And if this were not enough, before his arrest, he had accompanied the court to Auschwitz in 1964. For the first time, a German court had visited the concentration camp itself in order to become acquainted with the situation.

After his arrest Lucas remained silent; he distanced himself from the other defendants and gave the impression of having landed in this illustrious company merely by accident. This was all too much for the SS Rottenführer Stefan Baretzki who was accused of both beating prisoners to death and selections. On the trial's 137th day, he suddenly sprang to his feet:

> 'I wasn't mad, I wasn't blind when I saw Dr Lucas making selections on the Rampe. In a half hour, he sent 5,000 victims into the gas chamber and the bloke wants to play the great saviour!'[27]

Lucas at first denied but eventually, hesitantly, admitted that just three or four times he had selected Jews for the gas chambers. At this point, a fitter from Amsterdam, Abraham de la Penha reported to the public prosecutor in order to make a declaration. He had seen a photograph of Lucas in the newspaper and considered it his duty to give evidence:

> 'Lucas' decisions resulted in 150 sick prisoners being taken from the sick-ward and sent to perish in

the gas chambers. I watched that selection take place from my bed in the sick-ward ... .'[28]

Auschwitz Museum

Operating room Block 10

Nevertheless, Lucas' defending counsel asked for his client's release on the grounds that, under the circumstances applying at the time, the gynaecologist could not have behaved any other way. At the same time, the lawyer claimed that the selections ought to be construed in Dr Lucas' favour: he was on the Rampe purely in order to save as many as possible from death. He did his duty as a doctor: safeguarding people's lives. Why Lucas had concealed this illuminating fact for so long remained unanswered.

Johann Paul Kremer also deserves to be mentioned. Born in Cologne in 1883, this SS Hauptsturmführer, doctor of medicine and of philosophy, and professor of anatomy at the University of Münster was acting as camp doctor between 30 August and 18 December 1942. He kept a diary while he was working at Auschwitz, from which it became clear that he had performed medical experiments. He was involved with liver research, and the changes taking place in the body as a result of nutritional deficiency.

He had given orders to nurses to bring the worst starvation cases to the operating theatre, where he dissected them and removed the liver, the spleen and part of the lungs for research and preservation. He had also taken an active part in selections on the Rampe. Some excerpts from his diary:

'31 August: Tropical climate, thirty-eight degrees in the shadow; dust and countless flies! Excellent food at the officers' lodgings. This evening, for example, duck liver for forty pfennig, with stuffed tomatoes, tomato salad etc. The water is contaminated, we drink soda water here.'

'2 September: For the first time, out at three in the morning to attend a Special Action.[29] Compared to this, Dante's Inferno looks more like a comedy. Auschwitz has not been called a destruction camp for nothing!'

'3 September: Fall ill for the first time with something almost everyone in the camp gets: diarrhoea, vomiting and bursts of colic-like pain . . . .'

'5 September: Attended a Special Action this afternoon (Muzelmänner)[30] the most horrible of horrors! Hauptscharführer Dr Thilo is right: "We find ourselves at the *anus mundi*." This evening, attended another Special Action, from Holland. The men flock to take part in such actions for the special rations they receive in return: a fifth of a litre of jenever, five cigarettes, 100 grammes of sausage and bread. Today and tomorrow (Sunday) on duty.'[31]

Kremer testified at the Frankfurt trial and was able to speak frankly, having already been tried in Poland. He thought it quite understandable that the SS men came forward willingly for Special Actions, considering the advantages they offered in recompense. Kremer:

'It was wartime, cigarettes and schnapps were scarce. The SS men were always on the lookout for

Johann Paul Kremer
Auschwitz Museum

them. You made sure you got as many vouchers as possible, and ran off with the booze . . . .'

'You too?'

'Yes, me too. Everyone did it!'[32]

'6 September: Today, Sunday, an excellent lunch: tomato soup, half a chicken, potatoes and red cabbage (twenty grammes of fat), pudding, and a delicious vanilla ice-cream. After the meal, a welcome for the new garrison doctor Obersturmführer Dr Wirths. In the evening, around eight pm, out again for another Special Action.'

'17 September: At the Clothing Office in Berlin, ordered a duffel coat, according to tailor's measurements: overall size forty-eight, length 133, sleeve length eighty-one, chest 107, waist 100, hips 124. Today visited the women's camp with Dr Meyer.'

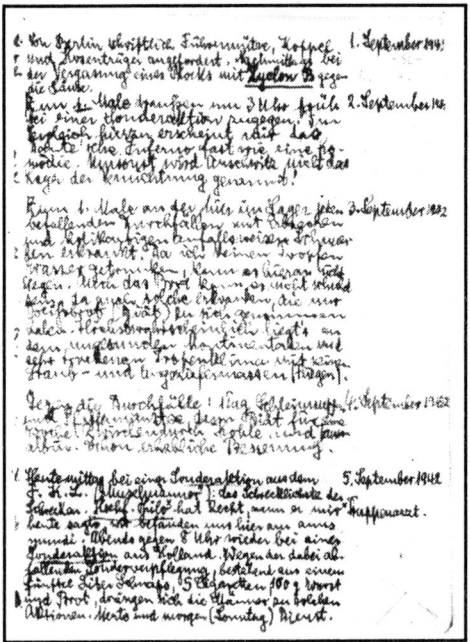

Page from the diary concerning
his activities at Auschwitz
Auschwitz Museum

'20 September: Today, Sunday afternoon, between three and six pm listened to a concert given by the prisoner-orchestra; lovely sunny weather. Conductor formerly conducted the State Opera in Warsaw. Eighty musicians. Lunchtime, minced pork, this evening baked tench.'

'23 September: Last night, attended the sixth and seventh Special Actions. This morning Obergruppenführer Pohl arrived with retinue at the SS quarters. A guard is posted at the door, who presents arms to me for the first time.'

'27 September: Today, Sunday afternoon, from four till eight pm a speech by Commandant Höss, music and performances.'

'30 September: Auschwitz has rows of streets with typhus. So got myself an injection against abdominal typhoid . . . .'

'7 October: Ninth Special Action (foreigners and

Muzelmänner). Wirths there again. Replaced Entress in the men's camp (selection, etc).'

'9 October: First packet of nine pounds of soft soap, value 200 marks sent to Münster. Raining.'

'11 October: Had second vaccination for typhus; in the evening a strong reaction (fever). Just the same, a night-time Special Action from Holland (1,600 people); horrible scene in front of the last bunker (Hössler)! This was the tenth Special Action.'

'17 October: Attended one punishment and eleven executions. Perfectly fresh material, removed spleen and pancreas after injection Pilvearpin. Drove to Nicolai with Wirths; informed me beforehand that I was to stay longer.'

'18 October: Cold weather; today, Sunday morning, attended eleventh Special Action (Dutch). Terrible scenes where naked women begged for their lives.'

'19 October: Went with Obstuf. Wirths and Mrs Höss to Kattowice to buy shoulder pads for my jacket. Back via Nicolai.'

'24 October: Gave lethal injections to six women from the Budge revolt (Klehr).'

'25 October: Today, Sunday, beautiful autumn weather, made a cycle trip via Rajsko to Budy. Wilhelmy is back from his trip to Kroatia (plum jenever).'[33]

Together with SS Oberscharführer Josef Klehr, a sanitary orderly, Kremer gave lethal injections to a number of prisoners, but he had selected those who were too ill to possibly recover from their sicknesses. At the close of the trial, Kremer testified:

'What we had been in civilian life was unimportant. Furthermore, as an SS officer, I had no say with Klehr. He was under the orders of the duty physician. I was just another cog in the wheel ... .'[34]

Within the Auschwitz complex, there was a work camp, Babice, dubbed by many of the witnesses as an 'island of peace'. This was due to SS Oberscharführer Dr Wilhelm Flagge, an

SDG non-commissioned officer, who like Münch, Delmotte and even, to a certain degree, Lucas — was a remarkable figure. The prisoner-physician Dr Wolken described how, in July 1944, Flagge had saved the lives of many prisoners.[35]

The prisoner-physician Dr Lingens-Reiner once asked Flagge how on earth he managed to withstand being in the SS, to which Flagge replied:

'Would you rather have a brute in my place?'[36]

He repeatedly confided with his family that he would rather be living on an island in the Pacific.

Dr Lingens-Reiner:

'How Dr Flagge managed to fix things in Babice is a mystery to me. It was clean there, the food was decent. The women called him 'Papa'. He even made sure that they got eggs from outside the camp. I told him: "Ach, you know, Herr Oberscharführer, it's all so completely pointless, what we're doing. If this war ends, they'll just do away with all of us. Not one witness will remain alive." Flagge answered: "I hope that there will be enough of us around to stop that from happening ... ." '[37]

And now the famous Dr Mengele. Hermann Langbein described him as 'a little man with a tanned face, dark hair, a slight tic in his left eye and a triangular gap in his upper front teeth.'[38] Dr Lingens-Reiner called him a thorough cynic:

'When a batch of newly arrived Jews was being classified into those fit for work and those fit for death, he would whistle a tune and rhythmically jerk his thumb over his right or his left shoulder — which meant gassing or work. He sometimes used the indirect method to select his victims in the isolation hospital. As prisoner-doctors, he ordered us to write out meticulous lists of patients complete with diagnosis and prognosis.

Collection Author

Auschwitz-Birkenau

If we put down a patient as having to remain in the hospital for three or four weeks, she was condemned. If we put down a shorter term, he shouted at us: "What! You claim to be a doctor and you mean to send this half-dead, wretched creature out of the hospital in less than four weeks . . . ?'' '39

Olga Lengyel stated:

'One could have called him handsome were it not for the expression of cruelty in his features. He was a specialist at the selections. No medical considerations governed his decisions. They seemed to be entirely arbitrary. He was the tyrant from whose decisions there was no appeal. Why should he trouble to select on the basis of any method? Nor did the state of health have anything to do with his selections. How we hated this charlatan! He profaned the very word "science"! How we despised his detached haughty air, his continual whistling, his absurd orders, his frigid cruelty . . . .'[40]

Fania Fénelon, the former prisoner who played in the camp female orchestra remembered:

'He was handsome. Goodness, he was handsome. So handsome that the girls instinctively discovered the forgotten motions of another world, running dampened fingers through their lashes to make them shine, biting their lips, swelling their mouths, pulling at their skirts and tops. Under the gaze of this man, one felt oneself become a woman again . . . .'[41]

Josef Mengele was born on 16 March 1911, and grew up in the city of Günsburg. In April 1930 he passed his high-school exams and decided to study medicine with an emphasis on anthropology and human genetics. Medicine at German universities was taught in accordance with the guidelines of the social Darwinist theories and the notion that some lives were worthless soon became academically accepted; the race was disintegrating, deteriorating through faulty breeding as a result of a liberally tinged promiscuity that was vitiating the nation's blood.

This ultimately lead to the establishment of a catalogue of 'positive' curative measures: racial hygiene, eugenic choice of marriage partners, the breeding of human beings by the methods of selection and extirpation on the other.

At the Nuremberg Party Convention of 1933, Hitler declared:

'National Socialism professes the heroic teaching of evaluating blood, race and personality as well as the eternal laws of selection and thus consciously puts itself in a position of unbridgeable contradiction in

Auschwitz Museum

Josef Mengele

opposition to the philosophy of pacifist-international democracy and its effects ... .'[42]

The 'aryanization' of the universities and scientific periodicals which came in the wake of the seizure of power was more than the forcible installation of competitors in positions for which they previously had striven in vain. Anti-Jewish feelings and convictions had to be inculcated in every German and this end could only be effected through science! The law of nature concerning the 'survival of the fittest' should be presented so as to admit no exceptions. The unfit was doomed to *Ausmerze* (extinction) and if he did not go voluntarily, he must be 'helped' out of existence. The law of nature, then, would be made to apply also to groups or, in a more mystical terms, to races. In the thirties, selection (*Auslese*) and extinction (*Ausmerze*) were the pivots of the racial doctrines that dominated German intellectual life.

In 1933, Dr Heinz Müller suggested in his preface to a book by the well-known statistician Bürgdorfer that

> 'A National Socialist biology must find the bridge to culture and politics just as National Socialist politics ought to be only biological, *i.e.*, that which takes the laws of life into account. To this principle, everything else in German life must be subordinated. The science of our people, too, on the basis of this Aryan biological value-gauge has to serve their struggle for existence and for preservation of their healthy life and the race defining it in that it prepares and hands over as a weapon and equipment to the materializer, the man of politics, the struggle of the people for existence ... .'[43]

Dr Achim Gercke, expert in race study in the Reich Ministry of Interior elucidated the principles he expected to follow in his work:

> 'First of all, we have the negative side in our work which, translated into race techniques means: extinction. In its last consequence, it amounts to sterilization of those hereditarily inferior. Let them

not bother us with the old and false humanitarian ideas.
    There is, in truth, only one human idea, that is
furthering the good, eliminating the bad! The will of
nature is the will of God. Let us look around . . . .
How does nature work for millenia with her creatures?
She sides with the strong, good and victorious one,
and separates the chaff from the wheat. We simply
fulfil the commandment, no more, no less . . . .'[44]

And in the same book, Professor Bauer, director of the Kaiser
Wilhelm Institute for Breeding Research and biologist of world-
wide reputation, stated:

> 'Every farmer knows that, should he slaughter the
> best specimens of his domestic animals without letting
> them procreate and instead continue breeding inferior
> individuals, his breed would degenerate hopelessly.
>   This mistake, which no farmer would commit with
> his animals and cultivated plants, we permit to go on
> in our midst to a large extent. As a recompense for
> our humaneness of today, we must see to it that these
> inferior people do not procreate!'[45]

One of the first 'scholars' who seems to have had considerable
influence on the young Mengele was Dr Ernst Rüdin. For many
years, he was Professor of Psychiatry at the University of
Munich, and later became director of the Kaiser Wilhelm
Institute for Genealogy and Demography.
    On the occasion of his sixty-fifth birthday, he was awarded
the Goethe medal for art and science by Hitler and honoured
by the following telegram from the Minister of the Interior, Dr
Wilhelm Frick;

> 'To the indefatigable champion of racial hygiene
> and meritorious pioneer of the racial-hygienic
> measures of the Third Reich, I send my heartiest
> congratulations.'[46]

Rüdin indeed became the champion of racial science and
edited a two-volume standard work on 'Genetics and Eugenetics
in the Folk Stage.' In reviewing the sterilization laws of the Third

Reich, he came to the following conclusion:

> 'Scruples and nagging of a political and philosophical nature against the (1934) law have almost ceased in view of the continuing onward march of National Socialist ideas and achievements. On the contrary! Not only at home but abroad as well, voices are heard which congratulate the German Reich on having found the leading man with assisting staff who dares to break also with racial-hygiene measures, the terror of the inferior kind of people.
>
> Racial Science is not a National Socialist invention, but a recognized international science.'[47]

Another advocate of the racial biology was Professor Theodor Mollison who claimed that he could tell if a person was of Jewish descent simply by looking at a photograph. This Mollison, an expert in the field of heredity and racial hygiene, awarded Mengele a Ph.D in 1935 for his thesis entitled: *'Racial Morphological Research on the Lower Jaw Section of Four Racial Groups'*.

In 1936 Mengele passed his state medical examination and accepted a position in Leipzig at the university's medical clinic. In the following year, after a recommendation from Mollison, he was appointed research assistant at the Third Reich Institute for Heredity, Biology and Racial Purity at the University of Frankfurt and joined the staff of Professor Otmar Freiherr von Verschuer who was an outspoken admirer of Hitler and who devoted much of his time to research into twins!

Verschuer, once a student of Bauer, eventually became Mengele's mentor. Thus we have the line Bauer — Verschuer — Mengele.

According to Posner and Ware;

> 'Mengele became the professor's favourite student; the two men developed a strong mutual respect. Von Verschuer almost certainly influenced Mengele's subsequent appointment at Auschwitz; and later, as wartime director of the Kaiser Wilhelm Institute for Anthropology, Human Hereditary Teaching and Genetics in Berlin, he secured funds for Mengele's experiments at Auschwitz.'

Without any doubt, Mengele was strongly influenced by people like Rüdin, Verschuer, Bauer and Mollison. In the spring of 1936, he told his friend Bruno Frank:

> 'With these scholars, we will reach the leadership in the scientific life of our nation. The time has arrived for a renewed scholarship and a renewed university. The dominant principle that is to be applied is not to introduce any drop of foreign blood into the German people that might decompose and impair its uniform cohesiveness but, in turn, not to cede a drop of blood of valuable German blood to an alien people ... .'[49]

In August 1940 Mengele became a member of the Waffen SS and when the war broke out, he was sent to occupied Poland where he was attached to the genealogical Section of the Race and Resettlement office. This department examined the racial suitability of those who would inhabit the newly conquered territories.

In January 1942, he joined the medical corps of the Waffen SS 'Viking Division', and eight months later, he was posted back to the Race and Resettlement office in Berlin and was promoted to the rank of SS Hauptsturmführer.

In May 1943, he was posted to Auschwitz and, according to Dr Benno Müller Hill, it was Verschuer who talked Mengele into going there:

> 'There is a big opportunity for science there. Many races there, many people. Why don't you go? It's in the interest of science ... .'[50]

And so the ambitious Mengele went to Auschwitz-Birkenau.

Here he performed most of his experiments in Blocks fifteen and twenty-two of the gypsy camp (*Zigeunerlager*). Three categories of experiments were performed: the first consisted of research into the origin and causes of dual births. The second was the search to discover the biological and pathological causes for the birth of dwarfs and giants. And the third was the study of the causes and treatment of a disease commonly called 'dry gangrene of the face'. This terrible disease, which was very rare, was fairly common among both children and adolescents in the gypsy camp.

Mengele performed most of his experiments in collaboration with prisoner-doctors who made all the medical examinations: blood tests, lumbar punctures, exchangeable blood transfusions of the twins, examinations of sight, hearing and other senses, measurements of height etc. Comparative drawings of the shape of the heads, ears, noses, hands and feet were made by a Jewish woman-prisoner, Dina Gottlieb, a painter from Prague whose artistic skill was a great asset to the enterprise. As Mengele's assistant she was granted privileges that ordinary prisoners never enjoyed.

The last phase of research consisted of analyses based on dissection of corpses which were made in the dissecting room in Crematorium II at Birkenau by the prisoner-physician Dr Miklos Nyiszli. Nyiszli on the experiments:

'When the convoys arrived, soldiers scouted the ranks lined up before the box cars, hunting for twins and dwarfs. Mothers hoping for special treatment for their twin children, readily gave them up to the scouts. Adult twins, knowing that they were of interest from a scientific point of view, voluntarily presented themselves in the hope of better treatment. The same for dwarfs. They were separated from the rest and herded to the right. They were allowed to keep their civilian clothes; guards accompanied them to specially designated barracks, where they were treated with certain regard.

Their food was good, their bunks comfortable, and possibilities for hygiene were provided. They were housed in Barracks fourteen of Camp F. From there, they were taken by their guards to the experimentation barracks of the gypsy camp, and exposed to every medical examination that can be performed on human beings (. . .).

The "*in vivo* experiments" were succeeded by the most important phase of twin study: the comparative examination from the viewpoints of anatomy and pathology. Here, it was a question of comparing the twins' healthy organs with those functioning abnormally, or of comparing their illnesses. For that study, as for all studies of a pathological nature, corpses were needed. Since it was necessary to perform a dissection for the simultaneous evaluation of anomalies, the twins had to die at the same time.

So it was that they met their death at the hands of Dr Mengele in the B section of one of Auschwitz's KZ barracks ... .'[51]

According to, Nyiszli there was no scientific value:

'Like the ethnological studies, like the notions of a Master Race, Dr Mengele's research into the origins of dual births was nothing more than a psuedo-science. Just as false was the theory concerning the degeneracy of the dwarfs and cripples sent to the butcher, in order to demonstrate the inferiority of the Jewish race ... .'[52]

With inextinguishable zeal, Mengele sought to fathom the mysteries of twins. The solution of these mysteries would enable Himmler to fulfil his racial ideals with twice the speed! Together, with hunchbacks and dwarfs, jokingly referred to in the corridors as 'Zirkus Mengele'.[53] They could be grateful for Mengele's scientific research. Nyiszli:

'When the convoys arrived, Dr Mengele espied, among those lined up for selection, a hunchbacked man about fifty years old. He was not alone; standing beside him was a tall handsome boy of fifteen or sixteen. The latter however, had a deformed right foot, which had been corrected by an apparatus made of a metal plate and an orthopaedic, thick soled shoe. They were father and son. Dr Mengele thought he had discovered, in the person of the hunchback father and his lame son, a sovereign example to demonstrate his theory of the Jewish race's degeneracy. He had them fall out of ranks immediately. Taking his notebook, he wrote something in it, entrusted the two wretches to the care of an SS trooper, who took them to number one crematorium ... . It was around noon ... .'[54]

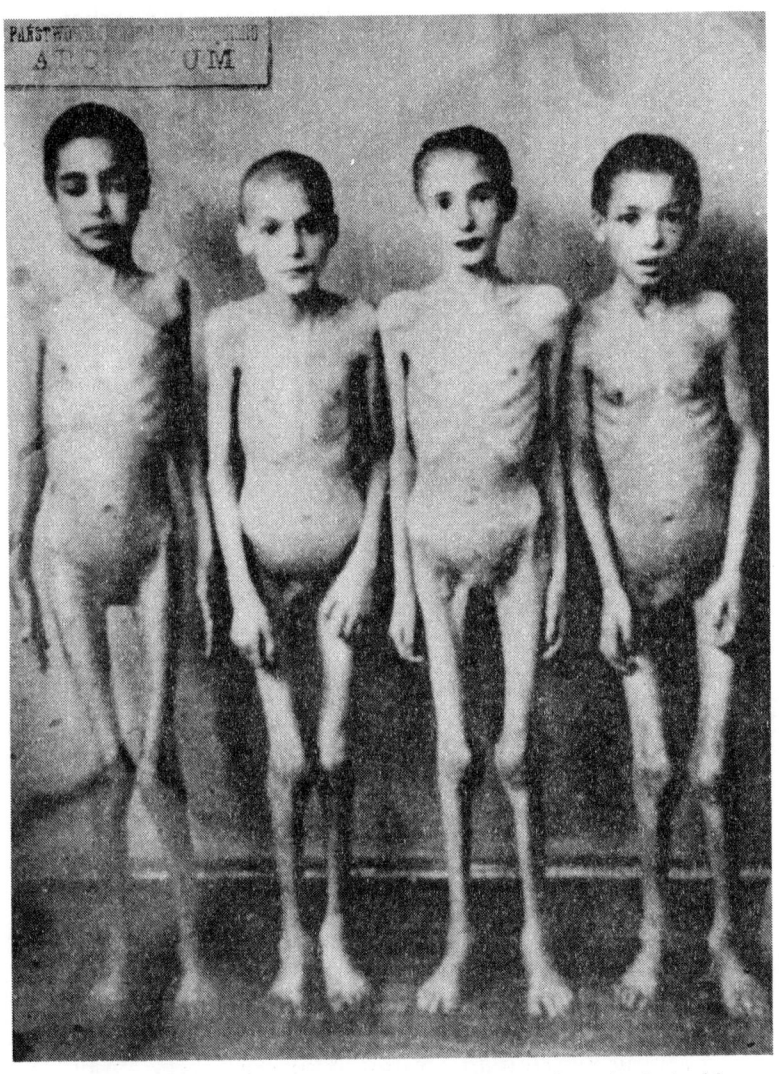

Auschwitz Museum

Dr. Josef Mengele's twins,
photograph taken by Mengele himself

Both father and son were murdered by Oberscharführer
Mussfeld, after which Nyiszli was to perform the dissection.
Magda Zalicovitz, a twin who survived Auschwitz, recalled:

'I was twenty-nine. We arrived at Auschwitz in a
cattle car; it was two o'clock in the morning. Our
family was together in a wagon, but then we were
separated. My little boy and I were told to go on the
left side, toward the crematorium. People were yelling:
"*Zwillinge, Zwillinge* (twins, twins)", when I saw a very
nice looking-man coming toward me. It was Mengele.
He was with two SS men and my brother Zvi. My
brother had told Mengele that he was a twin and that
he had a sister. They were looking for me, but I was
already on the way to the gas chambers. Pointing to
me, Mengele asked me: "Are you the twin of this
man?" I said "Yes". He noticed my child: "Who
is this little boy?" he asked. "It is my son", I said.
"Leave the boy with your mother," he
ordered . . . .'[55]

Her son was gassed and she was sent to the gypsy camp.
Zalicovitz:

'There was a block of doctors — anthropologists,
eye doctors, ear doctors . . . . They had a laboratory
where they performed all types of tests while you were
naked. They took X-rays, they gave us injections, they
drew blood, they examined our hair; they looked into
our eyes, especially our eyes.
The doctors told us that they were losing a lot of
soldiers in the war and that they wanted to increase
the German population. Mengele came every single
morning wearing an SS uniform, boots, very shiny
boots, a hat, and carried a stick . . . .'[56]

And Eva Mozes Kor remembers:

'I arrived at Auschwitz-Birkenau in late March or
early April of 1944. As we stepped down from the
cattle train, my father and older sisters (twelve and

fourteen), disappeared in the commotion. My mother was holding on to my sister Miriam and me. We looked alike and were dressed alike. An SS man approached my mother and asked if we were twins. ''Yes'', my mother answered. At that moment, we were torn out of mother's arms. She was pulled to the right where a tall SS officer was doing the selection. That was the last time I saw her ... .'[56a]

And what about Mengele? 'He was not polite, nor friendly, he was scary. Everybody in our barrack was so nervous before Mengele came on his daily inspections! When he found a dead twin, he would raise his voice in such a horrible scream that everybody froze in their place. By the way, I was puzzled why he got so upset when these twins died, since it was known that many twins were taken to the hospital and to the labs never to be seen again. We assumed that he killed them, which, of course, he did.

I understand it today, if they died in the barrack, that he lost some of his guinea pigs, and that the experiments would be spoiled. Mengele was good looking and some girls who were twelve or thirteen would pay attention to it. But there was also something very frightening in his eyes ... .'[56b]

And what about his politeness and friendliness? 'I could never talk about Mengele as a friendly or polite man! After all he didn't ask me politely to become a guinea pig, he made me his guinea pig! No, he was a very evil being with a lot of power and influence ... .'[56c]

According to Eva Kor, Dr König worked together with Mengele:

'He was tall, slim built, older than Mengele, he had light hair and wore glasses with wire rims. Hans König was always part of Mengele's entourage ... he was like Mengele's right hand person. König was more quiet and not as vicious in his relation to us; he carried out Mengele's orders ... .'[56d]

In 1984 Eva and her sister Miriam founded CANDLES (Children of Auschwitz Nazi Dead Lab Experiments Survivors), an organization of Auschwitz twins with the purpose to reunite survivors of the twin experiments, to research the experiments and their effect on the twins and to bring Mengele to trial for his crimes.

Although there is general agreement that Mengele died in Brazil in a swimming accident in 1979, CANDLES and her president Eva Kor refuse to believe it:

> 'I want you to know that all the twins believe that Mengele is alive. The truth will come out that the body from Brazil is a hoax. The rush-and-hush investigations of the bones is a crime against humanity ... !'[56e]

According to Gerald Posner and John Ware who investigated the whole Mengele affair, it *was* Mengele who died in 1979:

> 'The life, times and death of Josef Mengele were a squalid business from beginning to end. And what an ignominious end it was. On 21 June 1985, his bones, his skull, his bits and pieces were paraded before an eager audience on the twentieth floor of the Sao Paulo police headquarters. It all matched up: the broken left finger, the height — 174 centimetres — a tell-tale gap between his two upper front teeth. In one corner of the room his skull was displaced, and in another, a discussion was held about his degenerating skull spine.
>
> "This was present in a lower part of the column," said one specialist, pointing to his crumbling vertebrae. Elsewhere a doctor was trying to make a point about Mengele's hip. "We see here a montage of the hip bones," he said. "I want to show you what we found ... ." And so on.
>
> "Is there any doubt at all, Dr Levine, that this is Josef Mengele?" asked John Martin of ABC News.
>
> "Absolutely not," replied the forensic odontologist from New York.
>
> For the sake of the civilized world's peace of mind,

these scientists had performed one worthwhile experiment on an unworthy life . . . .'[56]

It will never be known how many prisoners died as a result of Mengele's experiments. On 17 January 1945 he liquidated his experimental laboratory, taking away with him all the material concerning the experiments conducted by him on twins, dwarfs and cripples. In the night of 17-18 January the rest of the documents together with the documents of the hospital office were burnt under the supervision of the SS.[57]

His experiments were cruel and sadistic but nevertheless, most survivors and colleagues remember Mengele as a hard worker who was unfailingly courteous and pleasant whether chatting with fellow officers or sentencing prisoners to their death. The polite smile and the friendly demeanour remain the most intriguing aspect of his personality.

Talking with Dr Münch about Mengele, the other side of 'the angel of death' appears. Münch:

> 'I admit that this will perhaps sound strange but I got on better with Mengele than with any of my other colleagues at Auschwitz. In contrast to most of the other officers, he showed human characteristics . . . in actual fact, he was a nice man, agreeable, or to be more precise, the least disagreeable. But I want to add straight away that we were not friends, let alone on familiar terms. We differed too much in character and opinion for that.
>
> Our first contacts arose from our work and from that, a somewhat stronger relationship grew. Perhaps the fact that we came from the same parts and spoke the same dialect had something to do with it. In his personal relations, he was polite and friendly. Furthermore, that is not just my experience but also that of many prisoners. Naturally, there will be others with a different impression, but I am considering my own personal experience. I had a similar relationship with Werner Rhode.
>
> Counting both Mengele and Rhode, I discussed the how and why of Auschwitz for hours; the conversations were often outspoken and far-reaching.

The starting point was always the machine of destruction within which we worked. For Mengele, the affair was straight forward. The Jews were inferior and deserved to be eradicated. Auschwitz was the logical consequence of history. Through the ages, the Jews had been persecuted, isolated and pushed into ghettos but they always succeeded in obtaining important posts within society, with all the attendant consequences. I took the opposite point of view and pointed to the criminal aspect but he was impervious to it. Take the selections for example. We discussed this too and he always had the same dictum: A doctor at the front also selects. Period!

It remains incomprehensible what went on inside the man. Sending entire transportations of people into the gas chamber didn't hurt him, he did it with religious fanaticism, but on the other hand, he confessed that he found it difficult dealing with individual cases. He was emotionally affected when he sent smaller children in to the gas chamber whom he had come to know after they had spent some time in the camp.

I know nothing about the experiments he carried out. I knew he was experimenting with twins, but I know no more. We didn't talk about it. I don't know whether he was working on orders or together with the Verschuer Institute. Indeed, the whole business is very vague. The strange thing is that almost no publications of these experiments exist. Caution here, I'm not saying that he didn't perform *any* experiments, I'm saying that practically nothing is known of them. I occasionally spoke with Nyiszli but he just told me that he performed dissections at the Crematorium on Mengele's orders. Not so long ago, I had a conversation with a colleague of Mengele who had worked with him at the Verschuer Institute. He assured me that he had known nothing of the experiments that Mengele performed. No papers about them ever appeared at the Institute. What I do consider nonsense, nonetheless, are the imputations that Mengele experimented with changing the colour of people's eyes. That is really *quatsch* (baloney).'[58]

Block ten, made up mostly of women prisoners was located in the men's camp. Unlike the huts in Birkenau and Auschwitz, it was two-storeyed. The windows were kept closed and shuttered so that communication with the outside world was impossible. This block was the main experimental centre, access to which required written permission from Dr Wirths. This rule was strictly adhered to and applied even to officers. There were separate research areas: those of Clauberg and Schumann, Wirths and his brother, and a special section for the Hygienic Institute.

The sterilization experiments were by far the most important. The driving force behind these was SS Oberführer Victor Brack whose name was already renowned in the world of euthanasia. Having occupied himself from 1939 to 1941 with wiping out 'degenerates', in March 1941, he concentrated on the possibilities of preventing their procreation. He wrote to Himmler:

'If people are to be rendered permanently sterile, this can be done only by X-ray dosages so high that castration with all its consequences ensues. These high X-ray dosages destroy the inner secretions of the ovaries and the testicles. Lesser dosages would merely suspend procreative capacity for a certain period of time. The symptoms in question include cessation of menstruation , symptoms of the menopause, changes in body hair, changes in metabolism, etc. It is necessary to call attention to these disadvantages.

The dosage can take various forms, and exposure to X-rays can be conducted inconspicuously. Men require a focal dosage of 500-600 r, women, a dosage of 300-350 r. Theoretically, with top voltage, thin filter, and close proximity and exposure of two minutes for men and three minutes for women should be sufficient.

But another disadvantage should be taken into account. Since it is impossible to screen other parts of the body with lead without attracting attention, other tissues are affected and so-called radiation sickness ensues. If the radiation has been too intense, the skin reached by the rays will, in the ensuing days or weeks, show symptoms of burning, varying with the individual.

One practical method, for example, would be to have the people who are to be processed step up to a window where they would be asked certain questions or have to fill out certain forms, detaining them for two or three minutes. The official behind the window could operate the equipment, in such a way that the switch simultaneously turned on two X-ray tubes, since exposure must be from two sides.

A two-tube installation could thus sterilize 150-200 persons a day. A large number of daily shipments is, in my estimate, out of the question anyway. I can only give a rough installation estimate of the costs — 20,000-30,000 marks per two-tube installation. The cost of adding a special building must also be added since substantial safeguards for the personnel concerned must be installed. In summarizing, it can be stated, without question that the present state of X-ray technology and research without question permits mass sterilization by X-ray ... .'[59]

Within six months Himmler had another proposal, from the dermatologist Dr Adolf Pokorny:

'Holding the opinion, as I do, that the enemy must not just be conquered but must also be destroyed, I feel it is my duty to bring the following to your question: When the article by Dr Madaus on pharmaceutical sterilization came to my attention, I immediately perceived the enormous importance of this drug for our nation. If, based on this research we could quickly develop a drug which produced relatively prompt sterilization, it would form a new and effective weapon. The thought alone, that three million Bolsheviks now in German captivity could be sterilized, leaving them able to work but unable to procreate, opens fresh perspectives (...).

Dr Madaus has claimed that the sap of the

Schweigrohr (Caladium sengium), taken by mouth or as injection, results in sterilization in especially male but also female animals. Should you agree with the main disposition of my thought, may I suggest the following:

1. Dr Madaus may no longer be permitted to speak in public about his research in any way (the enemy is listening!).

2. Production of the plant must be stepped up (simple, in greenhouses).

3. Immediate tests on people (criminals) to establish the dose and length of treatment necessary.

4. As quickly as possible, an accurate analysis of the sap, enabling a transition to artificial production . . . .'[60]

Himmler laid Pokorny's suggestions aside. He inclined more towards sterilization experiments using X-rays and operations and on 12 August 1942, he gave his fiat for sterilization tests at Auschwitz. The programme's direction fell to SS Sturmbannführer Dr Horst Schumann, a reliable SS physician who had been a leading figure in the euthanasia programme as director of the killing centre Grafeneck. Later, he became active in project 14 F 13 as a member of the medical commissions visiting the concentration camps. Survivors described this Air Force officer as a 'representative of the new German racist ideal with no feelings in regard to the prisoners'.[61]

He experimented on both men and women and the description of the tests leave no doubt that they were brutal, sadistic and unrestrained. Dr Alina Brewda, prisoner-physician:

'Schumann's guinea-pigs, healthy young men and women in their late teens or early twenties, were taken one by one to a room in Birkenau, where, after taking off all their clothes, they were placed in front of the X-ray machine. Two plates were fixed on the woman, one on the abdomen, the other on the back; the man had to place his sexual organ and scrotum on a china plate. The radiation was then turned on, the victim heard the noise of a motor and the radiation went on for five to eight minutes. How effective the X-ray strength was had to be gauged later. The ejaculation of the male semen was caused by putting a piece of wood up the rectum; this brought on an erection and the semen was caught on a strip of glass and was microscopically examined to see whether it was still potent. But even this was not found to be wholly reliable, for what is not potent today may become potent some months later. So surgical operations were resorted to for the removal of an ovary or a testicle, at times of both ovaries and both testicles, for microscopic analysis in a laboratory . . . .'[62]

A former Jewish prisoner testified:

'I had been working on road construction for four weeks, when suddenly one night the block clerk called out: "All able-bodied Jews, aged twenty to twenty-four, report!" I did not report. Twenty men were selected, and the very next day they had to report to a doctor. They returned the same day and had to resume work at once. No one knew what they planned to do with these twenty men.

A week later, another twenty Jews in the same age group were selected. But this time they were picked alphabetically. I was the very first one. We were taken to Birkenau, to a labour camp for women. A tall physician in grey Air Force uniform appeared. We had to strip, and our sexual organs were placed under a machine and kept there for fifteen minutes. The machine heated up the sexual organs and the surrounding parts and afterwards these parts turned black. After this performance, we had to resume work at once.

In the course of the next few days, most of my comrades experienced a discharge of pus from the sexual organs and they had great difficulty in walking. Nevertheless, they had to go on working until they dropped. Those that collapsed were taken to be gassed. I, myself experienced only a watery discharge, but no pus.

After two weeks, about October 1943, seven men of our group were taken to Auschwitz I. This distance had to be traversed on foot. They had great difficulty

Auschwitz Museum

Horst Schumann

in walking, due to the pain in the sexual organs. We
were taken to a hospital building and there we were
operated on. We received an injection in the back
which turned the lower part of the body numb while
the upper part remained quite normal. Both testicles
were removed. I was able to watch the proceedings
in the mirror of a surgical lamp. No consent for the
operation was obtained. We were merely told: "Your
turn", sent to the operating table without a word. The
director of the sterilization and castration experiments
was a Dr Schumann . . . .'[63]

Approximately 1,000 prisoners, male and female, underwent
X-ray sterilization or castration, and about 200 of these were
subjected to surgical removal of testicles or ovaries.

When the Russians marched in to liberate Auschwitz,
Schumann went to Ravensbrück were he continued his
experiments victimizing thirteen-year-old gypsy girls. When the
Russians also threatened to occupy Ravensbrück as well,
Schumann decided to run for it. Until 1950, he succeeded in
hiding under a false name, still practising as a doctor. That year,
the authorities almost caught him; in the nick of time he
managed to escape to Ghana where he was received by the
dictator N'Kruhmah and employed as physician in his personal
staff. Schumann's safety came to an abrupt end when
N'Kruhmah himself fell from power.

With credentials in his pocket, he fled to Upper Volta, where
he built up a large practice. Once again, peace was short-lived,
and this time there was no lucky escape. The German court
applied to Upper Volta for his extradition, which after lengthy
consideration, was granted.

In September 1966, Schumann, now sixty, returned to
German soil, where preparations were made for his trial. During
these preparations he fell 'ill', and on 23 September1970, he
was declared unanswerable. The 'terminally ill' Schumann
survived a further thirteen years in an affluent Hamburg suburb,
never having spent a day in jail for his crimes. Ironically, the
Ministry of Justice refused to explain this, pointing to the medical
confidentiality of the physicians who had examined him.[64]

Any discussion of the sterilization tests at Auschwitz can not
fail to include the surgeon Wladislaw Dering. In 1943 he was

incorporated in Schumann's staff and responsible for most operations during which the ovaries were removed. Dr Brewda:

> 'Then they brought in the Greek girl whom I knew was Bella, one of the two girls who already had an operation scar on the abdomen. I said to Dr Dering:
> "I suppose you know that one of her ovaries has already been removed. You are not going to make this girl a female eunuch, are you?"
> He replied: "That's not your business." He had earlier admitted that he had also removed the testicles of certain male prisoners. They were, of course, Jewish, just as all these girls were . . . .'[65]

Many patients remember him as a brute, and although forced to perform the operations, his only excuse was 'I have my orders. They will kill me. I have to do it!'[66]

In 1944 he was transferred to an SS clinic at Chorzow where he carried out medical research under Dr Clauberg until the end of the war. In the autumn of 1945, Dering left for England, where he opened a practice in a London suburb but in 1947 he was arrested and confined to Brixton prison. Dr Brewda had accused him of having carried out no less than 10,000 experiments, for which the Polish authorities had applied for his extradition. The British Ministry of Justice instituted a search inquiry but, after nineteen months, came to the conclusion that there was insufficient evidence to support his extradition.

Former Auschwitz prisoners were unable to recognize Dering, and testimonies claiming his innocence came from all over the world. He was released and left for Somaliland where he spent a few years practising surgery.

In 1954, he re-opened his practice again. In 1964, Leon Uris' book *Exodus* appeared and once again Dering's name was mentioned in connection with the Auschwitz experiments.

> 'Schumann removed fallopian tubes and Dr Dering carried out surgical experiments . . . .'[67]

At first sight, a rather insignificant remark in a book over 400 pages in length but Dering claimed that he had been libelled and went to court. Uris and his publisher William Kimber conceded that the number of operations, as stated in the book, was exaggerated but sought to substantiate that one hundred and thirty experimental operations on both men and women had been performed by Dr Dering. They called three prisoner-doctors[68] as well as eight of the ten girls who had been operated on for the removal of an ovary and six men who had one or both of their testicles removed in these operations during which, it was argued, Dr Dering had taken part. Dr Brewda:

> 'As the case largely concerned Dr Dering's actions and behaviour at Auschwitz, some of the questions were directed towards Jews and Aryans. It was stressed that not only was he known to have been anti-Semitic, but it was also obvious that his Jewish victims were not given a general anaesthetic, which would have been far more humane and would have alleviated their suffering, whereas the register clearly showed that general anaesthetics were available and had been given again and again to others .... '[69]

Dr Dering told the court that he had no choice and could not refuse to take part in the sterilization operations. If he had refused, it would not have saved the victims because the operations would have been performed by other doctors or by some unskilled person or — as Dr Schumann had threatened — he would send the victims to the gas chamber and get surgical aid to remove the X-rayed ovaries and testicles later. Furthermore, he claimed that Schumann and Clauberg had given him the choice: co-operate, or the bullet.

By the end of the procession of witnesses, the confusion was complete; there was as much to be said for him as against him. When giving their verdict, the jury awarded Dering one-half-penny as damages, the smallest coin in the realm. But the costs of the defence to about £16,000 were awarded against him. Inspired by these events, Uris wrote another bestseller *QB VII* (Queen's Bench Court Number VII), in which a doctor Kelno, although Uris denies this, takes the role of Dr Dering who died in 1966 of cancer.

* * *

PAŃSTWOWE MUZEUM W OŚWIĘCIMIU
ARCHIWUM

Auschwitz Museum

Carl Clauberg

Professor Carl Clauberg, a gynaecological researcher and practitioner of considerable distinction who did a lot of research in association with the University of Kiel, joined the Nazi Party in 1933 and became a loyal and dedicated Nazi with a profound commitment to Nazi versions of the German race and the German state.

In 1937, at the age of thirty-nine, he obtained his lecturer-professional status and started experiments to treat infertility. He developed several hormonal preparations such as 'Progynon' and 'Prolution' which are still in use today.

In 1940 he met Himmler who had learnt of Clauberg's research through the gynaecologist's successful treatment of infertility in a high-ranking SS officer's wife, and that became the start of a long relationship. According to Lifton, it was based 'on a malignant blending of bio-medical and political-racial ideologies'.[70]

At that first meeting, Clauberg explained his research aims: investigation of the causes and the treatment of infertility, but Himmler was more interested in sterilization. As a result of that conversation Clauberg directed his research energies toward the explicit goal of finding an effective method of mass sterilization. With financial support arranged by the Ahnenerbe, he started experiments on animals.

A year later Himmler suggested that he should conduct sterilization experiments at Ravensbrück concentration camp but Clauberg told the Reichsführer that Auschwitz would be more practical because of its proximity to Königshütte where he already had his clinical facilities.

In his private clinic he had already performed various experiments in an attempt to bring about permanent sterilization. Apart from X-rays, he used caustic fluids, which he projected into the womb.

Although he was an Auschwitz 'outsider', he went to Auschwitz in the summer of 1942 and 'rented' facilities: research subjects and prisoner-doctors. He began his research in Birkenau but in april 1943, he transferred his experimental setting to Block ten in the main camp. His method was to inject a caustic substance into the cervix in order to obstruct the fallopian tubes.[71] His test subjects were married women who had borne children. As assistant, he had Dr Johannes Goebel, chief chemist with the Schering pharmaceutical firm who worked on producing the necessary caustic substances as well as improving X-ray tracing material.

Clauberg first injected his test subjects with an opaque liquid in order to determine by X-ray that there was no prior blockage or impairment. He experimented with several substances but was very secretive about the exact nature of the one he used in order to protect a medical discovery from research competitors.

Himmler was very interested in Clauberg's experimental work. In July 1942, he ordered his secretary Rudolf Brandt to write the following letter:

'The Reichsführer SS ordered me to write to you and convey to you his desire that you go to Ravensbrück concentration camp for women at some time, after making arrangements with SS Gruppenführer Pohl and the camp physician, in order to perform sterilization on Jewesses by your method. Before you start with your work, the Reichsführer would appreciate receiving from you the approximate time that would be required to sterilize 1,000 Jewesses.

The Jewesses themselves are to know nothing about it. In the opinion of the Reichsführer you should be able to administer the injection in the course of a general examination. Extensive tests would have to be made to show the effectiveness of the sterilizations. For the most part, these could perhaps consist of X-ray photographs, to be made after a certain period of time, to be determined by yourself, which would establish what changes have taken place.

In one case or another, however, there might have to be a practical test, conducted in such a way that a Jewess is locked up with a Jew for a certain period of time, any success attained to be observed. May I ask you to give me your reactions to this letter . . . .'[72]

And so Dr Clauberg set to work in Block ten. The former prisoner Margaritha Neumann:

'Dr Clauberg ordered me to lie down on the gynaecological table and I was able to observe Sylvia

Friedmann who was preparing an injection syringe with a long needle. Dr Clauberg used this needle to give me an injection in the womb. I had the feeling that my stomach would burst with pain. I began to scream so that I could be heard through the entire block. Dr Clauberg told me roughly to stop screaming immediately, otherwise, I would be taken back at once to Birkenau concentration camp. After this experiment, I had inflammation of the ovaries . . . .'[73]

And a Greek girl testified:

'I was deported to Auschwitz on 6 April 1943, and arrived on the fourteenth. For the first six months, I did forced labour, digging and then I was sent to Block 10. Here, medical experiments were performed on me by several doctors, of which Dr Clauberg was one. There were tests done with X-rays and operations on the womb. As a result of these experiments, I bled heavily, I suffered from dizziness, nausea and severe pain in my genitals. Nevertheless, when the tests were over, I had to do forced labour again, this time carrying stones . . . .'[74]

To satisfy Himmler, he exaggerated the test results in his reports and, to justify his slow progress, he often referred to 'temporary difficulties'; his method was 'as good as perfected' but required 'a few refinements'.

In July 1943, he wrote to Himmler:

'The method I have devised for effecting sterilization of the female organism without operation has been virtually completed. It operates by a single injection from the cervix and can be performed during the usual gynaecological examination familiar to every physician. When I state that the method is "virtually complete" I mean:

1. Only certain refinements remain to be worked out.

2. Even today, it could be used regularly in our customary eugenic sterilizations in place of operation,

PAŃSTWOWE MUZEUM W OŚWIĘCIMIU
ARCHIWUM

Geheime Reichssache   Berlin W8, den 29. April 1944
                                       Voßstraße 4
                                       Fernruf: Ortsverkehr 12 00 54
                                       Fernverkehr 12 06 21

Kanzlei des Führers
der NSDAP.   An den
                                       Reichsführer-SS. und Chef der
                                       Deutschen Polizei
                                       Heinrich   H i m m l e r

Aktenzeichen: IIa/Kt.
                                       B e r l i n SW 11
                                       Prinz Albrecht Str. 9

              Sehr verehrter Reichsführer!

              Im Auftrage von Reichsleiter Bouhler überreiche ich
              Ihnen anliegend eine Arbeit des Dr. Horst S c h u -
              m a n n über die Einwirkung der Röntgenstrahlen auf
              die menschlichen Keimdrüsen.

              Sie baten seinerzeit Oberführer Brack um Durchführung
              dieser Arbeit und unterstützten dieselbe durch Zurver-
              fügungstellung des entsprechenden Materials im KL.
              Auschwitz. Ich verweise speziell auf den 2. Teil der
              vorliegenden Arbeit, der den Nachweis führt, daß eine
              Kastration des Mannes auf diesem Wege ziemlich ausge-
              schlossen ist oder einen Aufwand erfordert, der sich
              nicht lohnt. Die operative Kastration, die, wie ich
              mich selbst überzeugt habe, nur 6 - 7 Minuten dauert,
              ist demnach zuverlässiger und schneller zu bewerkstelli-
              gen als die Kastration mit Röntgenstrahlen.

              Eine Fortsetzung der Arbeit werde ich Ihnen demnächst
              überreichen können.

                                  Heil Hitler!

              Anlage.

                                                    Auschwitz Museum

Report on the medical experiments
as performed by Dr. Schumann

- 3 -

Fällen deutlich bemerkbar war. Möglicherweise wirken sich hier die häufigen Zuckergaben durch die fast aus reinem Milchzucker bestehenden biochemischen Tabletten aus. Versuche zu entsprechender Klärung sind angesetzt.

Bei einem Fall von Gelenkplastik wurde vorbeugend das Sepsismittel Kalium phosphoricum D 6 gegeben, da die Operationswunde besonders infektionsgefährdet war. Trotzdem trat am nächsten Tage Fieber bis 39° auf. Die biochemische Behandlung hat also das Eintreten bzw. Ausbrechen der Infektion nicht verhindern können, obwohl sofort und intensiv das Mittel kalium phosphoricum D 6 verabreicht wurde.

Bemerkenswert ist auch, dass von allen S c h w e r kranken nach kurzer Zeit die Einnahme der biochemischen Tabletten energisch abgelehnt wurde, weil es für sie eine Quälerei bedeutete, alle 5 Minuten, auch nachts, das Mittel einzunehmen.

A b s c h l i e s s e n d ist zu sagen, dass bei einer Gesamtzahl von 40 Fällen einem positiven Fall und vier mit Vorbehalt als positiv zu wertenden Fällen 35 Versager gegenüberstehen, von denen 10 tödlich ausgegangen sind.

Die Erprobung in Dachau wird weiter fortgesetzt.

Neben dem bisherigen Programm wird das Hauptaugenmerk auf die Erfassung möglichst gleichgelagerter Doppelfälle gerichtet, von denen der eine allopathisch, der andere biochemisch behandelt werden soll.

Gelesen:
Rascher kliniek
3.9.42
Hegemann

2. Im K.L. Auschwitz wurden 3 typische Fälle von Sepsis, die sich aus Zellgewebsentzündungen entwickelt hatten, mit Kalium phosphoricum D 4 nach Vorschrift behandelt. In keinem dieser Fälle konnte ein therapeutischer Einfluss auf den Verlauf der Krankheit beobachtet werden. Alle 3 Fälle endeten tödlich.
Die Versuche werden fortgesetzt.

which it is able to supplant.

As for the question you put to me not quite a year ago, Mr Reichsführer, namely, how long it would take to sterilize 1,000 women by this method, I can now give a preliminary answer: If the investigations I am conducting continue as hitherto — and there is no reason to assume that they will not — the moment is not far when I can say that: ''An appropriately trained physician, using appropriate equipment and perhaps ten assistants (the number depending on the speed to be attained) can very probably handle several hundred women a day, if not, indeed, 1,000'' . . . '[75]

Clauberg lied in his report, for to achieve complete sterilization, he was obliged to operate.[76]

Because of his ambition and the pressure from Himmler, he soon had considerable personal conflict with many of the other doctors and Wirths is claimed to have said that Clauberg, because of his experiments, had gone completely to the dogs and had become a severe alcoholic and a totally unscrupulous character . . . .'[77]

And his brother Helmut Wirths referred to Clauberg as 'one of the worst characters I ever met . . . .'[78]

Like Schumann, Clauberg continued his research at Ravensbrück in January 1945. When the Russians approached the camp, he too decided to flee. He was not so lucky as Schumann. Arrested by the Russians, he was given a trial, whose details are missing, and sentenced to twenty years hard labour. It looked as if the former SS Gruppenführer had disappeared behind the Iron Curtain for good. So it was to widespread astonishment that the following announcement appeared in a prominent German newspaper in 1956:

'Professor Carl Clauberg requires a number of excellent typists who, through unemployment or the availability of free time, would like to work for him two or three hours per day and particularly evenings. Apply immediately (from nine-ten am or seven-eight pm also Sunday) to the Academic Hospital, Surgical Department (ground floor, room one) in Berlin. Permanent position for the best, in which case they

would travel with me through Germany, all expenses
paid ... .'[79]

The advertisement was also seen by former prisoners who
clamoured for justice. Clauberg, who had been pardoned by
the Russians in 1955 and set down over the frontier, was arrested
in Kiel. After long hesitation, he had after all already been
sentenced by the Russians for his Auschwitz and Ravensbrück
past, the German courts decided to prosecute. The charge,
however, was limited; he was accused of having caused grave
bodily harm in 170 cases, four of which had led to death.
During the preparations for the trial, influential friends tried
to have him declared unanswerable, a much-practised stunt
which the German courts in this case did not fall for. However,
the trial was never to eventuate; a few days before it opened,
Clauberg was found hanged in his cell. The official inquiry
concluded that the cause of death was suicide. Once again,
Germany had been spared a dreadful confrontation with its past.
Attorney-General Dr Fritz Bauer:

> 'Most Germans are opposed to these trials. If people
> could say: there they are, the scapegoats, the bosses,
> the ones who must be sentenced, then they could
> consider themselves freed of their so-called guilt. But
> they don't react like that. People are against these
> trials. Clearly, more Germans identify with these
> people than are prepared to admit it.
>
> Though it might sound odd, I consider this to be
> a good sign. And the young generation is not simply
> a young generation. It is also the generation born of
> their fathers and mothers. Can you imagine what it
> means to these young people when they find out that
> their fathers were not the way during the war that they
> always had thought them to be ... ?'[80]

Dr Hans Münch was one of the very few SS physicians to
survive the criminal war trials after the war. As stated before,
he was not reluctant to talk about Auschwitz, his behaviour,
about his colleagues or his feelings of guilt. Münch about
Auschwitz:

'At the moment I arrived, I knew it was criminal. My first reaction was: I must get away, I don't want anything to do with this. I arrived with my wife at the station and there we saw the first prisoners. It was terrible and left an indelible impression on me. In the vicinity of the camp one could smell the crematoria and the whole atmosphere was perfectly suffocating. Naturally, I immediately asked what was going on and was told, without ceremony, that Jews were being gassed. I went straight to Weber and after a long talk with him, I decided to stay. A physician was needed with bacteriological experience and Weber assured me that I would not have anything to do with that horror.

From that moment on, I endeavoured in so far as it was possible, to help the prisoners. Our Hygienic Institute was a sort of enclave within the camp. Prisoners there received reasonable care and were not abused. There was even occasional friction with the other departments within the camp because we made too much food and provisions available to the prisoners. But I must state again that Auschwitz was a horror and the human reactions to it remain a riddle. To answer the question as to what my first impression was ... I remember it well. It was one of the first times that I stood by the camp's main entrance. I watched working parties leaving the camp. Grey columns of prisoners and Kapos who were beating and shouting ... a terrible experience.

And then it happened. In one of the groups, I thought I saw a friend from student days. His head had been shaved, he was in camp clothing and looked terrible. I was profoundly affected. My first reaction was that I had to save him somehow. The strange thing is that if one sees so much misery in such a short time, the whole mass will pass one by, but one is struck by the individual ... you see the misery of so many prisoners, but still, the one you know, that touches you ... .

I went straight to Weber and told him what had happened and of my intention to help my fellow-student. Weber made it clear that this was out of the

question. I couldn't just pull a prisoner out of the
working party! Nevertheless I did some more research
and it eventually turned out that the person I had seen
could not have been my fellow-student. Having gone
through the whole camp register, it seemed that I had
made a mistake .... .'[81]

It remained difficult for Münch to adapt; he well understood
what sort of hell he had ended up in. Escape was pointless;
service at the front was the alternative.

> 'Neither appealed to me. What I did resolve to do,
> and Weber felt the same, was to distance myself from
> the atrocities and to help the prisoners as much as
> possible.
> While I realize that it was just a drop in the ocean,
> I saved very many prisoners from the gas chamber.
> My dost difficult moment at Auschwitz came when
> Wirths wanted me to help him in making the selections
> from the arriving transports. I would have become
> directly involved and I had determined to avoid this
> at all cost .... . I discussed the affair directly with
> Weber, telling him that I did not want to do it. Mind
> you, formally Wirths was within his rights to demand
> it of me.
> Weber passed it on to Professor Mrugrowsky, the
> director of the Hygiene Institute in Berlin, and he in
> turn discussed the matter with Lolling and Wirths,
> as a result of which I was excused from the
> selections .... .'[82]

But suppose the matter had not ended in this way, and Münch
had been compelled to do the selections, what would he have
done?

> 'I really don't know ... I don't think that I would
> have done it. What would I have done? I don't
> know .... . Happily, I have been spared from this
> dilemma.'[83]

One of the reasons for his acquittal after the war was the fact that he had saved hundreds of prisoners and that no incriminating evidence had been given against him. Was saving prisoners a simple business?

'Yes and no. One of the greatest crimes an SS officer could commit was the favouring of certain prisoners. This was strictly forbidden. But it occurred on a wide scale. Auschwitz, as far as this was concerned, was held together by corruption and complicity.

The staff members were forbidden to employ the prisoners for their own benefit, but the practice was epidemic. We did it in Rasjko too. Officially, we had three cooks, and three prisoners went around wearing white suits and hats. In fact, two of the three were tailors, and we let them make clothes in a secluded room. We did a good job at camouflage.

The most difficult thing was, and many people don't believe this, saving prisoners who had been selected for the gas chamber. Even for an officer, like myself, this was impossible. A small example. One day, a prisoner came to me at his wits' end. His niece had arrived in Auschwitz shortly before and he had advised her to volunteer for the so-called "Clauberg-Kommando", having heard that women in that Kommando received excellent care. In fact these women were being experimented on, and after the tests, many women were sent to the gas chamber, and he asked me for help.

I was powerless to do so, but I decided to discuss the problem with Weber and the prisoner-doctor Alina (Brewda). Alina, a most remarkable woman, was looking after the women upon whom Clauberg had experimented in Block ten.

We decided to summon twelve women, any more was impossible, to our Institute under the pretence that we needed them for sputum tests, but in fact, to thereby obtain a stay of execution. And it worked. But the problem was that the women's names were still on the gas chamber list, and we couldn't go on doing sputum tests for ever. After the tests we would have had to transfer them back to be gassed. So we decided to carry out experiments on these women ourselves and keep them from the gas chamber that way. I discussed the matter in depth with Alina and Weber and we decided to develop a certain serum which should be tested on the women.

It looked very impressive on paper, but in reality it was nothing of the kind. However, the problem was in obtaining Wirth's consent and that of the camp superiors. Although they were originally against the idea, Höss didn't want us to do any more experimenting, we eventually got their approval. In this way, the women's names were removed from the death list and I could perform a number of entirely harmless experiments ... .'[84]

Dr Brewda confirmed this:

'Dr Münch, a young SS doctor, engaged on some harmless experiments in the large laboratory in Block ten where Kleinova and some other doctors were assisting him with blood and sputum tests ... .'[85]

Münch:

'Almost all these women survived Auschwitz and gave witness on my behalf during my trial ... .'[86]

But how could someone with Münch's attitude sustain himself in those surroundings? Perhaps an escape mechanism in the form of drink? Münch·

'No, I'm no drinker. Two glasses are more than enough for me. I know that a lot of drinking did go on. But I doubt if it was done out of guilt; probably just to forget the wretchedness. Alcohol flowed amply at Auschwitz but I never took part in drinking parties ... .' [87]

Was one not touched by the daily misery?

'Of course. Especially in the beginning. But no matter what you think, you get used to it. It is just like in an abattoir. When someone visits one for the first time and sees how the animals are slaughtered, it is a terrible experience, but after a while one doesn't see it anymore . . . but it was impossible to stave it all off. You saw this especially during your leave. When you got home, your own surroundings, far away from Auschwitz, when you played with your children, went for walks with them, then Auschwitz weighed heavy on you. The contrast became an oppression . . . .'[88]

Did the doctors often talk amongst themselves about their work, their feelings?

'No, apart from Weber, Mengele and Rhode, I never talked with colleagues about what we were doing. It may sound strange in hindsight, but that's how it was . . . .'[89]

What was discussed then?

'Matters such as understaffing, inadequate supplies, food shortages, and so on. One exchanged thoughts now and again only about such simple matters. But as I mentioned before, Weber and I always distanced ourselves as much as possible from the other personnel. Why? They weren't our type . . . .'[90]

And what is the lesson to be drawn from Auschwitz?

'That a person must never trust himself!'[91]

And what about feelings of guilt?

'The biggest mistake I made was volunteering my services to the Waffen SS. And that is something I have regretted to this day : . . .'[92]

Dr Ellis Hertzberger was deported to Birkenau in 1944. After a few weeks he was deported to Schwarzheide where he had to do hard physical labour. Because physicians were needed with bacteriological experience he was again deported and for the second time within a few months he arrived at Auschwitz. Here he did bacteriological research at Rasjko. Hertzberger:

'The treatment was good and the prisoners were hardly beaten but to say that the SS physicians at Rasjko were friendly . . . . No! Weber was not friendly at all. Of course he was responsible for the fact that there was enough food and no ill-treatment but it was self interest. We had to do research for the SS! I had little to do with Münch at Rasjko. I saw him occasionally and his behaviour towards the prisoners was correct, or rather, neutral. I got to know him better at Dachau concentration camp where I became head, I hate to use the word Kapo, of the bacteriological station in January 1945. Here I met Weber and Münch again.

I still remember . . . one day I was working when somebody entered the laboratory and grabbed me in the neck.

"Hello, you Hertzberger!"

It was Weber. He did not say: "Hello, you" but "Hello, you *Hertzberger*" so he used my name. Perhaps the first indication that the war would soon be over . . . . Anyway, the first thing he ordered me to do was to clean his brief-case because he had vomited on his way to Dachau.

I saw Münch almost every day and his behaviour was the same as in Auschwitz, polite and neutral.

In April 1945 we were told that we had to leave Dachau and the day before the departure I had to report to Münch. A most remarkable thing happened. He gave me a map and told me, if it was possible to escape, that we should hide in the neighbourhood of Bernbeuren, where he was living at the time. And if that wasn't enough, he gave me a pistol with one bullet! I was amazed. We didn't take the gun with us but buried it in our barrack. If it was discovered it would mean our death. I don't know why he gave

the map and the gun but I think that he really wanted
to help us. In 1980 I spoke with Münch, it was for
a German television programme. He couldn't
remember the incident but it became clear that he had
not given the gun and map because of self interest . . .
.'92a

Discussions with former SS physicians about feelings of guilt
led mostly to nothing. No one dared to admit his guilt openly.
All, Münch included, referred to the circumstances at the time.
Talking about guilt Münch reacted:

'Ach, what about the prisoner-doctors? Lots of them
must have an enormous guilt complex. I saw a
number who exploited their position at their fellow-
prisoner's expense . . . .'93

Former prisoner-physician Elie Cohen confirms this:

'In comparison with other prisoners, I was
favoured. Of course, I exploited the fact that I was
a doctor. I once called myself a collaborator . . . .'94

The feelings of guilt that Münch discusses with such difficulty,
Cohen philosophizes about with ease:

'I stood at the gas chamber; I beat nobody, but I
took part. But there must be a limit! A moment at
which one chooses death rather than life. Where is
that border? I find it terrible that a person will do
anything to survive. One clutches at straws . . . .'95

A few hours after his arrival at Auschwitz, Cohen knew that
his wife, child and parents-in-law had been gassed. Cohen:

'It is still incomprehensible to me, that I wanted
to live after hearing that they were dead. Why did
I do my best to do so? Yes . . . I feel guilty about that.
As if they had not existed! Egotism. I thought only
of myself. I didn't want to die . . . .'96

And finally Dr Lengyel:

'The Germans sinned grievously, but so did the rest
of the nations, if only through refusing to believe and
to toil day and night to save the wretched and the
dispossessed by every possible means. I know that if
people everywhere resolve that, henceforth, justice
must be indivisible, that no Hitlers must ever be
allowed to rise again, it will help (...).

I saw many internees cling to their human dignity
to the very end. The Nazis succeeded in degrading
them physically, but they could not debase them
morally. Because of these few, I have not entirely lost
my faith in mankind.

If, even in the jungle of Birkenau, all were not
necessarily inhuman to their fellowmen, then there
is indeed hope. It is that hope which keeps me
alive ... .'[97]

NOTES

Introduction

1. Todeslager. Sachsenhausen, Berlin 1948, p.81
2. Pseudo-medizinische Versuche im Konzentrationslagern. Jüdischer Pressedienst: Information des Zentralrates der Juden in Deutschland nr.2.3, June 1974, p.15 et seqq.
3. 'late homecomer' ... a designation of the BRD.
4. De Anti-fascist, 4e kwartaal 1977, p.23.
5. L. Poliakow: Auschwitz; Tilburg 1964, p.134.
6. Medical case 1, p.70 et seqq.
7. Quoted in: A. Mitscherlich, F. Mielke: Doctors of Infamy,New York, 1949, p.33.
8. M. Grey: Leur défense a Nuremberg, Paris 1976, p.109.
9. B.F. Smith: Reaching judgement at Nuremberg, New York 1977, p.46 et seqq.
10. See note 6.
11. W. Franken: German Science in the last century, Leeds 1947, p.48.
12. A. Mitscherlich, F. Mielke: Medizin ohne Menschlichkeit, Frankfurt a.M. 1960, p.13.
13. P. Berben: Dachau; the official history 1933-1945 London, 1975 p.125.
14. Letter from the 'Zentrale Stelle der Landesjustizverwaltungen Ludwigsburg' to the author dated 28 October 1976 and a letter from the 'Staatsanwaltschaft bei dem Landesgericht München' dated 17 January 1977.
15. NO 758.
16. Dachau-Prozess, case 00-50-2 November 1945, p.1498 et seqq.
17. At Rasjko near Auschwitz there was located the research institution for the south-eastern region of the Hygiene-Institute

of the Military SS called 'Hygienisch-Bakteriologische Untersuchungsstelle der Waffen SS, Südost' also designated as 'Hygiene-Institut der Waffen SS and Polizei Auschwitz.' Its organization was begun in the autumn of 1942 and it was opened in April 1943.'

18. Professor Marc Klein in: Témoignages Strasbourgeois, Paris 1947, p.448.

19. A Fiderkiewicz: Reminiscences concerning a prisoner-doctor's work in the tuberculosis blocks of the prisoners' camp hospital at Birkenau (1943-1944). From the history of KL Auschwitz, vol 2, Auschwitz 1976, p.282.

20. Quoted in Poliakow, op. cit. pp.161-162.

21. SS Hauptsturmführer Dr Bruno Nikolaus Weber was the director of the Hygiene-Institute and his substitute was Dr Münch. Weber was not tried and died in 1956.

22. Münch is wrong. Weber conducted medical experiments. See D Czech: The men's hospital camp at KL Auschwitz 11, Auschwitz 1976, p.80.

23. Again Münch is wrong. SS Obersturmführer Dr Hans Delmotte who was also a substitute for Dr Nikolaus Weber conducted medical experiments. See D Czech, op. cit. p.80.

24. Interview with Hans Münch, August 1988.

Chapter 1 — Himmler and his SS

1. H.R. Trevor-Roper: De laatste dagen van Hitler, Den Haag 1947, p.37.

2. ibid. p.110.

3. A. Speer: Inside the Third Reich, New York 1970, p.503.

4. ibid. p.147.

5. ibid. p.183.

6. F. Bernadotte: Het Einde, Den Haag, 1947. pp.40-41.

7. PS 3291.

8. Interview with Albert Speer, May 1976.

9. H. Hohne: Het zwarte korps onder de doodskop, Baarn 1967, pp.36-37.

10. ibid.

11. N.C.A. IV p.558 et seqq.

12. ibid.

13. ibid.

14. M.C., vol 1 p.870.
15. F. Kersten: Klerk en beul, Amsterdam 1947, p.37.
16. B.F. Heinrich Himmler; a Nazi in the making 1920-1926. Stanford 1971, pp.72-76. pp.91-92.
17. Trevor-Roper op. cit. p.41.
18. NO 751 C.
19. Nazi conspiracy and aggression. Washington 1947, vol. IV, pp.553-557.
20. M. Freund: Het Derde Rijk; geboorte, macht, en ondergang, Den Haag 1963, p. 295.
21. R. Manvell.H. Fraenkel: Himmler, London 1965, p.92.
22. G.S. Graber: History of the SS, London 1980, p.70.
23. Quoted in J. Kessel: De man die Nederland redde, Rotterdam, 1961, pp.112-113.
24. Lord Russell of Liverpool: De Gesel van het hakenkruis, Amsterdam 1960, P.17.
25. Quoted in H. Ahrendt: Banaliteit van het kwaad, Amsterdam 1969, pp.123-124.
26. J. Heydecker.J. Leeb: Op mars naar de galg, Amsterdam 1961, p.295.
27. PS 4050.
28. PS 1566.
29. PS 165-179 et seqq.
30. H. Desoille.M.M. Lafitte: Psychologie criminelle des Hitlériens, Paris 1972, p.4.
31. M.C., vol 1, p.72.
32. A. Gütt: Die Struktur der Volkgesundheit im Dritten Reich, Berlin 1935.
33. ibid. p.25.
34. E.A. Cohen: Het Duitse concentratiekamp; een medische en psychologische studie, Amsterdam 1952, p.222.
35. See note 11.

Chapter 2 — The Experiments at Ravensbrück

1. Lord Russell of Liverpool op. cit. p.158.
2. ibid. p.159.
3. ibid. p.180.
4. ibid. p.181.
5. ibid.

6. G. Tillion: Ravensbrück, Paris 1973, p.101.

7. NO 377.

8. Lord Russell of Liverpool op. cit. p.181.

9. ibid. p.183.

10. Speer op. cit. p.443.

11. NO 654.

12. PS 857.

13. H. Strong: 'Scientific Experiments'; a survey, Baltimore 1956, p.142.

14. PS 1453.

15. PS 1566.

16. PS 1569.

17. PS 986.

18. Arthur Nebe was in charge of SS Department No. 5: Suppression of Crime.

19. PS 1455.

20. PS 1456.

21. NO 487.

22. PS 1566 et seqq.

23. PS 4401 et seqq.

24. ibid.

25. NO 228.

26. PS 4316 et seqq.

27. Cohen op. cit. p.222.

Chapter 3 — Conti and Brandt

1. Interview with Albert Speer April 1976.

2. U. Bahnsen.J.P. O'Donnel: Die Katakombe; das Ende in der Reichskanzlei, Stuttgart 1975, p.180.

3. W. Treue: Mit den Augen ihrer Leibärzte, Bad Bernack 1956, p.279.

4. Interview with Albert Speer May 1976.

5. ibid.

6. H. Frank: Im Angesicht des Galgens; Deutung Hitlers und seiner Zeit auf Grund Erlebnisse und Erkentnisse, München 1953, p.274.

7. Lutz Graf Schwerin von Krosigk: Es geschah in Deutschland, Tübingen 1952, p.224.

8. See note 4.

9. PS 2577 et seqq.

10. See also: J. Michel: Dora, Paris 1976, p.185.

11. A. Speer: De slavenstaat, Amsterdam 1981, pp.213-214.

12. W. Treue op. cit. 283.

13. A. Speer: Inside the Third Reich, pp.160-162.

14. See note 4.

15. See note 4.

16. D. Irving: Hitlers Krankheiten. Stern Nr. 25, 1969, p.158.

17. ibid.

18. U. Bahnsen.J.P. O'Donnel op. cit. p.99.

19. PS 2601.

Chapter 4 — Euthanasia

1. G. Engel: Heeresadjudant bei Hitler 1938-1945, Stuttgart 1974, pp.56-57.

2. A. Hitler: Mein kampf, München 1935, p.297.

3. J. Denner: Euthanasie 1933-1945, Tübingen 1979, p.27.

4. PS 2413.

5. Quoted in W. Gehl: Der Nationalsozialistische Staat, Breslau 1933, pp.19-20.

6. G. Franke: Vererbung und Rasse, München 1934, p.125.

7. W. Berner: The teaching of ideology, New York 1959, p.48.

8. J. Menges: Euthanasie in het Derde Rijk, Haarlem 1972, p.VII.

9. K. Dorner: 'National-sozialismus und Lebensvernichtung', Tübingen 1967, p.15.

10. PS 630.

11. Menges op. cit. p.6.

12. PS 2417.

13. Menges op. cit. p.89.

14. NO 854.

15. PS 1858.

16. NO 470.

17. Anklageschrift Js 17.59, Frankfurt a.M. 1962, p.239.

18. NO 825.

19. Menges op. cit. p.30.

20. NO 828.

21. NO 82-01-501.

22. H. Bechmann: Euthanasia in Germany 1933-1941, New

York 1981, p.50.

23. This programme to kill the insane operated out of Bouhler's office in Hitler's chancellery at Tiergartenstrasse 4 — hence its code name T-4.

24. L.S. Dawidowicz: The war against the Jews 1933-1945, New York 1975, pp.180-181.

25. SS Standartenführer, Director of SS Department D-3 and in that function director of all camp physicians.

26. NO 2333.

27. NO 2799.

28. NO 3060.

29. ibid.

30. NO 3061.

31. H.G. Adler: Der verwaltete Mensch, Tübingen 1974, p.274.

32. PS 1913.

33. ibid.

34. PS 1921.

35. PS 2580.

36. PS 2583.

37. PS 2588.

38. J. Neuhäusler: Kreuz und Hakenkreuz, München 1946, p.346.

39. Menges op. cit. p.130.

40. Bechmann op. cit. p.289.

41. Neuhäusler op. cit. p.366.

42. Brandt received verbal instructions from Hitler at his HQ to stop the euthanasia programme; there is no written record of the order.

43. Engel op. cit. p.151.

44. Menges op. cit. pp.181-182.

Chapter 5 — The Buchenwald and Natzweiler Experiments

1. J. Hemelrijk: Er is een weg naar de vrijheid; zeven maanden concentratiekamp. Zeist 1965, p.193.

2. SS Standartenführer Enno Lolling.

3. E. Kogon: Der SS-Staat. Frankfurt a.M. 1946, p.154.

4. ibid. p.133.

5. ibid.
6. Zentrale Stelle der Landesjustizverwaltungen Ludwigsburg in a letter to the author dated 28 October 1976.
7. Kogon. op. cit. pp.186-187.
8. PS 6231.
9. Kogon. op. cit. pp.186-187.
10. J. Leber: A short history of the SS 1929-1945, London 1968, p.45.
11. PS 6881-6887.
12. Karl Genzken was SS Gruppenführer and director of the Health Department of the Waffen SS.
13. NO 265.
14. W. Poller: Medical Block Buchenwald. London 1961, p.99.
15. ibid. pp.226-227.
16. ibid. p.100.
17. D. Schubert: Medical Experiments in Buchenwald KZ. London 1974, p.14.
18. Kogon. op. cit. p.65.
19. M. Bar Zohar: La chasse aux savants allemands. Paris 1965, p.153 et seqq.
20. Institute for Bacteriological Research.
21. PS 9577.
22. PS 9571.
23. Haagen stood on trial in Metz (France).
24. R. Plant: The Pink Triangle. The Nazi war against Homosexuals. New York 1986. p.72.
25. PS 1453a.
26. Kogon. op. cit. p.361.
27. NO 921.
28. NO 185.
29. NO 807.
30. ibid.
31. NO 088.
32. PS 975.
33. PS 988.
34. PS 992.
35. Interview with Albert Speer, May 1976.
36. ibid.
37. NO 703.
38. PS 1081.
39. NO 3848.
40. ibid.

Chapter 6 — The Dachau Experiments

1. R. Vogelsang: Der Freundenkreis Himmler's, Musterschmidt 1972, p.8.
2. PS 1602.
3. PS 6748.
4. PS 2428.
5. PS 1971a.
6. PS 1971c.
7. PS 1971b.
8. PS 2428.
9. ibid.
10. ibid.
11. ibid.
12. PS 7018.
13. Romberg in a letter — via his lawyer to the author, June 1981.
14. 'The Paper-clip Project', BBC — documentary Film 1987.
15. ibid.
16. M. Bar-Zohar op. cit. p.161.
17. PS 6907.
18. PS 1618.
19. ibid.
20. NO 428.
21. Berben op. cit. p.127.
22. PS 675.
23. NO 262.
24. PS 681.
25. PS 697.
26. NO 323.
27. NO 611.
28. NO 1424.
29. Berben op. cit. p.134.
30. S. Payne Best: The Venlo incident. London 1950, p.161.
31. ibid.
32. ibid. p.163.
33. PS 921.
34. NO 164.
35. Grawitz committed suicide in April 1945 and was succeeded by Karl Gebhardt.
36. PS 8130.

37. NO 179.
38. ibid.
39. Doc. Beiglböck 32.
40. PS 8145.
41. PS 8887.
42. PS 912.
43. NO 914.
44. PS 8887.
45. ibid.

Chapter 7 — The Auschwitz-Birkenau Experiments

1. D. Hasmann: Auschwitz, Köln 1966, p.16.
2. R. Höss: Kommandant in Auschwitz, München 1965, p.44.
3. ibid. p.103.
4. H. Langbein: Menschen in Auschwitz, Vienna 1972, p.411.
5. Interview with Hans Münch, August 1988.
6. Langbein. op. cit. p.313.
7. R.J. Lifton: The Nazi Doctors; medical killing and the psychology of genocide. New York 1986, p.392.
8. Langbein. op. cit. p.414.
9. Lifton. op. cit. p.395.
10. R. Waitz: Auschwitz-Monowitz. Témoignages Strasbourgeois, Paris 1947, pp.469-470.
11. Interview with Elie Cohen August 1988.
12. ibid.
13. APMO Trial of Höss, vol. c.23.
14. E. Lingens-Reiner: Prisoners of Fear, London 1958, pp.125-126.
15. O. Lengyel: Five Chimneys, London 1959, p.159.
16. Lingens-Reiner. op. cit. p.7.
17. See note 5.
18. A. Fiderkiewicz: Reminiscences concerning a prisoner-doctor's work in the Tuberculous Blocks of the Camp Hospital at Birkenau (1943-1944), Oswięçim 1976, p.273.
19. NO 9402.
20. NO 9406.
21. ibid.
22. See note 11.
23. See note 5.

24. H. Jacobs/B. Stoop: Het Auschwitzproces; een bericht over de levenden en de doden. Amsterdam 1965, pp.68-69.

25. ibid. p.70.

26. G. Tillion: Ravensbrück. Paris 1973, p.84.

27. Jacobs/.Stoop op. cit. p.70.

28. ibid. p.67.

29. Selection at the Rampe.

30. Exhausted prisoners who would die soon.

31. NO 3408.

32. F.K. Kaul: Aerzte in Auschwitz. Berlin 1968; p.53.

33. NO 3408.

34. Kaul. op. cit. 159.

35. NO 3412.

36. Lingens-Reiner. op. cit. p.115.

37. ibid. p.116.

38. Langbein. op. cit. p.41.

39. Lingens-Reiner. op. cit. p.112.

40. Lengyel. op. cit. pp.152-153.

41. F. Fénelon: The musicians of Auschwitz. London, 1979, p.156.

42. Quoted in: A. Rosenberg: Der Mythus des 20 Jahrhunderts. München 1939, p.476.

43. F. Bürgdorfer: Völker am Abgrund. München 1933.

44. C. Köhn-Behrens: Was ist Rasse? München 1934, p.64.

45. ibid. p.35.

46. Allgemeine Zeitschrift für Psychiatrie und ihre Grenze 3, 1939, p.408.

47. Quoted in: M. Weinrich: Racial Science, New York 1946, p.33.

48. G.L. Posner.J. Ware: Mengele: The complete story, New York 1986, p.12.

49. B. Frank: Raumforschung und Raumordnung, Berlin 1941, p.28.

50. Posner-Ware. op. cit. p.18.

51. M. Nyiszli: SS-Obersturmführer Dr Mengele. Les Temps Modernes, Paris 1951, p.1666.

52. ibid. p.1681.

53. B.Castel: Le Cirque de Mengele. Paris 1976, p.102.

54. Nyiszli. op. cit. p.1854.

55. Interview with Magda Zalicovitz. Quoted in: Penthouse August 1986, pp.62-63.

56. ibid. p.62.
56a. Eva Mozes Kor in a letter to the author 19 February 1989.
56b. ibid.
56c. ibid.
56d. ibid.
56e. ibid. According to Mrs Kor the government of Israel has a report, the Menachem Russek Report (Russek is chief of Nazi criminal investigations for the Israel government), in which is stated that Mengele is alive. The government of Israel doesn't want to release the report because of pressure from Germany and the United States of America.
56f. Posner-Ware. op. cit. p.325.
57. APMO Trial of Höss, vol 3. p.138.
58. See note 5.
59. NO 203.
60. NO 035.
61. APMO Trial of Höss, vol 5. c.95.
62. R.J. Minney: I shall fear no evil; the story of Dr Alina Brewda. London 1966, p.112.
63. NO 819.
64. According to a letter to the author dated 27 December 1976.
65. Minney op. cit. pp. 129-130.
66. ibid. p.129.
67. L. Uris: Exodus, New York 1964, p.218.
68. Drs Brewda, Kleinova and Hautval.
69. Minney. op. cit. p.130.
70. Lifton. op. cit. p.274.
71. A. Fejkiel: Ethical and legal limits of experimentation in medicine in connection with Professors Clauberg's affair. Oswięçim 1976, p.102.
72. NO 213.
73. Quoted in Lifton op. cit. p.273.
74. Quoted in M. Novitch: Le passage des Barbares; contribution a l'histoire de la déportation et de la résistance des Juifs Grecs. S.l. s.a. p.102.
75. NO 212.
76. Novitch op. cit. pp.125-128.
77. Lifton op. cit. p.276.
78. ibid.
79. C. Bernadac: Verdoemde doktors, Baarn 1969, P.98.
80. Quoted in Jacobs-Stoop. op. cit. p.27.

81. See note 5.
82. ibid.
83. ibid.
84. ibid.
85. Minney. op. cit. p.116.
86. See note 5.
87. ibid.
88. ibid.
89. ibid.
90. ibid.
91. ibid.
92. ibid.
92a. Interview with Ellis Hertzberger March 1990.
93. ibid.
94. De Humanist Nr. 8.9 August-September 1988, p.16.
95. See note 11.
96. ibid.
97. Lengyel op. cit. pp.119-120.

BIBLIOGRAPHY

The Trials of the German War Criminals before the International Tribunal, forty-two volumes, Nuremberg 1947-1949.
Trials of Major War Criminals before the Nuremberg Military Tribunals, fifteen volumes, Washington, US Government Printing office 1949-1952.
Nazi Conspiracy and Aggression, ten volumes, Washington, US State Department 1946-1948.
War Crimes Trials, nine volumes, edited by David Maxwell Fyfe, London 1948-1952.
The Black Book: *The Nazi Crime Against the Jewish People*, New York 1946.
Archive of Państowe Muzeum w Oswiecimiu.

* * *

Adler, H.G. : *Der verwaltete Mensch*, Tübingen 1974.
Ahrendt, H. : *Banaliteit van het kwaad*, Amsterdam 1969.
Allainmat, H. : *Auschwitz en France*, Paris 1974.
Aziz, Ph. : *Les médicins de la mort*, 4 tomes, Genèva 1975.
Bahnsen, U..O'Donnel, P. : *Die Katakombe; das Ende in der Reichskanzlei*, Stuttgart 1975.
Bayle, F. : *Croix Gammée contre Caducée*, Neustadt im Pfalz 1950.
Bayle, F. : *Psychologie et éthique de national socialisme*, Paris 1953.
Berben, P. : *Dachau 1933-1945; the official history*, London 1975.
Bernadac, C. : *Verdoemde dokters*, Baarn 1969.
Bernadotte, F. : *Het einde*, Den Haag 1947.
Billig, J. : *L'Allemagne et le génocide*, Paris 1950.
Bleuel, H.P. : *Een staat van fatsoen*, Baarn 1972.
Brownbook War and Nazi-criminals in West Germany, Dresden 1965.
Butler, E..Young, G. : *Marshal without glory*, London 1951.

Castel, B. : *Le cirque de Mengele*, Paris 1976.

Cohen, E. : *Het Duitse concentratiekamp; een medische en pyschologische studie*, Amsterdam 1952.

Czech, D. : *Hefte von Auschwitz*, Oswieçim 1960.

Czech, D. : *Role of the men's hospital at KL Auschwitz-Birkenau*, Oswieçim 1976.

Delarue, J. : *Histoire de la Gestapo*, Paris 1962.

Desoille, H.. Lafitte, M.M. : *Psychologie criminelle des Hitlériens*, Paris 1947.

Dicks, H.V. : *Licensed massmurder; a socio-psychological study of some SS killers*, London 1972.

Engel, G. : *Heeresadjudant bei Hitler 1938-1945*, Stuttgart 1974.

Farago, L. : *Aftermath*, New York 1975.

Fest, J.C. : *The Face of the Third Reich*, Harmondsworth 1970.

Fiderkiewicz, A. : *Reminiscenses concerning a prisoner-doctor's work*, Oswieçim 1976.

Franke, G. : *Vererbung und Rasse*, Munich 1934.

Freund, M. : *Het Derde Rijk, geboorte, macht en ondergang*, Den Haag 1963.

Friedman, F. : *This was Oswieçim*, London 1946.

Frischauer, R. : *Himmler*, London 1953.

Garlinski, J. : *Fighting Auschwitz*, London 1975.

Graber, G.S. : *History of the SS*, London 1980.

Grey, M. : *Leur défense à Nuremberg*, Paris 1976.

Grunberger, R. : *A social history of the Third Reich*, Harmondsworth 1980.

Guerber, A. : *Himmler et ses crimes*, Paris 1947.

Hemelrijk, J. : *Er is een weg naar de vrijheid; zeven maanden concentratiekamp*, Zeist 1965.

Heydecker, J.J. and Leeb, J. : *Op mars naar de galg; het proces van Neurenberg*, Amsterdam 1961.

Hitler, A. : *Mein Kampf*, Munich 1935.

Höhne, H. : *Het zwarte korps onder de doodskop; de geschiedenis van de SS*, Baarn 1967.

Höss, R. : *Kommandant in Auschwitz*, Munich 1965.

Jacobs, H. and Stoop, B. : *Het Auschwitzproces; een bericht over de levenden en de doden*, Amsterdam 1965.

Kaul, F.K. : *Aerzte in Auschwitz*, Berlin 1968.

Kersten, F. : *Klerk en beul*, Amsterdam 1948.

Kessel, J. : *De man die Nederland redde*, Rotterdam 1961.

Kogon, E. : *Der SS-Staat*, Frankfurt a.M. 1946.

Langbein, H. : *Der Auschwitzprozess*, Frankfurt a.M. 1965.

Lingens-Reiner, E. : *Prisoners of fear*, London 1958.

Lengyel, O. : *Five Chimneys*, Chicago 1947.

Lauryssens, S. : *De man in de chacra*, Den Haag 1977.

Lettich, A.A.D. : *Trente-quatre mois dans les camps de concentration. Témoignage sur les crimes 'scientifiques' commis par les médecins allemands.* Thèse Faculté de médecine de Paris 1946.

Lifton, R.J. : *The Nazi doctors; medical killing and the psychology of genocide,* New York 1986.

Manvell, R. : *Heinrich Himmler*, London 1965.

Manvell, R. and Fraenkl, H. : *The incomparable crime, mass-extermination in the twentieth century*, London 1947.

Menges, J. : *Euthanasie in het Derde Rijk*, Haarlem 1972.

Mikulski, J. : *Pharmacological experiments in concentration camps Auschwitz-Birkenau*, Oswieçim 1976.

Minney, R.J. : *Geen angst voor ellende*, Baarn 1967.

Mitscherlich, A. and Mielke, F. : *Doctors of infamy*, New York 1949.

Mitscherlich, A. and Mielke, F. : *Medizin ohne Menschlichkeit*, Heidelberg 1947.

Neusüs, R. : *Die SS*, Hannover 1956.

Novitch, M. : *Le passage des Barbares; contribution à l'histoire de la Déportation et de la Résistance des Juifs Grecs, s.l., s.a.*

Nyiszli, M. : *SS-Obersturmführer Docteur Mengele. Les Temps Modernes*, Paris 1951.

Payne Best, S. : *The Venlo incident*, London 1950.

Platen-Hallermund, A. : *Die Tötung Geisteskranken in Deutschland*, Frankfurt a.M. 1948.

Poliakow, L. and Wulf, J. : *Das Dritte Reich und seine Diener*, Berlin 1956.

Poliakow, L. : *Auschwitz*, Tilburg 1964.

Poller, W. : *Medical Block Buchenwald*, London 1961.

Reitlinger, G. : *The Final Solution*, London 1956.

Rosencher, H. : *Medicine in Dachau*, British Medical Journal 1946.

Russell of Liverpool, Lord : *De gesel van het hakenkruis*, Amsterdam 1960.

Serenny, G. : *Into that darkness*, London 1974.

Smith, B.F. : *Heinrich Himmler, a Nazi in the making 1920-1926*, Stanford 1971.

Smolen, K. : *Auschwitz 1940-1945*, Oswieçim 1971.

Speer, A. : *Inside the Third Reich*, New York 1970.
Speer, A. : *De Slavenstaat*, Amsterdam 1981.
Témoignages Strasbourgeois. *De L'université aux Camps de Concentration*, Paris 1947.
Ternon, Y. and Helman, S. : *Histoire de la médecine SS*, Paris 1969.
Ternon, Y. and Helman, S. : *Le massacre des aliénés*, Paris 1971.
Ternon, Y. : *Le médecine SS*, Paris 1976.
Trevor-Roper, H. : *De laatste dagen van Hitler*, Den Haag 1947.
Vogelsang, R. : *Der Freundenkreis Himmler*, Musterschmidt 1972.
Wormser-Migot, O. : *Le système concentrationnaire Nazi 1933-1945*, Paris 1968.
Wighton, C. : *Heydrich, Hitler's most evil henchman*, London 1962.
Wulf, J. : *Martin Bormann, Hitler's schaduw*, Tilburg s.a.
Zbydow, K. : *SS im Einsatz*, Salzburg 1982.